Designing Quality
Survey Questions

Sara Miller McCune founded SAGE Publishing in 1965 to support
the dissemination of usable knowledge and educate a global
community. SAGE publishes more than 1000 journals and over
800 new books each year, spanning a wide range of subject areas.
Our growing selection of library products includes archives, data,
case studies and video. SAGE remains majority owned by our
founder and after her lifetime will become owned by a charitable
trust that secures the company's continued independence.

Los Angeles | London | New Delhi | Singapore | Washington DC | Melbourne

Designing Quality Survey Questions

Sheila B. Robinson
Kimberly Firth Leonard

Los Angeles | London | New Delhi
Singapore | Washington DC | Melbourne

FOR INFORMATION:

SAGE Publications, Inc.
2455 Teller Road
Thousand Oaks, California 91320
E-mail: order@sagepub.com

SAGE Publications Ltd.
1 Oliver's Yard
55 City Road
London EC1Y 1SP
United Kingdom

SAGE Publications India Pvt. Ltd.
B 1/I 1 Mohan Cooperative Industrial Area
Mathura Road, New Delhi 110 044
India

SAGE Publications Asia-Pacific Pte. Ltd.
3 Church Street
#10-04 Samsung Hub
Singapore 049483

Acquisitions Editor: Helen Salmon
Editorial Assistant: Megan O'Heffernan
Content Development Editor: Chelsea Neve
Production Editor: Jane Martinez
Copy Editor: Mark Bast
Typesetter: C&M Digitals (P) Ltd.
Proofreader: Alison Syring
Indexer: Diane Barrington
Cover Designer: Alexa Turner
Marketing Manager: Susannah Goldes

Printed in the United States of America

Library of Congress Cataloging-in-Publication Data

Names: Robinson, Sheila B., author. | Leonard, Kimberly Firth, author.

Title: Designing quality survey questions / Sheila B. Robinson, Kimberly Firth Leonard.

Description: Los Angeles : SAGE, 2019. | Includes bibliographical references and index.

Identifiers: LCCN 2018021358 | ISBN 9781506330549 (pbk. : alk. paper)

Subjects: LCSH: Social surveys—Methodology. | Questionnaires—Methodology.

Classification: LCC HM538 .R63 2019 | DDC 300.72/3—dc23
LC record available at https://lccn.loc.gov/2018021358

This book is printed on acid-free paper.

19 20 21 22 10 9 8 7 6 5 4 3 2

• Brief Contents •

• Detailed Contents •

• Preface •

This book began with a conversation between strangers on Twitter back in 2012. It took just three simple tweets for us to connect over a mutual frustration with poorly written surveys and the desire to do better ourselves. As we discussed our shared grievances and the many ways we thought surveys could be improved, we also dug more deeply together into research, resources, and tools to support our own work. We quickly realized there was a need to share what we were learning with others. Our initial online conversation led to many coauthored blog posts, conference presentations, professional workshops, and now this book!

It started with a little bird!

 Kim Firth Leonard @KimFLeonard · 2 Dec 2012
Also thinking about a possible blog post on the challenges of writing good survey questions. Share your tips, advice, resources, please?!

 Kim Firth Leonard @KimFLeonard · 2 Dec 2012
@KimFLeonard or lessons learned, examples, etc. and if anyone is interested in writing with me on this, would love to make it collaborative!

 Sheila B Robinson @SheilaBRobinson · 2 Dec 2012
@KimFLeonard We think alike! I've been planning series of blogs on surveys. Love thinking about this topic! Can we collaborate & cross post?

6:28 PM - 2 Dec 2012 · Details

Hide conversation

For the purpose of this text, we define **survey** or **questionnaire** (we use the terms interchangeably) as an instrument or tool used for data collection composed of a series of questions administered to a group of people either in person, through the mail, over the phone, or online. We believe the guidance in this text will apply to surveys of all scales and scopes.

Why This Text

Ours is a simultaneously data-hungry and data-saturated world—humans earnestly seek information about each other for a myriad of purposes. Companies aim to increase their market share by better understanding customers. Applied researchers such as those working in education, medicine, and program evaluation collect data to understand the relationships between actions and results, and to inform continuous improvement of programs. Organizations are accountable to a range of funders—government agencies, foundations, or donors—who want to know how their investments have made an impact. Organizations also continuously seek input from clients, employees, or beneficiaries to drive decisions about programs, practices, or policies. The near ubiquity of high-tech tools and resources for data collection, and more specifically for survey development, means that it is not only possible but expected that data be captured about everyone almost constantly.

Surveys are just like any other written work: the moment we finalize or submit whatever we've written, we inevitably spot a typo, a missing word, or some other mistake, no matter how many editing rounds we undertook. Often it is a small but important error: forgetting a bit of the instructions or an important but not obvious answer option. Sometimes it is something we know we should have anticipated (e.g., jargon we could have easily avoided using), and sometimes it is not (e.g., an interpretation issue that wasn't caught in pilot testing). Sometimes, it is a big mistake. For example, forgetting to ask a question we needed the answer to in order to answer a research or evaluation question or to inform a key programmatic decision. Or asking a question in such a way that when we analyzed the data, we scratched our heads and thought, *So what? These responses aren't useful after all!* And sometimes mistakes aren't realized until our trusty respondents let us know it with a comment or lack of response entirely.

Over 20 years ago, Floyd J. Fowler (1995), a preeminent survey text author, wrote:

> I believe that the design and evaluation of survey questions is the most fertile current methodological area for improving survey research. Poor question design is pervasive, and improving questions design is one of the easiest, most cost-effective steps that can be taken to improve the quality of survey data. (p. vii)

Although this remains true, a lot has changed since Fowler's text was written, including giant leaps in the technology used to create and administer surveys and an ever-increasing demand for data gleaned from surveys. Yet poorly crafted surveys continue to appear almost everywhere, including market research, program evaluation, behavioral research, and other applied research sectors.

Many good resources on survey design do exist (and are referenced throughout this text). However, most existing and current survey texts give question design inadequate attention, emphasizing instead other topics such as sampling and analysis procedures. Beyond introducing the most common question types and a few rules indicating what not to do in constructing questions, other survey research texts lack in-depth instruction or advice on how effective questions can be composed, and have limited discussion of or opportunities for practice in developing survey questions. Even Fowler's 1995 foundational text *Improving Survey Questions* falls short of the kind of detailed and current guidance we wished for in doing our own work. We insist that it is crucial to pay greater attention to the questions themselves. As the heart of any survey, it is the questions that drive how useful the resulting data will be.

What This Text Is

We hope that this text supports researchers in crafting quality questions and compiling those questions into surveys that will result in useful data. Survey researchers have long understood that even seemingly minor changes in question wording can result in large differences in responses and employ a variety of strategies to prevent survey error.

> The most successful surveys are those built purposefully—designed with the knowledge of how to construct quality questions with appropriate response options. Sufficient planning is required, as are multiple rounds of review and revision, and ideally, intentional testing efforts. Successful surveys are built after reviewing relevant research, studying existing successful measures (when available), and most especially, careful consultation with those we wish to have respond to our survey.

This text covers the complete survey design process broadly and the question design phase of that process with particular depth. Our survey design process is introduced in Chapter 1. It is worth noting that the design process we outline appears far more linear than is typical in real contexts. In fact, many of the stages or steps of the process are interrelated, and the design process is often iterative. One of the greatest challenges we encountered in writing this text was determining the order in which to cover various parts of the survey development process. For example, planning for administration should be considered throughout the survey design process; we reluctantly relegated it to the end of this text because we felt the rest of the design process was important for the reader to understand first.

We built this text on all that current research and literature has to offer on survey question construction, on our own experiences designing and administering surveys, and on the experiences of other experts and practitioners currently working with surveys in applied research and evaluation contexts. We hope that it will bridge a distinct gap in the resources available for survey researchers—specifically addressing question wording and design beyond the basic, oft-repeated, and highly general advice. We incorporate the guidance and principles outlined by such well-known authors and survey researchers as Bradburn, Dillman, Fowler, Krosnick, Presser, Schuman, Schwarz, Sudman, and Tourangeau as well as many (perhaps less familiar) others. In doing so, we delve into the cognitive and psychological processes involved in answering survey questions to help the reader understand how people read, understand, and attempt to answer questions as well as understand what can potentially go wrong when surveys are not carefully designed.

In addition, this text addresses more current challenges in survey question design, including the following:

- Creative approaches to question design to keep respondents engaged and avoid survey fatigue

- Considerations for different survey administration modes (e.g., online, mail, telephone, in person)

- Current practices and principles for culturally responsive survey design

- Current language considerations for demographic and other common questions (e.g., how to ask about gender identity or sexual orientation)

- Discussion related to challenges of human memory, social desirability, and other factors that influence survey responses

What This Text Is Not

In focusing on survey question design, this text does not include in-depth coverage of a number of survey-related methodological issues, including sampling, analysis of survey results, and testing for reliability and validity. Although we do touch on a variety of related issues, including response rates and incentives, we've also suggested resources throughout the text for further reading and more complete coverage of particular topics.

Who Can Benefit From This Text

This book is intended for undergraduate and graduate students grappling with their first, second, or even third research methods course, as well as applied researchers and other practitioners who use surveys as a key data collection tool. Survey research is so abundant that the guidance in this text is certain to help researchers in many fields, including education, psychology, sociology, counseling, human development, statistics, measurement, and program evaluation. We hope that students and practitioners find this text complements those more focused on sampling and analysis and that the text comes to occupy a spot within easy reach in their professional libraries.

We also hope that organization leaders and program managers will find this a particularly useful guide in gathering data to understand their clients or beneficiaries and to improve programs. We recognize that organizations are increasingly using surveys to capture information and that many of those charged with doing so are not experts in survey development. Although we don't believe that advanced degrees are required in order to produce an effective survey, knowledge of survey fundamentals and skill in question design will positively influence the quality and usefulness of data collected with a survey instrument. With an understanding of how people respond to questions, and by following the guidelines we lay out in this text, even those new to creating surveys can construct effective questionnaires that result in high-quality, usable data that inform a broader research effort.

Because this text is meant to help *anyone* who designs a survey—from college students to seasoned researchers—no prior research methods or design knowledge is needed to understand or benefit from our guidance.

> We believe everyone working to collect and analyze data is a researcher. Although some reserve the title *researcher* for those with advanced degrees or who conduct more formal studies, in this text we recognize that many students as well as those working in applied fields including program evaluation take on the role of survey researcher as they seek to collect data in less formal circumstances and in small, local contexts.

Navigating This Text

This text walks readers through the WHY, WHAT, HOW, and WHEN of survey design, with an emphasis on crafting quality questions. The main body of the text is broken into three parts, following our survey design process.

- Chapter 1, "WHY Quality Surveys and Questions Matter," introduces and discusses the concept of quality in survey and question design, and outlines our purposeful survey design process.

- Part I, *WHAT to Consider Before Drafting Survey Questions*, covers the knowledge and activities necessary prior to drafting survey content itself.

  o Chapter 2, "Planning and Predrafting," covers the importance of establishing a given survey's purpose, discusses what surveys can measure, and outlines the advantages and limitations of surveys as a research tool.

  o Chapter 3, "Understanding Respondents," describes how respondents experience a survey and walks readers through the cognitive processes people use to answer survey questions.

- Part II, *HOW to Develop Survey Questions and Response Options*, is the heart of this text. It covers in great detail the many types of survey questions, including special purpose and sensitive questions, as well as how to design quality question stems and aligned response options.

  o Chapter 4, "Sourcing and Crafting Questions," includes an introduction to sourcing survey questions, whether they are developed by researchers or sourced from existing measures; introduces basic question types; and offers guidance about how to develop open- and closed-ended questions.

- o Chapter 5, "Constructing Response Options," serves as a companion to Chapter 4 and leads the reader through current and relevant research on many of the decision points researchers encounter in developing closed-ended questions and appropriate response options.

- o Chapter 6, "Special Purpose and Sensitive Questions," covers some of the most challenging types of questions to design and include in surveys, including questions with special purposes (e.g., filtering questions), potentially sensitive or threatening questions, and demographic questions.

- Part III, *Knowing WHEN a Survey Is Ready for Use*, provides guidance about finalizing survey questions and pulling questions together into a complete survey instrument, as well as planning for administration.

- o Chapter 7, "Finalizing Questions and Using Pretesting Strategies," covers pretesting and finalizing questions and considerations for how best to pull questions together into a survey tool in order to maximize response. We introduce our Checklist for Quality Question Design in this chapter.

- o Chapter 8, "Pulling It All Together to Maximize Response," covers many of the considerations key to ensuring that the administration phase of a survey is successful. We also address the importance of planning ahead for analysis and use in this final chapter.

Key features of this book will help readers apply the guidance we've included. First, vocabulary terms appear in bold wherever they are first introduced in the chapters; definitions of each of these terms are included in a glossary. Second, call-out boxes include particularly noteworthy ideas, along with topics that deserve special attention:

- "Design Details" focus the reader on especially salient topics in the design process.

- "Real-World Questions" are examples of poorly constructed questions and inappropriate or inadequate response options and scales culled from surveys we have taken over the years.

- "Stories From the Field" provide even more real-world experiences for the reader collected from practitioners who share lessons learned about survey design.

- "Mini-Interviews" are brief interviews with expert practitioners on key survey design topics.

Third, materials at the end of each chapter, which may be used in academic or practitioner-focused courses, include the following:

- "Discussion Questions" are designed for group discussion and reflection on the content.

- "Design Drills" are exercises that challenge the reader and support application of the information included.

- "Extended Learning" includes suggested additional readings for further study.

Finally, our comprehensive question design assessment tool—the Checklist for Quality Question Design—is introduced in Chapter 7 and included in the appendix to provide a handy summary of the guidance outlined in the text and to support students and practitioners alike as they compose surveys.

A Note About Language

As with any piece of writing, we have had to make certain decisions about our language use—those words and phrases we so carefully choose for communicating with readers. Two decision points are worthy of brief explanation here.

First, we write in the first person, and the reader will note generous use of pronouns such as *we, us,* and *our* throughout the text. At times these pronouns are used to refer to ourselves as the two authors of this text. Mostly, however, they are used to include *you,* the reader, when we collectively refer to *all of us* as survey researchers. Because it was way too awkward for us (as authors) to use the third-person "Sheila and Kim" or "Kim and Sheila" in certain places, our decision was to trust you, the reader, to be able to distinguish among the two purposes for the first-person pronouns. And we are quite confident that you will be able to do so.

Second, we have made considerable effort to avoid the need to use singular, gender-specific pronouns, such as *he* or *she,* and were quite successful throughout most of the text. In the few places we felt the writing absolutely called for these, however, we have tried to alternate their use. We recognize that this may not be an ideal solution.

• Acknowledgments •

We share deep gratitude for the support and contributions of many family members, friends, and colleagues, including the following:

- Helen Salmon, our SAGE acquisitions editor, for being open to our initial ideas, guiding us through the process, and being unfailingly kind and patient with us

- Chithra Adams and John Nash for their expert review of our material on design thinking

- Amy Germuth for her insight and feedback on some of our earlier ideas and material

- Two dear evaluation friends and colleagues—Stephanie Evergreen and Kylie Hutchinson—for their consistent encouragement, support, and advice

- Sione Aeschliman for her incredibly helpful developmental edits that brought us much clarity

- The colleagues and clients we have learned with and from; many of the lessons shared in this text are the result of researchers we've worked with working through the challenges of survey design

- Those who contributed original material for important text features—Stories From the Field, Mini-Interviews, and illustrations

- Our dear spouses—Larry Nagle and Scott Leonard—for their love, patience, and moral support; for tolerating our obsession with survey design; and for taking care of us, our houses, and our families while we were consumed with writing this text

SAGE and the authors are grateful for the input from the following reviewers:

Adrienne E. Adams, *Michigan State University*

Anne K. Hughes, *Michigan State University*

Joseph C. Kush, *Duquesne University*

Joni M. Lakin, *Auburn University*

Chris M. Ray, *North Dakota State University*

Lori Wilkinson, *University of Manitoba*

Allison K. Wisecup, *Radford University*

• About the Authors •

©Michelle Ames

Sheila B. Robinson, EdD, is an educator, program evaluator, and professional development workshop facilitator whose survey design experience began with assessment design in K12 public education. She is often an invited keynote speaker and workshop presenter at professional conferences, a consultant with educational and other organizations on survey design and program evaluation, and an adjunct professor of graduate courses in both program evaluation and professional development design and evaluation. Sheila is an active member of the American Evaluation Association (AEA); she is past chair of AEA's Pre-K12 Educational Evaluation Topical Interest Group, lead curator for AEA's blog Tip-a-Day by and for Evaluators, and coordinator of AEA's Potent Presentations Initiative. Sheila and her husband Larry live in Rochester, New York.

©Britta Marie Photography

Kimberly Firth Leonard, MPA, has built, administered, and taught others about surveys for more than a decade, primarily in the context of program evaluation. Kim is currently a senior research officer at the Oregon Community Foundation where she manages evaluations of several large grant-making initiatives, each of which includes at least one survey-based data collection component. Kim is an active member of the American Evaluation Association (AEA) and was president of the Oregon Program Evaluators Network in 2013. Kim lives in Portland, Oregon, with her husband Scott, daughter Hazel, and two dogs and a cat.

Sheila and Kim have been coauthoring blog articles on survey design since 2013 (look for their articles on sheilabrobinson.com and actionabledata.wordpress .com) and have led several successful preconference and skill-building workshop sessions to packed rooms at the American Evaluation Association (AEA) annual conference.

1

WHY Quality Surveys and Questions Matter

Questioning is more important today than it was yesterday—and will be even more important tomorrow—in helping us figure out what matters, where opportunity lies, and how to get there. We're all hungry for better answers. But first, we need to learn how to ask the right questions.

—Warren Berger, American journalist and author

What Is a Quality Survey?

Let's start with a thorough discussion of what we mean by survey. We define a **survey** as an instrument or tool used for data collection that is composed of a series of questions. Others call these **questionnaires**; we use the terms interchangeably. Surveys include primarily **closed-ended questions** with distinct sets of **response options**, or answer choices. Though many surveys do employ **open-ended questions**, these do not typically make up the majority of questions included (see Chapter 4 for a detailed discussion of specific question types).

Surveys are administered to a group of **respondents**, people who answer those questions. Surveys may aim to collect data from a whole **population** or **census** (as in the United States Census, a survey administered to every household in the United States) or from a specific subgroup of people, known as a **sample** (as in the American Community Survey, a survey administered only to select households in U.S. communities). Choosing whether to administer a survey to an entire population or to a sample of that population is a critical survey design decision. Sampling in and of itself is a topic with its own literature base and set of theories and is beyond the scope of this text; however, we offer a number of suggested readings on the topic at the end of this chapter.

Surveys are ideally used to capture information not already available through existing data sources. Surveys can measure respondents' attributes (e.g., demographic characteristics), behaviors, abilities (e.g., knowledge and skills), and thoughts (e.g., attitudes, beliefs, feelings, awareness, opinions, or preferences). Chapter 2 includes a more detailed review of each of these measurement areas (as well as the advantages and limitations of surveys more generally). The distinguishing characteristic of a survey is that the questions are consistently administered, typically in person, through the mail, over the phone, or online. This contrasts at least somewhat with more flexible data collection techniques like interviews.

DESIGN DETAILS
INTERVIEWS AND SURVEYS

We distinguish interviews from surveys, though they can share many similarities. Both are characterized by sets of questions, typically asked in the same manner to each respondent. Both can include open- and closed-ended questions. Here are a few characteristics that distinguish surveys from interviews.

- Surveys may be administered in several modes—the more typical paper or online modes, or in person or by phone with a researcher reading questions. Although the latter seems much like an interview, we still consider these surveys, so long as the instrument used—the questionnaire itself—and how it is administered is structured and standardized.

- Interviews can range from semistructured to highly unstructured, letting the conversation flow between interviewer and interviewee.

For interviews, researchers are also typically prepared to use **probes**. Probes are additional subquestions we ask such as "Can you tell me more?" or "What exactly do you mean by that?" They are designed to elicit additional information from respondents by encouraging them to add to, expand on, or revise their initial answers.

- Interviews are typically composed primarily of open-ended questions.

Just as with survey design, there is an art and science to developing and conducting interviews. Although the guidance included in this text may well apply to interviews, there is a significant body of literature specifically on interviews for data collection, including *Interviewing as Qualitative Research: A Guide for Researchers in Education and the Social Sciences*, by Irving Seidman (2013).

Surveys are ubiquitous in modern society, used not only by social science researchers and evaluators but also by marketers, businesses, government, and the media, among others. Most of the examples we include in this text could be considered "special purpose surveys"—those that serve a specific research purpose (Fowler, 2014)—though the bulk of the advice included could apply to any type of survey.

What Makes Survey Questions *Quality Questions*?

At the heart of a quality survey are, of course, quality questions. According to Bradburn, Sudman, and Wansink (2004), "A good question is one that yields a truthful, accurate answer" (p. 325). Quality questions are relevant and engaging to respondents because researchers have taken the time to carefully craft them to reflect respondents' ability and willingness to answer, and their unique cultures and context. This can only come from an effort to empathize with and understand respondents, which requires knowledge of how respondents comprehend, interpret, and draw from their memories the information we seek. Quality questions are designed with an understanding of the anatomy of open- and closed-ended questions, of how to use language to elicit response, and of how to arrange questions into a coherent measurement tool. Stanley LeBaron Payne (1951), author of one of the earliest texts on survey design, opined, "A 'good' question, among other things, is one which does not itself affect the answer" (p. 72).

> "
> *A good question is one that yields a truthful, accurate answer.*
> —Bradburn, Sudman, & Wansink

What Makes a Survey a *Quality Survey*?

Quality surveys yield rich, nuanced, useful data that help answer one or more research or **evaluation** questions (see Chapter 2 for more on research and **evaluation questions**). Through quality questions, quality surveys effectively engage respondents in providing accurate and useful data. But a survey is more than just a simple set of questions. Sudman, Bradburn, and Schwarz (1996), prominent survey researchers and authors of many foundational texts on developing surveys, offer "a dual conception of the survey" (p. 1) that we find helpful:

> On the one hand, a survey is a social encounter. On the other hand it is a series of cognitive tasks to be performed by respondents. . . . A survey is a special type of conversation . . . [and] is also a voluntary social encounter between strangers. Thus understanding the rules that govern conversations and social encounters in general should help us understand how survey questions are being understood and answered. (p. 2)

We take to heart the notion that a survey is a form of conversation and social exchange and that respondents are rarely, if ever, *compelled* to answer questions for us. This drives us to use a "respondent-centered" design process. Taking respondent needs, interests, and abilities into account allows us to maintain integrity as researchers; we respect and care for our respondents' well-being and avoid burdening them with unnecessary or unduly difficult questions. Surveys must be more than a quick list of everything a researcher would like to know about respondents dashed off in a series of questions. Instead, we think of surveys as conversations built on a foundation of shared language. To frame that conversation such that we are able to gather the needed information, we must thoughtfully employ a *purposeful* survey design process that takes into account an understanding of and empathy for our potential respondents.

Why Does Quality Matter?

Despite the increasing availability of copious amounts of existing data and incredible computing ability to mine that data, surveys are often still the best way to capture the specific information needed for a particular research effort. In particular, surveys are a critical and valuable tool in applied research (and thus, most behavioral and market research). Collecting data about human behavior (such as through direct observation) can be quite expensive and problematic. The proliferation of web-based survey design tools (e.g., SurveyMonkey, SurveyGizmo, Google Forms) have made surveys easier and more cost-effective to develop and administer, greatly increasing their use. In fact, surveys have now become the first line of defense in data collection.

Surveys commonly pop up on retailers' websites when we visit online, and survey links are printed on receipts from brick-and-mortar stores (often accompanied by offers of entry into sweepstakes or the promise of coupon codes). Medical offices and other businesses mail surveys to our homes after in-person visits, and survey requests from banks, airlines, hotels, and others are regularly delivered via email, and occasionally still by telephone.

The rapid rise of the survey in recent years, however, has resulted in an increase in **survey fatigue** that "occurs when survey participants become tired of the survey task and the quality of the data they provide begins to deteriorate" (Lavrakas, 2008). This phenomenon is well documented, especially on college campuses where "colleges must prove themselves to accreditors and legislators, and, within campuses, departments contend for scarce resources . . . students have come down with survey fatigue, the main symptom of which is **nonresponse**" (Lipka, 2011).

Chris Lysy, Fresh Spectrum

Despite this, surveys remain one of the most facile means by which we can gain access to and insights about others, especially in great number. Researchers must therefore take great care in deploying surveys in order to combat nonresponse and ensure that respondents provide high-quality data. This now requires even greater attention to crafting high-quality questions and survey tools than is typical; researchers must work with a deft hand, using a purposeful design process to maximize useful survey responses.

Why Do We Need a Purposeful Survey Design Process?

We have identified seven key reasons for a purposeful survey design process. These are culled from our review of existing research as well as from our own experiences.

1. Surveys are inherently imperfect tools and are easily fraught with error.

2. Self-reports are problematic.

3. Surveys are often developed without the benefit of formal study or practice.

4. Surveys developed internally are increasingly common and require extra attention.

5. Question wording can dramatically impact responses and data quality.

6. Today's survey researcher must work to ensure cultural relevance.

7. Survey fatigue and nonresponse negatively impact data collection.

Surveys Are Inherently Imperfect Tools and Are Easily Fraught With Error

Though all researchers strive to ensure the tools they use capture reliable and valid information, no survey or question is entirely immune from error. Further, the existing survey literature has clearly established that even seemingly minor changes in question wording can result in large differences in responses (see, for example, Bradburn et al., 2004; Sudman et al., 1996; Tanur, 1992; Tourangeau, Rips, & Rasinski, 2000).

Experts before us have categorized several kinds of survey error in a variety of ways. Dillman, Smyth, and Christian (2014) provide an excellent description of four kinds of potential **survey error** (coverage, sampling, nonresponse, and measurement), whereas Fowler (2015) describes potential error in two broader categories—errors related to who is answering the question and errors related to the answers themselves. We use Fowler's broader categories to think about possible error because most other types of error fit neatly into this simpler typology. Errors related to who is answering questions may also be described elsewhere as errors related to the interviewer, especially for in-person and telephone surveys. The concepts of coverage, sampling, and nonresponse from Dillman et al. (2014) belong in this broader category. Fowler's (2015) description of errors related to the answers themselves is quite similar to Dillman's description of **measurement error**, defined as "the difference between the estimate produced and the true value because respondents gave inaccurate answers to survey questions" (Dillman et al. 2014, p 3). Answer-related errors include problems like **bias** and respondent reliability. It is this latter type of error we are most interested in combatting through the advice in this text because this is where the order and phrasing of questions and response options becomes critical. In addition to the Dillman and Fowler texts, other types of survey error are covered in depth in other survey texts (see, for example, Alreck & Settle, 2004; Czaja & Blair, 2005).

Self-Reports Are Problematic

Surveys are generally (if not always) self-reports of behaviors, attitudes, perceptions, opinions, knowledge, skills, or attributes. Unfortunately, self-reports can be rife with inaccuracies, over- and underestimations, as well as outright fabrications, particularly when questions are poorly worded or configured. Respondents' own perceptions or their sense of others' perceptions of them may get in the way of accurate reporting. Dillman et al. (2014) break down measurement error into two types: response variance and response bias. One type of response bias, called **social desirability bias**, can make respondents reluctant to tell the truth about any behaviors or attitudes that could be perceived by others as negative or unflattering, or they may be more likely to overestimate responses about positive behaviors and underestimate responses about negative ones (see Chapter 6 for more on social desirability bias).

Response **variance** is typically the result of the fallible human memory. People don't always have the ability to remember things (e.g., events, feelings, opinions, attributes) exactly as they happened. This is true even when people *think* they are remembering things correctly. This phenomenon can result in responses to the same question varying over time. In other words, reliability in responding accurately can be low. People also tend to exaggerate similarities and differences and over- or underestimate occurrences of behaviors. Humans rely on a complex set of implicit biases to make decisions about how they respond to questions and have tremendous difficulty accurately sorting events and behaviors into specific time periods (for a more detailed discussion of how memory impacts survey responses, see Chapter 5). However, many of the challenges inherent in survey responses and the resulting datasets can be mitigated with good question design practices.

Surveys Are Often Developed Without the Benefit of Formal Study or Practice

Research (especially of the "applied" variety, such as program evaluation) is increasingly done by those without formal training or preparation in research methods or survey design. In the general quest for data-informed decision making on various aspects of our work in organizations, people in many types of positions (especially organizational leaders, e.g., directors, department heads, principals) are increasingly expected to gather their own data. And surveys are often the first tool grabbed from the toolkit, especially for those not exposed to or experienced in using other methods to capture data.

It can be helpful to think about why this is problematic by using a driving meta-phor. The experience of being a passenger does not automatically result in the ability to drive a car well. We need a certain amount of study and practice behind the wheel to achieve proficiency. That said, it doesn't take years of study or a graduate degree to learn how to drive, and the same goes for survey design. Effective surveys are devel-oped by those who have engaged in *some* study and practice (although we readily admit that we do not have the one-size-fits-all prescription for the "right" amount of study and practice). In fact, the quest for well-crafted surveys evolves as new tools and specific issues around question design arise (e.g., the ever-evolving considerations for how to ask sensitive questions, such as those about gender identity and sexual orienta-tion). Thus, it is vital to continue to hone survey design skills. After all, if we learn to drive as teens but then move to a new city and don't drive for several years, we likely need to relearn some aspects of road safety and perhaps catch up with new laws and the latest in auto technology.

Surveys Developed Internally Are Increasingly Common and Require Extra Attention

Survey design work that is done internally—within organizations and usually about the work of those organizations—brings its own set of complications (as well as being subject to the other concerns discussed in this section). Sometimes these efforts are more informal, as with surveys used as a quick and easy means to collect perception data from people internal to the organization. And sometimes surveys are developed internally that are used for research about people *external* to the orga-nization. These are typically intended to be as robust as surveys developed by more experienced external consultants. However, when surveys are created internally, even with the right technology in the hands of someone with sufficient expertise and prac-tice, soliciting input from outsiders (or better yet, desired respondents) is especially critical. Otherwise, it is easy to get lost in the familiarity of organizational culture and dynamics, use language that makes sense to people within the organization but not to intended respondents, or to misinterpret responses due to internal perceptions.

Question Wording Can Dramatically Impact Responses and Data Quality

It is critically important for any survey designer to understand the role and extent of the cognitive and communicative processes that respondents go through when answering survey questions. The psychology of asking and answering questions was for a long time largely absent from research, evaluation, and survey textbooks, with just a handful of researchers tackling these issues.

In the 1940s and early 1950s, researchers began experimenting with survey wording and finding that changes in wording produced significant changes in survey results (Schuman & Presser, 1977, p. 152). It soon became clear that for survey researchers to obtain the highest-quality data, potential respondents must be able to easily compre-hend, process, and interpret survey questions. In fact, "vagueness and ambiguity can lower response quality and increase measurement error in the survey data" (Lenzner,

STORIES FROM THE FIELD
SIMPLE QUESTIONS ARE NOT ALWAYS SIMPLE

Sometimes, a seemingly simple survey question just doesn't work. I was once asked to analyze data from a brief survey of open-ended questions asked of a small number of practitioners across a few departments in my organization. The department director had quickly crafted the survey in anticipation of an upcoming meeting where she expected the practitioners to be in attendance and knew she had easy access to them. The first question on the survey was "In what areas do you feel you have expertise?" The purpose of the question was not stated, and no additional direction or elucidation was offered. From the answers received, it was clear to me that the question could have been asked for any number of reasons, and I wondered, *Did the director want to build a database of department members with expertise in different areas? Was there simply a need to get a general sense of departmental knowledge or experience? Something else entirely?*

Let's take a quick look at how a simple question like this can be so problematic. The word *expertise* is wide open to interpretation. What did the director mean by *expertise*? After all, each of these practitioners (the survey respondents) had degrees in their field. Some held multiple degrees, and some had decades of experience. Despite this, many survey respondents crossed out the word *expertise* and substituted *experience* or *strength*. I wondered, *Did they not consider themselves experts? Did humility get in the way of their willingness to identify areas of expertise? Were they concerned that by admitting expertise, they might be called on to teach or train others?* Without talking with respondents about how they approached the question, we will never know.

Perhaps the even bigger issue here is about measurement. What was the director trying to measure when she crafted this question? Was she trying to learn (1) whether people have simply had *training or exposure* in certain areas? (2) whether they have a certain level of *confidence* in a certain area? (3) whether they feel they have enough knowledge or skill to *practice* in a certain area? (4) whether they have the ability to *teach or train* others in that area? or (5) something different? Measuring these would require different questions and speaks to the importance of establishing a purpose for each survey question before crafting the question itself.

And so, after analyzing the resulting data from this question, I wondered, *What do we really know now?* The answer unfortunately was . . . not very much.

—Sheila B. Robinson

2012, p. 2). Examples of vague or ambiguous terms include *sometimes, often, many people,* and *significantly* (for more on these types of "**vague quantifiers**," see Chapter 5) as well as deceivingly familiar terms such as *family, farmer,* and *athlete*. Does an unmarried cohabiting couple "count" as a family? Does a gardener selling some produce by the side of the road count as a farmer? Does a casual weekend bowler count as an athlete? Each word can have multiple and varied interpretations. Even a simple-sounding survey question such as *How many times have you read a magazine in the last six months?* contains a key phrase that is widely open to interpretation. What counts as *read a magazine* could range from glancing through a few pages, to skimming or reading just one article, to reading the issue cover to cover, and everything in between.

This focus on question wording became part of a newer paradigm of survey research that emerged in the 1980s and 1990s and changed the focus on survey error from "a statistical model that focused on the *effects* of survey errors . . . [to a] social scientific model that focuses on the *causes* of survey errors" (Tourangeau, 2003, p. 4; emphasis in original). This shift had survey researchers looking to cognitive psychology and related fields to understand how survey respondents decide whether to participate in surveys and how they go about approaching the complex process of answering survey questions. This is referred to as the Cognitive Aspects of Survey Methodology (CASM) movement. CASM began when survey researchers and cognitive scientists convened in 1983 for some rich dialogue and idea exchange on how their worlds could collide and result in some collaborative research. Although one might assume that these two disciplines were closely aligned for years (after all, survey researchers understood as early as the 1940s that question wording could impact responses), this was actually a groundbreaking movement.

Tourangeau (2003) describes CASM with one key sentence: "Reporting errors in surveys arise from problems in the underlying cognitive processes through which respondents generate their answers to survey questions" (p. 5). Hence, Chapter 3 is devoted to unpacking these key cognitive processes and their relationship to respondents' answering questions. At the heart of cognition and shared understanding is language. Sudman et al. (1996) remind us:

> The vehicle through which survey questionnaires are delivered is language. Understanding how people comprehend speech and written materials deepens our understanding of the way in which questionnaire design affects people's answers. Language comprehension is based not only on formal structures like syntax, but more importantly, on pragmatic factors that deeply affect meaning. (p. 2)

This makes it quite clear that comprehensibility plays a huge role in survey design and that "survey data quality is reduced if questions are difficult to understand and exceed the processing effort that respondents are willing or able to invest" (Lenzner 2012, p. 17).

Today's Survey Researcher Must Work to Ensure Cultural Relevance

Challenges and opportunities related to **cultural responsiveness**, relevance, and competence are also important to consider when developing surveys. Researchers are increasingly called on to be attentive to the way that our work operates within and can influence cultural contexts. This means that we must take greater responsibility for ensuring that surveys are reflective of and relevant to our intended respondents. Although language considerations are critical, there is much more to attend to than just translating a survey into respondents' preferred language. Among other things, researchers must answer the following questions as they plan and design a survey:

- If the survey needs to be translated into another language, how can we ensure the translation is valid?

- Does the survey reflect the language used by the respondents, including slang, colloquialisms, and regional dialect?

- Are there subjects that are taboo or inappropriate to ask about in the desired respondents' culture? Or ways of asking questions that would not be well received due to cultural norms (i.e., etiquette)?

- What assumptions or expectations do we have as researchers about the way that respondents will engage with the survey? How can we be sure these don't prevent us from capturing, analyzing, and using data in a responsive, respectful manner?

- How could those fluent in the language be engaged in helping to develop the survey? Helping to analyze or interpret results? How can we otherwise respectfully vet our work with those from the respondent community?

- When using or building on existing validated tools, with what populations were the tools validated? What limitations might those tools have for the population we wish to learn about through our research?

We further discuss cultural responsiveness in survey design in Chapter 3, leaning on the theoretical framework of **culturally responsive evaluation (CRE)**, and have woven cultural considerations related to survey question development throughout this text.

Survey Fatigue and Nonresponse Negatively Impact Data Collection

There is tremendous competition for respondents who are oversurveyed and burdened by the constant barrage of requests for perceptions and feedback. Surveys must feel brief and be easy to navigate for the respondent in order for the researcher to have any chance of combating nonresponse and achieving an acceptable **response rate**. Every question must count and yield the most useful data possible. The following tweet was part of a conversation in response to a request posted on Twitter for survey respondents and illustrates a reasonable reaction to a survey with too many questions. Researchers are now forced to cull lengthy lists of potential survey questions, using only those so well designed that they will serve to directly inform key study questions.

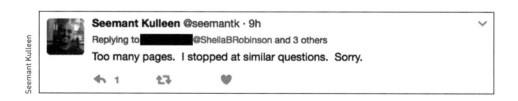

Seemant Kulleen

Seemant Kulleen @seemantk · 9h

Replying to ███████ @SheilaBRobinson and 3 others

Too many pages. I stopped at similar questions. Sorry.

Further, key research on survey fatigue indicates that not only do respondents feel oversurveyed based on the *number* of surveys they are asked to complete, but also based on the *relevance* of the surveys to their lives (Porter, Whitcomb, & Weitzer, 2004, p. 65). It is now incumbent upon survey researchers to consider how they can address this issue of relevancy with potential respondents and minimize respondent reluctance. Not only does this mean ensuring the survey is culturally responsive, it may also require providing specific incentives for response. A commitment to sharing the results or information about how the results will be used in ways that potentially impact those respondents can also go a long way in motivating respondents. For more on respondent willingness and ability to participate in survey research, see Chapter 3.

DESIGN DETAILS
RESPONSE RATES

Response rates, though important, should be considered only one indicator of the quality and usefulness of survey data. It is commonly believed that the higher the response rate, the more likely the data are representative of the population the researcher intended to learn about or from, and are therefore more accurate. Some studies have provided evidence that lower response rates may not mean less representative data, and even that extraordinary efforts to raise response rates can result in more skewed data (Krosnick [1999] outlines several). Even the venerable Pew Research Center (n.d.-a) states that "fortunately, low response rates are not necessarily an indication of nonresponse bias."

Despite it being more complicated to understand the degree to which survey respondents represent the population intended to be reached through the survey, calculating response rates is still valuable. The American Associates for Public Opinion Research has a handy "best practices" list (see https://www.aapor.org/Standards-Ethics/Best-Practices.aspx) and has developed the standard in calculating response rates. An Excel workbook is available on their website to calculate response rates.

Survey researchers must also determine what characteristics of the population are important given the survey topic, and what can be known about both the population and the sampled respondents. Researchers can then strive to collect pertinent information in order to learn as much as is feasible about the representativeness of the respondents for a given survey (such as through use of demographic questions).

The key reason for using a purposeful approach to survey design is that an effective, successful survey is much, much more than a simple set of questions, quickly drafted after a brief brainstorm and delivered to a group of potential respondents. Consider the case made for customized survey designs (those tailored to the circumstances of an individual survey) in *Internet, Mail, and Mixed-Mode Surveys: The Tailored Design Method* by Dillman et al. (2014):

Our response to those seeking answers to specific situations . . . is that there is not a simple set of design procedures that if applied to every situation will be most effective in reducing survey error. The populations to be sampled and surveyed, the kinds of questions that need to be asked, the resources available for doing the survey, and other constraints imposed by survey sponsorship differ greatly across individuals and organizations who wish to do surveys. (p. 16)

In other words, there is no single way to determine a sample, no perfect set of survey questions, and no ideal administration mode for all scenarios. Determining what methods and questions to use for a given survey requires a purposeful design process as well as a deep research-based understanding of surveys themselves.

> There is no single way to determine a sample, no perfect set of survey questions, and no ideal administration mode for all scenarios.

Applying Design Thinking to Survey Research

We have chosen the term *design* as a helpful heuristic in keeping with our intent to develop surveys with the mindset of a designer. Many modern designers, whether their work is on products or services, think of design as a "human-centered" or "user-oriented" process. In fact, there is an entire field and associated process of "user-experience design" that is rooted in human-computer interaction (HCI) and devoted to improving user experiences regarding usability, accessibility, and even pleasure and satisfaction. Our position is that a survey design process focused at least as much on our respondents' experience as on our own (or our clients') information needs will result in richer and more useful data. Before delving into our survey design process, we offer a brief introduction to the concept and phases of a design thinking approach and delineate how each phase dovetails with survey design.

The question development process (and larger survey development process) can be greatly enhanced by applying principles of design thinking. **Design thinking** is both a process and a mindset or way of thinking. Design thinking can be broadly applied to problem-solving challenges in a multitude of circumstances; objects of design can be as diverse as a chair, a school curriculum, a hiring process, or a city garden. Design thinking is generally composed of a set of phases during which designers attempt to deeply understand end users and their experiences, especially in the context of the identified problem. Design thinking calls for making sense of insights gleaned from these efforts, brainstorming solutions to the problem at hand, building prototypes, testing designs, and using feedback to make revisions and refinements. The hallmark of design thinking is a human-centered approach in which the designer puts ego and self-interest aside to design a "product" that best meets users' needs. Regarding survey design, we think of this human-centered approach as a "respondent-centered" approach; a respondent-centered mindset encourages us to put our respondents' needs, interests, and contexts ahead of our own.

Elevating respondents' interests in the survey design process may feel counterintuitive to researchers. Researchers are much more accustomed to having our information needs drive such processes. However, survey questions that are poorly understood, misinterpreted, or skipped by respondents pose serious problems. We have both had experiences with surveys that did not work for various reasons and resulted in a lack of useful data. Some survey efforts failed and others resulted in low response rates. Looking back, we can see that in some cases we clearly had designed poor questions, often because we did not know or understand our respondents well enough.

Design thinking phases generally include these: empathize, understand, brainstorm, prototype, and test. There are variations of these phases in the design literature, and some phases are also known by other names. We describe each next, along with their specific connections to survey design.

DESIGN DETAILS
DESIGN THINKING PHASES

1. Empathize

2. Understand

3. Brainstorm

4. Prototype

5. Test

Empathize

The first phase in design thinking is *empathize*, during which we get to know as much as we can about potential respondents in order to inform question design.

> Empathy is the centerpiece of a human-centered design process. The Empathize mode is the work you do to understand people, within the context of your design challenge. It is your effort to understand the way they do things and why, their physical and emotional needs, how they think about the world, and what is meaningful to them. (Hasso Plattner Institute of Design, n.d.)

Much of what we know about how people generally respond to survey questions is a result of research on survey design and response. Key studies we have reviewed from the CASM era as well as from more recent times include those that explore the following:

- Question wording

- Response options and rating scales

- Cognitive tasks associated with answering questions

- Survey fatigue
- Nonresponse

Comprehensibility is the defining characteristic of a high-quality survey question (as we explore more deeply in Chapter 3). The more we can learn about our respondents, the better we can craft questions they will be able to comprehend and answer. We suggest gathering as much detail as possible about the specific respondent pool *before* drafting survey questions. What are their demographic characteristics? Knowing about their age, gender, occupation, race/ethnicity, education level, literacy level, income, access to technology, interest in the topic, or even willingness to respond to a survey, along with other attributes, can significantly inform the design process. This can mean the difference between low-quality data and a highly successful survey research effort. Here are some additional questions to consider:

- What are the literacy levels of respondents?
- How are their days structured (at work or at home)?
  - Will they feel they have the time to complete a survey?
  - When are they most likely to be able and willing to complete a survey?
  - How much time might they be willing to devote to completing a survey?
- What are their interests? Do those interests relate to the survey topic?
- What do they value? Do those values relate to the survey topic?
- How much do they care about the survey topic? What aspects of the topic might they most care about, given the context (e.g., home, work, community) in which they will be surveyed?
  - Will they be interested in providing data?
  - Are there reasons they may want or not want to participate in a survey?
  - Will they be interested in the results of the study?
- What is their relationship to the researchers, if any? What is their relationship to the organization conducting the survey (i.e., are they employees, customers, clients, fellow community members)?
  - Do they know us as internal or external to the organization?

Designers typically use in-depth observation and interview strategies to learn more about their end users. Survey researchers may not be afforded the luxury of time or resources to empathize with potential respondents as deeply as we would like. However, we are often able to read about the target population as a result of previous research efforts or to ask questions of them, or of those who do interact with them more regularly. In survey research the empathy phase may be fairly straightforward, especially if we know our respondents well or share key characteristics with potential respondents. For example, this may be the case when conducting surveys from inside

💡 DESIGN DETAILS
EMPATHY MAPS

In doing the research for this text, we stumbled on a wonderful idea that can easily be adapted for survey design. In a design blog post, "Interaction Designer" Matthew Weprin (2016) introduces "empathy maps" as a way to gather and organize information about end users (e.g., survey respondents). In doing so, he lays out the steps for building the map using chart paper and sticky notes.

How to Build an Empathy Map

1. Draw the map and its four quadrants: Says, Thinks, Feels, and Does.

2. Sketch your user in the center and give them a name and a bit of description about who they are or what they do.

3. Diverge, with each team member writing one observation per sticky note and applying it to the appropriate quadrant of the map.

4. Annotate unknowns (assumptions and questions) for later inquiry or validation.

5. Discuss observations and fill in gaps collaboratively. (Weprin, 2016)

Alternatively, the four quadrants can be labeled Think & Feel, Hear, Say & Do, and See, with additional space for Pain & Gain as recommended by Dave Gray (n.d.), the reputed creator of this idea. Empathy maps can capture the answers to questions such as these:

•   What are our respondents' preoccupations, worries, or aspirations?

•   What is their attitude in public, appearance, or behavior toward others?

•   What are their pain points, their fears, frustrations, or obstacles?

•   What are their wants, needs, or measures of success? (Gray, n.d.)

Weprin (2016) suggests that this mapping process be completed as a team and, where possible, that respondents be included in the creation of the map or checking the accuracy of assumptions used to develop the map. He also advises that readers go beyond just listing job titles (e.g., our respondents are teachers or accountants) and consider respondents' "actual tasks, motivations, goals, and obstacles."

an organization to be used inside the organization. However, even when it seems we are close enough to the respondents to understand them adequately, researchers must take care not to make assumptions or jump to conclusions about respondents. In particular, we need to know about respondents *in the context of the specific survey topic.*

Readers of this text may be thinking that this is where we test out some of our question ideas on potential respondents. Some may be familiar with the terms *piloting* or **cognitive interviewing** and think that is what we are describing in this section. Not so. The focus on empathy is squarely on knowing and understanding respondents *in preparation for developing appropriate questions for them.* This is part of the survey design process that *precedes* drafting questions. Pretesting survey questions using various strategies such as those mentioned earlier comes later in the design process (and is discussed in Chapter 7). Finally, empathy can even influence the look, feel, and layout of a survey as well as inform decisions about how and when a survey is administered.

STORIES FROM THE FIELD
WHEN PUTTING RESPONDENTS FIRST YIELDS SUCCESS

Throughout my career in public education, I've worked with school principals for decades and am intimately familiar with their responsibilities and workloads. When I needed the answers to three key open-ended survey questions from a group of 16 busy principals, I knew that an online survey wouldn't do the trick. Even if I thought that composing a few brief paragraphs in response to these questions would only take them 15 to 20 minutes at the most, I knew their world of countless emails, voice mails, and office interruptions on top of their school management and personnel supervision responsibilities well enough to know that sitting down at a computer, clicking on the link, and taking a survey would not rise to the top of the priority list. However, I also knew from previous interactions with them that they cared about the project and that if I asked for that same 15 to 20 minutes of their time for a phone call, they would agree to participate. And they did. My respondent-centered survey design decision resulted in a 100% response rate!

—Sheila B. Robinson

STORIES FROM THE FIELD
EMPATHY IN SURVEY DESIGN

My colleague and I evaluated the services provided by youth centers. As part of the funding requirements, we had to administer a survey to youth who had received services. The survey asked questions about life in general as well as about specific mental health outcomes like substance use, violence, and trauma. Since the survey was mandated by the funder, we could not change the questions. However, we wanted to learn how youth respondents would feel about the survey, so we piloted the survey to youth program staff. Some of the feedback we received was that some of the questions made the staff feel uncomfortable. The youth program staff were worried that some questions could possibly trigger painful memories and may be traumatic to youth responding to the survey. We (the evaluators) attended a training on trauma-informed interviewing. As part of the training, we learned several strategies that we could use to make respondents comfortable such as recognizing and responding appropriately to signs of distress and selecting an appropriate room in which to administer the survey. We also shared these strategies for trauma-informed interviewing with youth program staff. If we had not piloted or talked to the youth program staff, we would not have learned about trauma-informed interviewing. Empathy can not only be useful in designing questions but also in survey administration. An empathetic researcher should be ready to learn new skills or provide resources based on insight gained through empathetic need finding.

—Chithra Adams

The first story on the preceding page illustrates a time when a key survey design decision (in this case, about administration mode) resulted in a positive outcome. This same decision would not necessarily have been made in a different context such as a much larger respondent pool, and the decision was counter to what the researcher initially preferred (an online survey in which respondents typed their own answers). The point is that *the design decision was made based on known characteristics of the respondents* and that was key to the successful outcome. In the second story, empathy was also used to alter the survey administration conditions in a very different context but also in response to a known characteristic of respondents.

Understand

The second phase in the design thinking process is *understand*. In the literature on design thinking and design processes, this phase is also known as *define*.

> The Define mode of the design process is all about bringing clarity and focus to the design space. It is your chance, and responsibility, as a design thinker to define the challenge you are taking on, based on what you have learned about your user and about the context. (Hasso Plattner Institute of Design, n.d.)

After developing empathy for respondents through various efforts to know more about them, we next must make sense of insights gained along the way. In this phase, we reflect on our research or evaluation questions and revisit the clearly articulated survey purpose and information needs in the context of what we now understand about potential respondents. This sense-making phase may also include reviewing relevant literature or even existing surveys on the topic and potential **constructs**— or underlying concepts—(see Chapter 2 for more on constructs) we hope to measure.

If we have made special efforts to empathize with respondents by observing them in the field or interviewing them, this is where we review, analyze, and interpret notes, transcripts, or other data collected in service to understanding their experiences. If we already have a thorough knowledge of respondent characteristics, this is where we might list, prioritize, and begin to think about what these characteristics will bring to bear on question and overall survey design.

Brainstorm

The third phase in design thinking is *brainstorm*. In some of the design thinking literature, this is also known as ideate, or idea generation. In survey design, this is where we generate and start drafting questions, taking into account what we know about respondents as well as our survey purpose and information needs. As with any good brainstorming session, during this phase "anything goes." What sets this session apart from other types of brainstorming is that we have gone through two previous phases—*empathize* and *understand*—that have grounded us in the experiences of respondents. This positions us well to generate a more focused set of questions than would otherwise be generated without those phases and should help limit necessary pruning of ideas and questions in later stages of the process.

During the brainstorm phase, we are free to generate possible questions with little regard to specific question types. In other words, we don't attend to whether questions will be open- or closed-ended, and we don't necessarily craft rating scales or other types of response options. Whereas designers use the question stem "How might we . . . ?" as they generate ideas for a solution to a perplexing problem, we use it to come up with survey questions. For example,

- How might we ask respondents about their shopping habits?

- How might we find out about their opinions of the new policy?

- How might we understand their experiences at the event?

- How might we figure out if they intend to change their practice?

- How might we ask questions of respondents in ways that limit bias?

Researchers must avoid getting mired in the details of question wording, question order or sequencing, and other design considerations during this phase. New question ideas and considerations may surface while brainstorming that would otherwise be missed if we jump too fast into the details. We strongly encourage survey designers to stay flexible and creative during this phase and avoid rushing the process.

Prototype

The fourth phase of design thinking is *prototype*. A prototype of a product or service is typically designed to be taken to a set of potential users for their feedback and input. In survey design, this phase looks like building a survey draft—our prototype. To do so we draw on what we have synthesized from understanding and brainstorming. Question ideas are refined and then we determine whether they should be open- or closed-ended given the information needed. If closed-ended, specific question types are established, and response options are developed. This is an important early step in ensuring that our survey measures what we really want to measure—that our questions have **face validity**. This requires that the constructs we want to measure are clear and well defined. In other words, we want to **operationalize** them. This typically requires review of relevant existing research about a given concept (e.g., if satisfaction is to be measured, the researcher needs to review and incorporate existing research about how satisfaction is operationalized). At this stage we also begin to ensure that question stems and response options are appropriately aligned (i.e., mirror one another in focus and language; see Chapter 5 for fuller treatment of the development of response options).

During prototyping, questions may be added, or questions generated during the brainstorming phase may be divided into multiple questions. Or questions may be pruned as our understanding of how best to capture the desired information is refined. Questions should also be prioritized based on work from earlier phases to balance information needs with feasibility constraints. In other words, knowing what we know about potential respondents, how long a survey can we create? Generally, fewer questions should be asked than initially brainstormed or drafted. However, it is more important to consider the length of *time* it will take respondents to complete the survey than the *number* of questions included. And because question responses can be influenced by the order in which questions are posed to respondents, it may be useful to build multiple prototypes, or different versions of our survey, in which questions are alternated in order to test this phenomenon. Building multiple prototypes to test may be especially important for larger-scale projects or if the survey includes potentially sensitive questions. In general, we want to introduce more sensitive or potentially threatening questions only *after* more innocuous questions are posed. In addition, we begin surveys with more general questions prior to asking more specific questions. There are also order considerations for **demographic questions**. All of these choices have implications for survey results, and some of these **order effects** are discussed in Chapter 8. Once we receive feedback on a prototype, we may redesign the survey accordingly to incorporate any relevant feedback before moving into a testing phase.

Test

The fourth phase in design thinking is *test*. In survey research, we often refer to this as "pretesting" because we are testing the instrument and its component questions *before* we administer it to our desired respondents. Such testing solicits even more user input to inform potential revision or redesign before a survey is finalized. Common survey research pretesting practices include piloting and cognitive interviewing. For a detailed description of these pretesting strategies, see Chapter 7.

Whether we share survey drafts with a few willing colleagues who offer honest feedback, or invest considerable resources in more formal and larger-scale pretesting, valuable information can be gleaned from this step that cannot be learned any other way. We can ask for reactions and initial impressions, not only of questions but also of format. Although pretesting is clearly time-intensive when thoroughly executed, we cannot overstate its worth in a purposeful survey design process.

An Iterative Process

Design thinking may appear to be a linear process, but it is also an iterative one. Although empathizing is a natural antecedent to understanding, and brainstorming must precede prototyping and testing, a designer frequently returns to earlier phases throughout the process, as more and more information is derived from each phase. As we make sense of our learning during the define phase, we may engage in additional activities to build more empathy for respondents. As we build prototypes or receive feedback from pretesting them, we make revisions based on this new learning. In some cases, this may even cause us to return to the respondent population to seek more of an understanding about them. Being empathetic to respondents means that the researchers are open to possibilities and willing to change, learn new skills, and use new software tools. Design thinking requires flexibility and adaptability. It also means practicing design restraint. Thorough empathy and understand phases may leave the researcher with a wealth of information about respondents; therefore, it will be important to identify which aspects of respondents' lives will influence how survey questions will be answered and focus on these during the design process.

A Purposeful Survey Design Process

Numerous authors of survey texts have conceptualized a survey research process in series of stages, steps, or phases. We examined many examples of these before crafting our own process specific to survey question design. In doing so, we noticed the following across the various process frameworks:

- There is no one "right" way to conduct survey research.

- Many authors (including us) at least agree on some *key parts* of the process.

- It is all but impossible to suggest *how long* each part of a survey research process will take, for each survey effort and research project is unique.

- Parts of the design process are interrelated, and the process is typically iterative in practice, despite being presented (as we have) as a more ordered, linear process.

At its most fundamental, we conceptualize the broader survey research process as having four main parts: 1) design, 2) administration, 3) analysis, and 4) use. This text focuses on the survey design process, that is, the process of developing survey instruments, and particularly survey questions. We consider the design process as inclusive of everything that needs to happen prior to survey administration, including any pretesting of survey questions necessary. Our survey design process is described next and summarized in the boxed outline. This text does not include a great deal of advice about administration, analysis, and use, though considerations are peppered throughout, and Chapter 8 covers preparing for administration, analysis, and use (e.g., determining survey administration mode). Many other survey research texts cover survey administration and data analysis far more thoroughly than we can here. Use of survey results specifically has not been tackled as thoroughly, but many texts support use of research and evaluation results more broadly (e.g., Patton's [2008] *Utilization-Focused Evaluation*).

The survey design process has three major components with a few subcomponents under each:

1. Planning and predrafting
   a. Determining and articulating survey purpose
   b. Understanding what surveys can measure
   c. Understanding survey respondents

2. Developing questions
   a. Sourcing questions
   b. Crafting question stems and response options

3. Finalizing
   a. Pretesting
   b. Preparing for administration, analysis, and use

Planning and Predrafting

In this step, we clarify research goals and articulate **research questions**. We determine what will be measured, confirming that a survey is the right tool to capture the data we need. We use design thinking phases of empathizing, understanding, and brainstorming to get to know our respondents in the context of our information needs, and begin a list of more detailed topics for questions that may end up on our survey.

Developing Questions

In this step, we use the valuable information gathered in the planning and pre-drafting stages to actually select and/or draft survey questions. We determine the extent to which we will need to consider whether a suitable survey instrument already exists or whether we will need to design an original measurement tool. We use design thinking strategies to prioritize questions brainstormed during the planning/predrafting step, and build a prototype of a survey that will be shared in the testing step to determine the comprehensibility and appropriateness of the questions, among other considerations.

Finalizing

In this step, we pretest survey questions using strategies such as peer review, piloting, or cognitive interviewing to ensure that respondents understand questions and can interpret and answer them as we intend. We can also use feedback from respondents to refine and revise questions in preparation for administering the survey. One additional strategy is to use a quality assessment tool, such as our Checklist for Quality Question Design, introduced in Chapter 7.

This step also calls for planning for analysis and use of survey responses and planning for administration details, including mode (e.g., in person or self-administered, telephone, mail, or online) and timeline. These decisions are based on what we know about respondents and the context in which the survey is being administered. We should determine how results can (and cannot) be used and consider what analyses will be needed. Ideally, we begin considering administration, analysis, and use intentions and needs far before we are done developing a survey tool. This is a great example of how the survey design process can be highly iterative rather than linear; analysis plans may evolve over time as the survey is developed and the researcher determines what types of questions are needed.

An Iterative Process

Though the process appears linear (and our text roughly follows the order presented), it is critical to note that the entire process is typically iterative. For example, though a researcher may begin with determining survey purpose, then develop questions, and then employ a pretesting strategy, pretesting may reveal that she needs to know more about respondents and their specific characteristics or context and rework some

Purposeful Survey Design Process	Location in Text
1. Planning and Predrafting	
a. Determining and articulating survey purpose	Chapter 2
b. Understanding what surveys can measure	Chapter 2
c. Understanding survey respondents	Chapter 3
2. Developing Questions	
a. Sourcing questions	Chapter 4
b. Crafting question stems and response options	Chapters 4, 5, 6
3. Finalizing	
a. Pretesting	Chapter 7
b. Preparing for administration, analysis, and use	Chapter 8

questions before returning to conduct additional pretesting. Additionally, there are a few pieces in particular that are hard to place in a linear order. Understanding respondents is often an evolving effort, and researchers are wise to do at least some planning (or at least *thinking*) about administration and use of results early in the process.

We intentionally introduced design thinking before introducing our survey design process. Understanding design thinking will impel the reader to keep the survey design process focused on respondents, which is critical to crafting effective surveys. Design thinking can be thought of as a set of fluid phases that, in a sense, *overlay* the survey design process and inform our thinking throughout (see Figure 1.1).

FIGURE 1.1 ● How Design Thinking Informs Survey Design

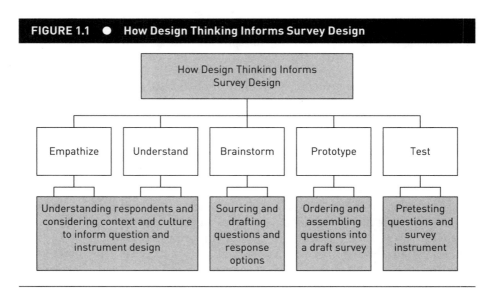

Discussion Questions

- What are the implications of survey fatigue for data collection using surveys? How might researchers work to limit survey fatigue?

- What phase of the design thinking process seems easiest to apply to survey design? Most challenging? Where might a survey researcher devote the most time and effort?

- How can understanding your desired respondents help in designing quality survey questions? How might a survey researcher access information needed to understand desired respondents?

- What are the advantages of the prototyping and testing phases?

 # Design Drills

1. Find a question in a publicly available survey (such as a retail customer service survey or a student survey from your school) that is problematic. How is it problematic? What do you think went wrong in its design? Are any of the reasons for purposeful survey design outlined in this chapter illustrated by this question? If so, how?

2. Review the following questions and identify the problem. Rewrite the question with necessary improvements (making any assumptions necessary about what information might be desired by the researchers).

    a. Was the information you received timely, relevant, and appropriate?

        _____ YES

        _____ NO

    b. Do you think it's wise to cut spending on Program A and increase spending on Program B?

        _____ YES

        _____ NO

    c. How useful was this program for you?

        _____ Excellent

        _____ Very good

        _____ Fair

        _____ Poor

    d. What is your age?

        _____ under 30

        _____ 30–35

        _____ 35–40

        _____ 40–45

        _____ 45–50

        _____ over 50

3. Research Scenario, Part 1 (additional parts are found in subsequent chapters): You are tasked with capturing information that will help assess the effectiveness of a new and ongoing program to support low-income senior citizens. The program is based at public libraries in several small towns and cities across a large geographic region. Assuming for a moment that a survey of participants is the best way to capture critical data for this project, draft a brief memo or email to your research teammates or supervisor making a case for a purposeful survey design process. Include a proposal for how you might work to understand your desired respondents as part of that process, noting why that will be important for this project.

4. Your survey: In this chapter we learned that designers use the question stem "How might we . . . ?" as they generate ideas for a solution to a perplexing problem. We provided examples of how this might be used to help draft survey questions. For example, "How might we ask respondents about their shopping habits?" Or "How might we ask questions of respondents in ways that limit bias?" For a survey you are currently developing, or expect to develop, generate a few additional "how might we" questions specific to your research scenario that could help you draft questions with a respondent-centered mind-set.

 ## Extended Learning

- A thorough treatment of sampling can be found in the following:

  - Alreck, P. L., & Settle, R. B. (2004). *The survey research handbook* (3rd ed.). Chicago: Irwin.

  - Babbie, E. (1990). *Survey research methods* (2nd ed.). Belmont, CA: Wadsworth.

  - Ornstein, M. (2013). *A companion to survey research.* Thousand Oaks, CA: Sage. (Provides a good overview of applied sample design and the design of purposive samples.)

  - Rea, L. M., & Parker, R. A. (2014). *Designing and conducting survey research: A comprehensive guide* (4th ed.) San Francisco: Jossey-Bass.

  - Weisberg, H. F., Krosnick, J. A., & Bowen, B. D. (1996). *An introduction to survey research, polling, and data analysis* (3rd ed.). Thousand Oaks, CA: Sage.

- Additional details about survey error can be found in Czaja, R. F., & Blair, J. (2004). *Designing surveys: A guide to decisions and procedures* (2nd ed.). Thousand Oaks, CA: Sage. Dillman, D., Smyth, J. D., & Christian, L. (2014). *Internet, phone, mail, and mixed-mode surveys: The tailored design method* (4th ed.). Hoboken, NJ: Wiley.

- For more on use-focused evaluation, see Patton, M. Q. (2008). Utilization-focused evaluation. Thousand Oaks, CA: Sage. Patton, M. Q. (2011). *Essentials of utilization-focused evaluation.* Thousand Oaks, CA: Sage.

- For more on design thinking:

  ○ Tim Brown's blog: Design thinking, http://designthinking.ideo.com

  ○ *The field guide to human-centered design*, available at http://www.designkit.org/resources/1

  ○ Cameron Norman's blog: Censemaking: Contemplating complexity, designing social innovation, https://censemaking.com

  ○ Hasso Plattner Institute of Design, *An introduction to design thinking process guide.* Available at https://dschool-old.stanford.edu/sandbox/groups/designresources/wiki/36873/attachments/74b3d/ModeGuideBOOTCAMP2010L.pdf

WHAT to Consider Before Drafting Survey Questions

The first part of this text is devoted to the planning and predrafting stage of the purposeful survey design process described in Chapter 1. As we illustrate in these chapters, developing an effective survey requires a fair amount of planning and preparation. Dedicating time at this stage of the survey design process is key to designing a survey that will yield rich, nuanced, and useful data. We cannot overstate the importance of this work being done *prior* to drafting questions. In fact, our frequent experience of the absence of these steps was largely what compelled us to write this book. Working with people who developed surveys without careful consideration and attention to planning and predrafting efforts, resulting in datasets that were sorely lacking in useable information, compelled us to spend considerable time and energy detailing this stage of the survey design process, despite the natural tendency to want to jump directly to brainstorming questions the moment we decide a survey is needed.

Purposeful Survey Design

1. **Planning and predrafting**
   a. **Determining and articulating survey purpose**
   b. **Understanding what surveys can measure**
   c. **Understanding survey respondents**
2. Developing questions
   a. Sourcing questions
   b. Crafting question stems and response options
3. Finalizing
   a. Pretesting
   b. Preparing for administration, analysis, and use

Chapter 2, "Planning and Predrafting," covers the important steps of determining and articulating the purpose of a given survey effort, which requires a solid understanding of what can be measured with a survey. This starts with confirming that a survey is indeed the right tool for a given research effort. This chapter sets the researcher up for the survey design process and emphasizes the importance of careful planning, as Sudman and Bradburn (1982) illustrate:

> Too often questionnaire writers are so caught up in the excitement of question writing that they jump rapidly into writing questions before they have adequately formulated the goals of the research and thoroughly understood the research questions. Many questionnaires constructed by inexperienced people look as if the researchers did not know what they were trying to find out until they saw what they had asked. (p. 13)

Chapter 3, "Understanding Respondents," provides in-depth coverage of the respondent experience, including challenges they may experience in answering survey questions as well as a discussion of cultural considerations. This chapter is focused on what survey researchers can do to empathize with and understand respondents prior to developing questions to help ensure a high-quality measurement instrument.

2

Planning and Predrafting

Wisely and slow. They stumble that run fast.

—**William Shakespeare**, *Romeo and Juliet*

Why Survey?
The Importance of Establishing Purpose

Surveys are conducted for a plethora of purposes. A survey may be the only source of information, or it may be part of a multimethod research effort. The stakes may be relatively low, as in a survey that provides information to help an organization understand its client's interests. Or the stakes may be much higher. Survey results may inform whether a program continues to be funded or is altered in a substantial way (as happens when surveys are used for program evaluations). All surveys should be developed purposefully from the outset, regardless of the centrality of a survey to a given research effort or its potential use for decision making. An unclear or unarticulated purpose is the most common challenge we see in our experience providing consultation to others about survey design. When the purpose of a survey is not particularly clear, it is not surprising that survey questions themselves are unfocused or unclear.

It is wise to begin survey development, or any data collection effort for that matter, by articulating or confirming the key research questions that the data to be collected will help answer. Research questions are the "big-picture" questions that drive and focus a given research effort. Most research efforts aim to answer one or a small handful (often just two or three) of research questions (though more specific subquestions may help identify additional detail desired). It is important to distinguish these questions from questions that are asked in a survey (or in an interview or focus group). It is almost never appropriate to simply pose the research questions to survey respondents. Usually these questions are much too broad to generate useful responses, and, because they are the questions pursued by the researcher, respondents in fact would not be able to answer them. Ensuring that each individual survey question is in service to these broader research questions helps prevent the capture of unnecessary data and supports the capture of the most useful information possible.

Chris Lysy, Fresh Spectrum

💡 DESIGN DETAILS
RESEARCH AND EVALUATION QUESTIONS

Research questions are high-level questions of inquiry into specific concerns or issues of interest and make up the fundamental core or central element of a study. Research questions focus the study, guide the selection of study methodology, and inform all stages of inquiry, analysis, and reporting. Similarly, evaluation questions focus a program or policy evaluation on the aspects of the program or policy under investigation. Neither high-level question types are intended to result in single data points, in the way that an individual survey question would, and therefore wouldn't be asked directly to respondents.

Consider the following example: a researcher is studying the use of a new therapeutic technique, to determine how well it is supporting improved behavior in patients. The research question might be something like this: "How well is 'Technique X' supporting improved behavior in patients?" A survey of patients could serve as one of several data sources for the research project, but the researcher is unlikely to simply ask patients, "How well is 'Technique X' supporting improved behavior for you?" Instead, the researcher is going to operationalize (or further define) some of the key concepts. For example, what is meant by *supporting*? What is considered "improved" behavior? What specific behaviors will be explored? Researchers can measure these by asking multiple questions about various ways in which "Technique X" is used and experienced by the patient, and about specific ways in which their behavior may (or may not) have changed.

Further, we have found it extremely useful to establish and articulate, in writing, how the survey will help support the broader research purpose and help answer the research questions. In fact, identifying and articulating the purpose for conducting a given survey may be the single most important piece of design advice we can offer. We recommend including the following when articulating survey purpose:

- How the resulting dataset will inform the answer to one or more research questions (i.e., its relationship to the broader research effort)

- Who will use the information captured by the survey

- How the information gathered will be used, including any decisions that rest on the results of the survey

- What form the information will need to be in to maximize its usefulness

> Articulating the purpose for conducting a survey may be the single most important piece of design advice we can offer.

Identifying and articulating the specific purpose for conducting a survey helps focus the process of creating, prioritizing, and selecting questions. As survey questions are generated, revisiting the survey purpose from time to time helps keep the focus of the research *needs* at the forefront, as opposed to addressing *interests* that may not serve the articulated purpose. Pursuing interests that go beyond the survey purpose and research information needs contributes to scope creep, or mission creep, the expansion of a research project beyond its original goals. It is generally considered harmful to the effort, increasing respondent burden and potentially survey fatigue. For example, researchers may need to understand certain characteristics of people who attend a program, such as where they live, their ages, or why they chose to participate in the program. These may be important given decisions program managers must make about potentially expanding, reducing, or changing the program. It may be of *interest* to know whether the people who attend have a certain level of education, but this may not be *relevant* to the research question(s) or the decisions program managers must be ready to make in this case. Asking questions about education levels *in this case* would only contribute to respondent burden. The point is to clearly delineate *needs* from *interests* based on the research question(s). The survey purpose will also help drive decisions about the format, administration mode (e.g., in person, by mail, online), and length of the survey (more about that in Chapter 8).

What Will Be Measured?
Understanding Constructs and Indicators

Armed with clear research question(s) and an articulated survey purpose, we can start to consider more specifically what constructs our survey can potentially measure. Many researchers make a distinction between "concepts" and "constructs," and we could devote considerable space here to attempting to understand their differences. Some even use one term to define the other. However, in this text, and for our purposes, we use the term *construct* and define it rather broadly as "something to be measured that cannot be directly observed."

Researchers need to define and operationalize constructs in order to measure them in a meaningful way. A piano is not a construct, nor is a cat. These are things that *can* be directly observed. Intelligence, health, prejudice, intent to change, interest in a topic, and awareness or understanding of a social problem are examples of constructs. These are things that *cannot* be directly observed in a person and for which we must identify **indicators**. Indicators tell us the state or level of something. The dots or bars on our smartphones, for example, indicate the level of service we have at any given time or place. Physicians use indicators during a physical examination as evidence of the construct we call "health." Such indicators may include heart rate, blood pressure, cholesterol levels, and body-mass index. These indicators have been identified because health cannot be directly observed. Doctors cannot simply look at us and determine that we are 74% or 92% healthy!

Babbie (1990) refers to constructs, or that which social scientists attempt to measure, as being "rich in meaning," and as such, they "must be reduced to oversimplified, inevitably superficial, empirical indicators. [They have] *no real meanings*, no ultimate definitions" (p. 119; emphasis in original). Consider how people have struggled to define *intelligence*. There is not necessarily a single correct way of measuring constructs like intelligence. It is the researcher's goal to measure constructs in ways that will help answer research questions. Babbie (1990) further contends, "We can never make *accurate* measurements, only *useful* ones" (p. 120; emphasis in original).

> **"**
> *We can never make accurate measurements, only useful ones.*
> –Babbie

Let's consider the following example to illustrate these points: a research project aims to understand whether participants in a training session were *satisfied* with the training. *Satisfaction* is a construct. Although a literature search on satisfaction would help a researcher to learn how others have operationalized this construct, it is also possible to identify reasonable indicators that could be measured and provide useful information without reviewing other conceptualizations of satisfaction. The degree to which this is possible depends somewhat on the construct and the context for the research. For example, if the construct to be measured is more complex, like self-esteem or environmentalism, it would be far more valuable (or even necessary) to operationalize (and therefore measure) the constructs in the same way as other researchers—in a research-informed manner.

For our example, how might the construct *satisfaction* be measured in the context of a training session? If participants were satisfied, possible indicators may be that

- they liked the training,

- their time was well spent in the training session,

- they found the materials or resources helpful or useful,

- they felt the instructor was knowledgeable about the topic, and

- they would recommend the training course to a colleague.

Indicators will vary in strength and predictive ability. A dissatisfied participant probably will not report liking the training; hence, liking the training is a stronger indicator. Another participant may agree that the presenter was knowledgeable, but the participant was not satisfied with the training for some other reason (e.g., the content was not relevant). In this case, feeling that the presenter was knowledgeable is a weaker indicator because it does not possess predictive ability. There are certainly many other indicators of satisfaction a researcher could potentially identify.

In gathering information about participant satisfaction, a researcher would likely want to measure other related constructs as well. It may be useful to know whether participants intend to change their practice after a training session, for example. The construct *intent to change* can be operationalized in the same manner as satisfaction. To do so, researchers determine what participants might report if they had an intent to change their practice as a result of the training (i.e., the potential indicators of an intent to change). Once what must be measured is clear, crafting actual questions to measure those constructs (asking about indicators) is much more productive and purposeful.

The following story provides a "real world" example of this stage of survey design. As the researchers in this story refined their questions, they held their survey purpose in mind as they revisited what they wanted to measure. In addition, they empathized with and attempted to understand their respondents to inform the design process and build their prototype.

STORIES FROM THE FIELD
ASKING ABOUT ECONOMIC STATUS IN A SURVEY: AN ODYSSEY

The Institute for Community Health (ICH) is a nonprofit consulting organization that specializes in participatory evaluation, applied research, and strategic planning. We help health care systems, governmental agencies, and community-based organizations improve services and create meaningful impact. We recently encountered a survey design problem that was unexpectedly tricky.

Once upon a time, we set off on a trip to help a client understand *if their program was reaching vulnerable members of low-income communities*. Little did we know, when we started, what a long and winding journey it would be!

At first, we assumed we would define "low income" as "below the federal poverty level (FPL)." We designed a survey that included the following question:

What is your household income? $ _____

(Continued)

(Continued)

To determine whether a person fell above or below the FPL, which varies based on household size, we also had to include:

How many people in your household? _____

However, we found a number of problems with this set of questions.

Household income may be difficult to calculate for some households. Do you know the income of everybody you live with? Do you share all expenses? Do you count the income of your adult child? Do you count the income of someone who only lives there part of the year?

Household size is also a tricky thing to ask for some households! In particular, people may not know how to calculate their household size if they have members who do not live there permanently, or with people who contribute to the household's income but do not live there. This is most common among the economically vulnerable households we expected to be identifying.

Poverty and vulnerability are relative to the cost of living. A household at the FPL is better off in rural Alabama than in New York City, for example.

In our experience, many respondents skip survey questions about income. This could be for the reasons above, but also because of taboos about money and financial vulnerability.

Finally, we didn't need this much information!

We thought of a number of tweaks and repairs to help fix these questions, but we eventually realized that we only needed to know whether a respondent was vulnerable due to their low income. This is fundamentally a yes/no question. So we moved on to the next waypoint in our journey.

We next proposed the following proxy measure for low income.

Do you get ANY of the following benefits: SNAP/food stamps, WIC, SSI, SSDI, TANF, housing assistance, Medicaid:

O Yes
O No
O Unsure
O I prefer not to answer

We reasoned that in order to receive the benefits above, applicants are put through a rigorous vetting process. In looking at the end results, we would be taking advantage of that vetting. Clever, right? We thought so . . . until we piloted the survey with our clients and grantees.

At that stage, we were faced with an unexpected detour. Our client felt stigma around public benefits would prevent people from answering. Further, they felt some of the respondents could be undocumented immigrants who, even when eligible for benefits, are often reluctant to apply.

Despite these indications that this phrasing was not the destination we were looking for, we lingered for a little while here, attempting the following fix:

Just based on your income, are you or would you be eligible for any of the following benefits: Food stamps, cash assistance, housing assistance, or [state-specific Medicaid name]?

O Yes
O No
O Unsure
O I prefer not to answer

Perhaps the less said about this half question/half monster, the better.

Coming to our senses, we decided to refocus on the *actual* domain we were trying to assess: vulnerability. The following is based on validated measures of social determinants of health.

In the past 12 months, have any of the following been true? (*check all that apply*)

☐ You worried whether your food would run out before you got money to buy more

☐ You worried about losing housing or were homeless

☐ The electric, gas, water, or oil company threatened to shut off services in your home

☐ None of the above

☐ I prefer not to answer

This final question both measures the actual construct we needed to know about (vulnerability) and is responsive to the contexts where it is fielded.

At the beginning of our odyssey, we thought we were looking for the answer to a standard demographic question—income—which had an easy answer. However, through the many stops we made along the way, we learned not to take even the "easy" questions for granted. By the time we reached our ultimate destination, we had gained a new appreciation for the importance of a) staying connected to the underlying question and b) the process of piloting.

—Carolyn Fisher, Martina Todaro, and Leah Zallman

Wait, Do You Really Need a Survey?

As survey enthusiasts, we sometimes wish we could choose to employ a survey for every research project. It is important, however, to recognize that surveys are not always the best data collection tool for a given research effort. The research question(s), information needs, respondent population, and other considerations may mean another data collection approach is more appropriate. Just as in home remodeling, auto repair, or surgery, great care must be taken to ensure that appropriate tools are selected for the job at hand.

Under the right circumstances, surveys can be just the right tool for the job. As we discussed, it is virtually impossible to know if a survey is the right tool without first establishing *why* the research is being conducted and what is expected to result from it (e.g., knowledge creation, program decisions, customer acquisition). In addition, it is vital to ensure that existing data or a different method of data collection effort would not do a better job of meeting the research needs.

DESIGN DETAILS
PUTTING USE FIRST

We cannot allow readers to go any further in this text without a brief "lecture" about the importance of considering respondent burden and ensuring that we collect *only the data needed* for a given research effort. We can think of countless occasions on which we, or researchers we were working with, wanted to capture more information than was needed to answer the research question(s). It is always tempting to ask an extra survey question or two ("We may as well ask 11 or 12 questions, as long as we're asking 10 questions"). And sometimes researchers experience a sort of "research FOMO" (or fear of missing out) thinking, *If we don't ask* all *the questions we can think of now, we might* *not have an opportunity to do so later.* Researchers should resist this inclination in order to limit the burden we place on respondents as much as possible but also because it is simply unethical to gather information that isn't needed. This practice can be viewed as highly intrusive in some circumstances and contributes to the already present challenges of survey fatigue and nonresponse. Researchers should aim to capture only the information necessary to answer the stated research or evaluation questions. Of course, this requires being quite certain about what exactly is needed to answer those questions before administering any survey.

Is a New Data Collection Effort Necessary?

New data should not be collected when the desired information is already available elsewhere and analysis of that data (i.e., **secondary data** analysis) is feasible. Exploring existing data prior to conducting any new data collection effort is worthwhile for several interrelated reasons. As previously mentioned, researchers should only collect data that is truly needed, minimizing respondent burden as much as possible. Researchers should also avoid adding to the existing oversurveying (and subsequent survey fatigue) problem.

The capture and review of secondary data can be especially valuable for research efforts when such data exists and is accessible to researchers. Examples of secondary data use include **case record review** (typically, but not always, managed on paper), analysis of data from administrative databases (typically managed electronically), and use of existing datasets such as from the U.S. Census or American Community Survey. There is almost never a need to use a survey to capture data that already exists in other datasets. Of course, use of secondary data comes with its own challenges as well. There may be multiple barriers to access, and sometimes existing datasets don't contain exactly the information desired. Processing and analyzing this data can be tedious if datasets are especially large or complicated or if data entry was problematic (i.e., resulting in datasets with missing data, duplicated data, or data organized in ways that do not make sense to us).

Is Another Data Collection Tool a Better Fit?

Researchers should consider whether another data collection option might be a better fit. Surveys are often misused and overused, so it is important that researchers consider carefully whether other tools or methods could be more appropriate for a given research effort. It may seem ironic for a book about how to design surveys to promote the consideration of other tools, but we cannot overstate how critical it is to ensure that a survey is indeed the *right* choice, and not just the easiest or default option. Even professional researchers occasionally forget that surveys are only one method of collecting **primary data** (i.e., data collected firsthand, directly from respondents themselves). Colleagues have approached us many times requesting help with survey design only to discover through conversation with us that in fact a survey was not actually the best option given the nature of the information desired, potential respondents, resource constraints, cultural considerations, and other relevant circumstances. The following paragraphs describe some of the most common alternative data collection methods (in addition to secondary data analysis), though this discussion is certainly not exhaustive.

Interviews and focus groups. Interviews and focus groups share key characteristics with surveys. Typically, all three methods employ protocols consisting of questions and framing language (e.g., introductory information). However, unlike surveys, interviews and focus groups support the capture of detailed qualitative data. Interviews and focus groups are ideal formats for asking open-ended questions and can be much more unstructured, letting the conversation flow between interviewer and interviewee. Interviews and focus groups also allow for the flexible use of probes. Although in some cases it may be useful to include subquestions that act like probes in a survey, these can be tricky to anticipate and deploy and are not usually used to capture qualitative data.

Interviews and focus groups can also allow the researcher to capture data on facial expressions, tone of voice, body language, and other nonverbal cues that can enhance a rich dataset and allow for deeper insight into the phenomenon being studied. Whenever qualitative data are desired or there is need to clarify a particular question's response in the moment (usually a clue that it isn't possible to develop adequate closed-ended response options for that particular question), researchers should consider an interview, focus group, or other qualitative method. That said, these methods come with the distinct disadvantages of being very time-intensive both to administer and to analyze the resulting data. As a result, fewer respondents can typically be reached through these methods than through a survey, lowering sample size and thus reducing potential generalizability of the resulting information.

Observation. **Observation** is especially useful when the researcher needs to see firsthand a behavior or practice in action and does not want to rely on the authenticity or accuracy of self-reported data. Although observations are best for accurately measuring behavior, they are often logistically impossible for research studies due to a number of factors, not the least of which is concern for privacy. Resource limitations also often prevent observation from being a viable data collection option, especially because multiple observers may be needed to gather the necessary data over a long period of time, observers need proper training in order to achieve a degree of **reliability**, and the fact that some behaviors are infrequent or not easily observed by another (e.g., how could an observer tell if someone is actually *reading* or just *looking* at a magazine?). Observations are therefore more time-consuming, more labor-intensive (e.g., they include the necessity for the observer to travel to and from sites), and costlier than surveys. Sample sizes are typically limited for observation as well, because researcher time is needed for observing behavior, recording information about that behavior, and analyzing that information.

Tests of ability or knowledge. Tests of ability or knowledge are considered by some to be a type of survey, because survey questions can measure knowledge when written appropriately. Such tests or assessments of knowledge are sometimes used in pre-post designs for evaluation of professional development (staff development) or training courses. In these cases, change in responses can determine the degree to which participants have learned the course content. In contrast, performance tests are tasks in which people are expected to demonstrate their knowledge, ability, or proficiency with a given task that is performed for a reviewer or evaluator. Instead of indicating knowledge through an answer to a question, in a performance test the respondent is asked to actually display or use the knowledge.

DESIGN DETAILS
SUMMARY OF DATA COLLECTION ALTERNATIVES

There are several alternatives to surveys, including the most common methods described in this text:

- *Secondary data analysis* methods such as case record review allow researchers to tap into existing information to answer research questions. Although the greatest advantage in these methods is that no new data collection is required, the information available is sometimes limited, or a great deal of restructuring of information is required in order to analyze the data.

- *Interviews and focus groups* allow for the collection of richer, more nuanced, and detailed qualitative data, but typically fewer respondents can be included and analysis can be time-consuming.

- *Observation* is necessary when a researcher needs to see behavior in action and does not want to rely on self-reported data, but observation data can be labor-intensive both to collect and analyze.

- *Tests of knowledge* are actually similar to surveys but intended to measure actual knowledge or ability (versus perceived knowledge). If well-constructed, these can be quite accurate, but context matters—catch research subjects on the wrong day and their memories can fail them.

- *Performance tasks* allow for observation of ability, demonstrated by the research subject. These can result in rich and highly valid information, but they can also be challenging to develop and administer.

It is important to note that the data collection methods described in this text as alternatives to surveys are certainly not the only possible methods for a given research effort. There are many other methods, including emerging methods such as those from the fields of participatory research and evaluation that researchers may want to consider. Typically, the best way to learn about possible alternative methods is to look for and be open to what methods other researchers have used (or not used) for related topics.

In the following two stories, each of us tells about a time when we needed to carefully consider whether a survey was the right tool, before diving in and crafting questions. In Kim's story, a survey turned out to be the best tool for data collection, whereas in Sheila's story, she helped a group determine that a survey was not the right tool after all.

Once researchers have determined that a survey is indeed the best tool for a given data collection effort, it is important to have a solid understanding of what *can* be measured with a survey, along with the distinct advantages and limitations of using surveys.

What Can Be Measured With a Survey?

Surveys typically capture self-reported information. In other words, surveys ask respondents to answer questions about themselves and their experiences. As such, surveys can capture the following types of information about or from respondents:

- Attributes (e.g., demographic characteristics such as age, ethnicity, or gender)
- Behaviors (e.g., what people do, such as shop, exercise, engage in hobbies)
- Abilities (e.g., knowledge or skills)
- Thoughts (e.g., attitudes, beliefs, feelings, awareness, opinions, or preferences)

STORIES FROM THE FIELD
WHEN A SURVEY WAS THE ONLY FEASIBLE OPTION

I was once tasked with analyzing case record information from child welfare workers in order to describe and assess the use of kinship placements (i.e., placement of a child with a relative or fictive kin) as an alternative to foster care. Though case record review or secondary analysis based on existing database records would have been the ideal data collection methods for this effort, neither was feasible. Existing data systems were in the middle of a massive technical transition that meant data was unable to be extracted in a useable format. And existing case records were sitting several states away, and not always understandable to those who weren't the case workers themselves.

And so we devised a survey. Case records were randomly selected and case workers asked to complete a survey for each of their records, reporting the particular details needed for the analysis, including details that weren't tracked in existing online systems. One might consider this a case record review rather than a survey—simply a creative use of an online survey tool to capture case record information. But in many ways it fit the definition of a survey and was the best possible tool for the job at hand.

—Kimberly Firth Leonard

STORIES FROM THE FIELD
WHEN A SURVEY WAS NOT THE RIGHT TOOL

There came a knock on my door one day. It was a district office administrator who needed to use a survey for a new committee he was leading and was pointed in my direction by a colleague who knew me as the resident "survey expert." Excited as always to assist in a survey design process, I readily agreed to meet him and his committee co-chair to get started. As I walked into the conference room, the co-chair had already opened up a textbook related to the committee's topic and was pointing at a list of questions asking if I thought they would be "good questions" for their survey. I laughed and asked if they could start by taking a few steps back and helping me to understand the nature of the committee and why they felt they needed a survey. It turned out that in fact, they did not. The committee was newly formed, and the chairs themselves lacked a common understanding of its purpose and goals. After a lengthy conversation outlining these as well as identifying the group's information needs and available data sources (their potential survey respondents), they agreed that a survey would not be appropriate after all. Instead, other data collection strategies such as conducting a focus group or interviewing a few key informants would better serve their needs at the time. Lesson learned? Don't get ahead of yourself by drafting questions before making sure a survey is the right choice!

—Sheila B. Robinson

Attributes

Most surveys feature one or more questions about attributes. Attributes are inherent characteristics or qualities such as age, race, ethnicity, nationality, education, employment, religion, gender identity, and sexual orientation. Questions that measure these are called demographic questions (see Figure 2.1 for examples). Attribute questions can also capture information beyond the more common demographic questions, about other quantifiable characteristics. For example, how many years' experience respondents have in an occupational field, what departments they work in, or what organizations they belong to are all examples of attributes that could be captured with well-crafted survey questions.

Despite the common compulsion to capture *all* possible information about attributes, especially classic demographic information (e.g., age, gender, race/ethnicity), it is important to limit the number and type of these questions in surveys. This is especially true for surveys that are intended to be anonymous. It can be possible to identify specific respondents from the combination of answers to questions about attributes. It is worth noting too that there are significant complexities associated with asking questions about more sensitive attributes such as race/ethnicity, gender identity, and sexual preference, and it behooves a survey researcher to carefully consider the most appropriate, respectful, and up-to-date ways to ask these questions. This will depend on the population or sample being surveyed. For more detailed information about demographic questions, see Chapter 6.

FIGURE 2.1 ● Questions That Measure Attributes

What is your age?

- ○ 20 or younger
- ○ 21–30
- ○ 31–40
- ○ 41–50
- ○ 51–60
- ○ 61 or older

What is your educational level?

- ○ Did not complete high school
- ○ Earned a high school diploma or GED
- ○ Earned an associate's or other 2-year degree
- ○ Earned a bachelor's or other 4-year degree
- ○ Earned a master's degree
- ○ Earned a doctorate (PhD, EdD, JD, PsyD) or other terminal degree
- ○ Earned other educational credential (please identify the credential)

Behavior

Questions about behavior include those that ask how often or how many times respondents regularly engage or have engaged in certain behaviors of interest (see Figure 2.2 for examples). We can ask which behaviors respondents engage in or do not engage in (e.g., exercise) along with when and where the behaviors take place (e.g., mornings, at a gym). Which behaviors are of interest are determined by the research topic and research question(s) and may range from the seemingly mundane to the unusual. Washing one's hair, consuming alcohol, arguing with a loved one, purchasing groceries, or attending cultural events are just a few of the myriad examples of behaviors that could be of interest to a researcher. Respondents can typically be trusted to report on their own behaviors via a survey so long as questions are written well enough that respondents are able and willing to answer them accurately, and especially when the survey topic is *not* of a sensitive or threatening nature (e.g., sexual behaviors, use of illicit drugs). For example, respondents must understand exactly what the researcher is looking for regarding questions such as "How often do you drink alcohol?" In this example, respondents may wonder if the researcher is looking for how many days per week or month alcohol is consumed, or how many individual drinks are consumed. Given the question "How often do you read a magazine?" respondents may wonder if the researcher is looking for occasions when they have glanced at a magazine, read an article or two, or read a magazine cover to cover. Any of these could reasonably fall within an individual's interpretation of "read a magazine." Well-designed questions are clear, leave little room for interpretation, and do not put respondents in a position of having to guess the researcher's intentions (for more on respondent ability and willingness to answer questions see Chapter 3). Survey designers must also be clear about which dimensions of behavior to measure, for example, frequency, duration, and intensity. Even measuring just the *frequency* of a behavior demands additional design decisions because it can be broken down into more specific categories:

- Relative frequency (e.g., questions that use "vague quantifiers" such as *sometimes*, *often*, *rarely* [see Chapter 5 for more on vague quantifiers])

- Grouped absolute frequencies (e.g., questions that offer intervals such as 1–3 times, 4–6 times, 5 or more times)

- Rates (e.g., 3 or more times per month, a few times per year) (Schaeffer & Dykema, 2011).

FIGURE 2.2   ●   Questions That Measure Behavior

On average, how many times a week do you exercise? Exercise is defined as sustained physical activity for the purpose of achieving or maintaining a desired level of fitness with a duration of at least 30 minutes.

- ◯ Less often than 1 day per week
- ◯ 1 day per week
- ◯ 2 days per week
- ◯ 3 days per week
- ◯ 4 days per week
- ◯ 5 or more days per week
- ◯ I do not exercise at all

How many times in the last 3 months did you visit an indoor shopping mall?

- ◯ None
- ◯ 1 time
- ◯ 2–3 times
- ◯ 4–5 times
- ◯ 6 or more times

Abilities

Surveys can also measure respondents' abilities, skills, or knowledge of a particular subject. However, most of the time when surveyed about abilities, skills, or knowledge, respondents are really providing information about their *perception* of their own abilities, skills, or knowledge (see Figure 2.3 for examples). This is an important distinction;

in many cases, we are not truly measuring abilities but rather *perceived abilities*, and as such, these questions are actually measuring respondent's thoughts.

In many cases, measuring perceived abilities may be sufficient for a given research effort. However, if a true test of abilities or skills is desired, another research method is likely necessary. Surveys *can* test respondents on *knowledge*, if questions are well-crafted enough to elicit this information. Pre- and posttest surveys may measure respondents' knowledge prior to an event and again following that event. In particular, knowledge questions may follow a professional development (staff development), training, or continuing education course as providers seek to understand the effectiveness or impact of course activities on participants' learning. Knowledge questions can also be part of a **needs assessment** (another type of research effort that often employs surveys) to determine if training is necessary.

FIGURE 2.3 ● Questions That Measure Abilities (Knowledge)

How many states are in the contiguous United States?

    O 50

    O 48

    O 44

    O 40

Which of the following is an example of a root vegetable?

    O Tomato

    O Carrot

    O Zucchini

    O Cucumber

How would you rate your word processing skills?*

    O Excellent

    O Very good

    O Good

    O Fair

    O Poor

* This question measures *perceived* abilities and therefore might more accurately be described as a question that measures thoughts.

Thoughts

Surveys commonly ask respondents about their perspectives on a topic—their attitudes, beliefs, feelings, awareness, opinions, or preferences about a particular matter. We have collapsed these possibilities into what we call thoughts. Examples of questions about respondents' thoughts include political polling questions about feelings regarding elected officials or employer surveys asking for input about new policies in the workplace (see Figure 2.4 for additional examples). Surveys about public awareness of particular issues like health concerns or social problems also contain questions about respondents' thoughts. Awareness may also be further distinguished from knowledge. For example, a respondent may be *aware* of AIDS as a medical condition and public health concern but may have very little actual *knowledge* about AIDS, such as how it is contracted, its symptoms, or treatments.

Although composing questions that ask about respondents' thoughts may seem easy on the surface, there is much to understand about how people form attitudes, how they articulate them with regard to answering questions about them, and the degree to which they can be influenced by question wording and construction. Attitudes can be fleeting and transient and change over time, or be deeply held and enduring. Though quite common, questions about respondents' thoughts may be the most challenging of all to compose. Chapter 3 includes information about respondent ability and willingness to answer questions that is critically important to consider during the process of drafting and testing survey questions about thoughts.

Schaeffer and Dykema (2011) offer an excellent roundup of question types along with relevant examples. They claim that a list or "compendium" of question types and response dimensions would include the following:

- Questions about events and behaviors (that is, questions that ask about target objects that occur in time, whether the event is external or internal, performed by the respondent or occurring in the respondent's environment)

- Evaluations or judgments (absolute or comparative) about objects (such questions are often used to measure "attitudes," which we consider a theoretical construction rather than a type of question)

FIGURE 2.4 ● Questions That Measure Thoughts

In general, how would you rate your experience?

    ○ Excellent

    ○ Very good

    ○ Good

    ○ Fair

    ○ Poor

I feel supported by my direct supervisor.

    ○ Strongly agree

    ○ Agree

    ○ Neither agree nor disagree

    ○ Disagree

    ○ Strongly disagree

- Internal states or feelings (such as worry or happiness)

- Accounts (such as reasons for leaving a job)

- Classifications (such as whether one has a defined benefit retirement plan)

- Other social characteristics (such as age and marital status)

- Descriptions of the environment (such as how many FTEs are employed at the place you work)

Many classification questions and social characteristic questions are associated with underlying events or behaviors (e.g., one signed up for the retirement plan, got married, gave birth, etc.). (pp. 924–25)

These authors' list of question types align well with our categories of attributes, behaviors, and thoughts.

What Are the Advantages and Limitations of Surveys?

Surveys are the most common data collection tool for good reason. Surveys can be used to collect large amounts of very specific information from large pools of respondents with a relatively small investment of time, fiscal, and other resources as compared to other data collection strategies. However, surveys cannot capture all possible types of data, in all scenarios, from all people. So, how do we know when a survey is the right tool for a given research effort? We must first understand what surveys can measure (as we have just done) and then consider the general advantages of using a survey, know and understand their limitations, and determine if a survey is indeed the *best* tool for our data collection needs.

Advantages

There are many reasons to consider surveys; here are six that particularly resonate with us. Surveys can do the following:

- Capture needed information with relatively limited resources

- Capture a large dataset formatted for ease of analysis

- Be used to generalize about a larger population from a smaller sample of respondents

- Be used to compare responses between subgroups (e.g., different income levels, genders)

- Be used to collect data across multiple sites or over time to aggregate or compare information

- Be administered in multiple modes

Surveys can capture needed information with relatively limited resources. Surveys typically require less time and other costs than needed to conduct multiple interviews, observations, or focus groups. Especially with an online survey, the main administration cost is for a subscription to the survey tool. There is no need to pay for postage as would be needed for a postal mail survey, or rent a space or pay additional research staff as might be needed for an in-person survey. Surveys also have the potential to gather data from hundreds, thousands, or even tens of thousands of people simultaneously. However, additional survey costs may include hiring a statistician, if the researcher does not have the capability to perform necessary analyses.

Surveys can capture a large dataset formatted for ease of analysis. Surveys typically generate standardized data amenable to quantification and relatively easy to analyze. This is especially true when using an online survey tool (e.g., SurveyMonkey or SurveyGizmo), which eliminates the need for data entry as well as some preliminary analysis because basic calculations such as response frequencies are often automatically generated. Most online survey tools also allow for easy export of responses into spreadsheets.

Surveys can be used to generalize about a larger population from a smaller sample of respondents. A survey with a high-quality sample of a given population (i.e., one that is adequately large and representative of the population being studied) can be used to generalize information about a whole population. Many public health surveys are good examples of surveys using a targeted, representative sample of respondents to monitor the health status of whole populations. For example, the National Health Interview Survey (NHIS) collects data on a broad range of health-related topics from a large sample of U.S. households. Another example, the American Community Survey (ACS), which regularly gathers more detailed information than its cousin, the U.S. Census, is a longer survey sent to a sampled population (rather than the *entire* population as with the U.S. Census). See https://www.cdc.gov/nchs/nhis/index.htm for more information on the NHIS, and https://www.census.gov/programs-surveys/acs for more information on the ACS.

Surveys can be used to compare responses between subgroups (e.g., different income levels, genders). With adequate sampling and demographic information, it is also possible to understand whether respondents from different populations or with different attributes answer questions differently. In fact, this is one of the most common ways in which survey data are analyzed.

Surveys can be used to collect data across multiple sites or over time to aggregate or compare information. Because of their typically rigid design (e.g., not allowing for probes or follow-up questions as might happen during less structured interviews), surveys can also easily be repeated across time or locations. This means that results can also be compared across locations, populations, or points in time, so long as surveys are conducted consistently and adequate information about the context of each survey administration (e.g., when collected or about what location/population) is captured.

Surveys can be administered in multiple modes. Surveys can be administered in person, over the phone, through the mail, online, or even through a combination of administration modes. With a sharp decline in survey response rates in recent years, many researchers have shifted their thinking about survey administration modes to focus on what mode(s) might reach the most respondents (i.e., what the population would most likely have access and respond to) versus the researcher's preference. This thinking is, of course, in line with a respondent-centered approach to the survey design process.

It is important to note that a high-quality survey designed with well-crafted questions, appropriate and sufficient sampling procedures, and effective administration methods is required for these advantages to come to fruition for any given survey effort.

Limitations

Research typically aims to capture factual, objective information. Thus, it is important to consider whether survey respondents are able to be accurate and honest in their responses. This has implications for what can be captured via a survey, especially given that researchers often have little or no ability to clarify or confirm the information gathered, because many surveys do not ask for identifying information (e.g., respondent names) that would allow for such follow-up. There are types of information that surveys are not well designed to measure and a number of circumstances in which a survey is not the best choice. For example, surveys may not be the best option under the following circumstances:

- When exacting information about a target population's behavior or abilities is needed

- When a substantial amount of qualitative data is needed

- When respondents' nonverbal cues (e.g., facial expressions or body language) are important

- When data are needed from populations not able to respond to a survey

Exacting information about a target population's behavior or abilities is needed. It is important to note that although surveys are often used to measure behavior, they cannot *directly* measure behavior. Questions such as "How many times per week do you consume alcohol?" "How often do you exercise?" or "How well can you ballroom dance?" are examples of questions that actually measure thoughts (i.e., respondents' perception, including memory of how often or how well they do these things), not the behaviors themselves. Direct measurement of behavior requires observation, or a test of performance that allows a subject (respondent) to demonstrate a given behavior while an observer is present.

It is also much trickier for respondents to report on the behavior of others. After all,

> Our own behaviors provide a rich set of experiences, including information about what we wanted to do, what we actually did, and how we felt while doing it as well as information on where the event took place and who else was present. (Sudman et al., 1996, p. 203)

Asking respondents about others is generally ill-advised because we are often not in a position to accurately assess and report others' behaviors. The problem emerges because "when asked about the behavior of others, [respondents] may draw on their impression of 'what kind of person' the other is, basing the estimate on an implicit theory of personality" (Schwarz & Oyserman, 2001, p. 142).

Reports about others' behaviors, often referred to as proxy reports, may be sought because the target person is not available for an interview or because the researcher wants to validate a respondent's reports against the perceptions of a familiar other, often another household member. Researchers sometimes assume that these proxy reports are more accurate than self-reports. However, controlled experimental studies provide little support for this conclusion. . . . In many cases, respondents may not be fully aware of the others' behavior. Moreover, others' behaviors are even more poorly represented in memory, unless they were extreme and memorable (Schwarz &Oyserman, 2001, p. 144).

A substantial amount of qualitative data is needed. If the researcher needs to capture information that is highly **qualitative** in nature—that which cannot be easily boiled down to specific response options, as would be found in closed-ended questions—a more qualitative method for collecting data such as interviews, focus groups, or a less traditional method may be called for. Interviews and focus groups allow the researcher to take the conversation where it naturally goes and respond to participants' initial answers with probes and subquestions that elicit richer, more detailed responses. Although some probes or subquestions can be designed into surveys with the use of **skip logic**, filtering questions, or conditional **branching** (whereby the particular response to a single question directs the respondent to move to a different or additional set of questions), these are preselected based on a specific set of response options offered versus in the moment as the interviewer or focus group moderator hears a response and chooses to follow up and elicit more data.

Another consideration, especially for self-administered surveys whether on paper or online, is that respondents are often not willing (or able) to provide lengthy or detailed written answers in response to multiple open-ended questions. This happens for a variety of reasons, not the least of which is both the time it takes to organize one's thoughts and to articulate them coherently in writing, along with the willingness to expose one's writing ability to researchers. A more detailed discussion of using open-ended questions in surveys can be found in Chapter 4.

Respondents' nonverbal cues (e.g., facial expressions or body language) are important. When the research question entails understanding *how* people experience attributes, situations, or programs (e.g., winning the lottery, having depression, fighting cancer, being in a drug rehabilitation program), it may be helpful or even necessary to capture facial expressions, tone of voice, laughter, sighing, or crying along with body language such as gesturing and shifting. In these cases, in-person interviews or video-based methods will be necessary. Although it may be possible to capture notes about nonverbal cues as respondents work through questions during a survey administered in person, it is typically best to design a more qualitative method to allow for integrated capture of this key information along with responses to whatever questions the researcher is posing.

Data are needed from populations not able to respond to a survey. Consulting existing literature about the specific target population will be critical in determining the most appropriate methods for capturing information from or with these populations. Special considerations are often necessary when studying children or other vulnerable populations, and surveys are not typically best in these scenarios because they are difficult to adapt for populations with specialized needs. Although there is no hard and fast rule about the exact age at which children can be successfully surveyed, some researchers (see, for example, Borgers, de Leeuw, and Hox [2000]) suggest that children under 4 years of age not be surveyed at all. It is important to note that anytime a researcher intends to use a survey with children, extensive cognitive pretesting of both questions and instructions is absolutely necessary. Borgers et al. (2000) offer a brief literature review and specific suggestions for surveying children ages 4 to 16. The following story tells of a time a researcher attempted to collect data for a program evaluation through a survey of young children and the lessons learned in doing so.

One final consideration when determining whether a survey is appropriate is whether the research effort requires asking particularly sensitive questions. In these cases, it is important to consider whether respondents are both likely to and able to answer honestly. It may be best to use a more qualitative approach (e.g., interviews) that allow for greater rapport building and the use of probing questions. We discuss sensitive questions in greater detail in Chapter 6.

STORIES FROM THE FIELD
LESSONS LEARNED FROM SURVEYING YOUNG CHILDREN

As a graduate student earning a certificate in program evaluation along with my doctoral degree, I had the experience of conducting an exploratory evaluation of a zoo expedition program that targeted children in Grades 1–3 (roughly ages 6–8). Along with the program designers and a few literacy experts, I designed student surveys after benchmarking surveys for Grades K–3 audiences used at other institutions. Surveys were designed to assess students' understanding of key concepts before and after visiting the expedition exhibit.

We conducted a small pilot of these student surveys to see if they could easily be understood by students. The pilot helped us realize the importance of always reading the questions aloud to the children word for word. The zoo staff member who initially read assessments aloud paraphrased the questions while reading, which led to misconceptions among students. Moving forward, the survey was treated as a script so that all staff members reading the questions would not run into this problem. Students in Grade 1 classes that participated in the pilot did appear to understand all questions, so we moved forward with this part of the study.

We learned a number of important lessons once we moved forward with the evaluation. We observed that students were very social during the pretest survey and were often sharing answers. On a question that asked children to circle all answers that applied to them, they would keep circling responses in order to have more than their friends, and then they would share out loud how many of these they circled. This affected the amount of growth we were hoping to measure with the posttest survey. A small percentage of children also reported a loss of knowledge on the posttest survey, which would indicate errors in understanding the survey questions. Others may have selected the "best" answer (or most answers, depending on the question) because they wanted us to see growth in their learning.

Although the results from this exploratory evaluation certainly began to answer our key questions, the biggest takeaway will be how to better collect data in the future, especially from young children, for this expedition program.

—Peter Kalenda

Discussion Questions

- Why is it valuable to develop a purpose statement for a given survey?

- How is a survey different from other data collection tools? How can researchers be sure that a survey is the best option for a given data collection need?

- What might be advantages and limitations of surveys that are not discussed in this text?

- What are some potentially sensitive questions or topics that might not be obvious to survey researchers?

 Design Drills

1. Research Scenario, Part 2 (additional parts are found in other chapters): You are tasked with capturing information that will help assess the effectiveness of a new and ongoing program to support low-income senior citizens. The program is based at public libraries in several small towns and cities across a large region. Your research team has determined that asking participating senior citizens about their behaviors and thoughts related to the program will provide important data for the project. Is a survey appropriate? Explain your answer. If unsure, what additional information would help you make that determination? What other data collection methods might you consider, and how would you determine whether those are more appropriate than a survey?

2. Your survey: Draft as detailed a purpose statement as possible for your ongoing or anticipated survey project, being sure to connect it to any broader research questions.

3. Your survey: Identify 1–3 constructs you anticipate needing to measure given your research question(s) and survey purpose. Identify potential strong and weak indicators for each.

4. Create your own research scenarios, one for which a survey would be appropriate, and one for which a survey would not be the best tool. Write research questions for each scenario. Exchange scenarios with a colleague or classmate and see if you are in agreement with each other about the use of surveys for each scenario.

 Extended Learning

For an extended example of operationalizing constructs to inform survey question design:

- Johnson, R. L., & Morgan, G. B. (2016). *Survey scales: A guide to development, analysis, and reporting.* New York: Guilford Press.

For more on surveying young children:

- This article contains a literature review and secondary analysis on surveying children:
    - Borgers, N., de Leeuw, E., & Hox, J. (2000). Children as respondents in survey research: Cognitive development and response quality. *Bulletin de Méthodologie Sociologique, 66,* 60–75.

- This article describes the development of a survey instrument for adolescents ages 11–18:
    - Arthur, M. W., Hawkins, J. D., Pollard, J., Catalano, R. F., & Baglioni, A. J., Jr. (2002). Measuring risk and protective factors for substance use, delinquency, and other adolescent problem behaviors: The communities that care youth survey. *Evaluation Review, 26*(6), 575–601. doi:10.1177/019384102237850

- This article describes a survey for children ages 5–10:
    - Foster, T., & Maillardet, V. (2010). Surveying young patients. *Emergency Medicine Journal, 27*(3), 221–223. doi:10.1136/emj.2008.065615

Recommended texts and blogs for interviews and focus groups:

- Focus groups:
    - Krueger, R. A., & Casey, M. A. (2014). *Focus groups: A practical guide for applied research* (5th ed.). Los Angeles: Sage.
    - Morgan, D. L. (1996). *Focus groups as qualitative research* (2nd ed.). Newbury Park, CA: Sage.
    - Roller, M. R., Lavrakas, P. J., & ProQuest (Firm). (2015). *Applied qualitative research design: A total quality framework approach.* New York: Guilford.

- Interviews:
    - Brinkmann, S., & Kvale, S. (2014) *InterViews: Learning the craft of qualitative research interviewing* (3rd ed.). Thousand Oaks, CA: Sage.
    - Seidman, I. (2013). *Interviewing as qualitative research: A guide for researchers in education and the social sciences* (4th ed.). New York: Teachers College Press.
    - Spradley, J. P. (2016). *The ethnographic interview* (Reissue ed.). Long Grove, IL: Waveland Press.

- Both focus groups and interviews:
    - *Research design review: A discussion of qualitative and quantitative research design issues*; blog by M. Roller: https://researchdesignreview.com

Understanding Respondents

I am not what you see.

I am what time and effort and interaction slowly unveil.

—Richelle E. Goodrich, American poet and author

All too often, survey researchers begin the process of developing questions by essentially asking themselves, *What do I need to know from respondents?* After all, the research questions that drive the need for a survey were likely developed by the researchers themselves, whether alone or in concert with fellow researchers. In contrast, through a respondent-centered design, we approach the process of survey design by asking, "What might respondents want to tell us? What questions might they be able and willing to answer that would help answer the research or evaluation question(s)?"

Composing high-quality survey questions first requires that researchers consider what it takes from respondents to answer those questions, the cognitive processes involved, as well as factors related to respondent willingness and ability to answer questions and the context or cultural factors that may influence the respondent. This is part of the empathy phase of the design thinking process introduced in Chapter 1. As Tim Brown (2009), president and CEO of the global design company IDEO, reminds us, "Empathy is the mental habit that moves us beyond thinking of people as laboratory rats or standard deviations" (p. 49).

Cognitive Tasks Involved in Answering Questions

In Chapter 1, we introduced the Cognitive Aspects of Survey Methodology (CASM) movement, the intersection of cognitive psychology and survey research focused on the mental work that survey respondents must do to answer questions. CASM researchers explored ways in which respondents are influenced by various aspects of the survey administration process and paid particular attention to how the questions themselves influence responses. In this chapter, we delve into how our respondents understand, process, and answer survey questions. This includes discussion of the **cognitive load**, or total amount of mental effort it takes for respondents to read, make sense of, and answer questions, along with the profound role that human memory plays in answering questions.

Tourangeau, Rips, and Rasinski (2000) devote an entire text to the study of *how* respondents answer survey questions, probably the most comprehensive work to date on this particular aspect of survey research. *The Psychology of Survey Response* is organized around four major components of a survey response process:

- Comprehension

- Retrieval

- Judgement

- Response (p. 8)

Problems with any of these components can result in survey error; hence it is critical that survey researchers are familiar with what each component entails. **Measurement error**, the difference between what we are able to measure with surveys and the actual or true values, is particularly likely to result from poorly designed questions.

Comprehension

Respondents must use mental processes to read and understand a question (along with any relevant instructions), inferring the main idea of the question and identifying what the researcher is looking for regarding a response. Problems with comprehension arise when respondents 1) do not notice, do not read, or misinterpret instructions; 2) encounter unfamiliar vocabulary in a question stem or response options; 3) interpret words or phrases differently than the way the researcher intended; or 4) find a question worded in an overly complex or detailed way. Each of these conditions can interfere with respondents' ability to answer a question accurately.

Retrieval

Retrieval "requires recalling relevant information from long-term memory. This component encompasses such processes as adopting a retrieval strategy, generating specific **retrieval cues** to trigger recall, recollecting individual memories, and filling in partial memories through inference" (Tourangeau et al., 2000, p. 9). A retrieval strategy might be the particular way in which we attempt to remember something. For example, if you were asked to think of as many animals as you can, you might think in terms of classification. Perhaps you might start by naming mammals, then reptiles, and then birds. Or you might think about the alphabet and name as many animals as you can that start with the letter *A*, then *B*, and then *C*. Retrieval cues stimulate memory. Our school teachers likely took advantage of this phenomenon when teaching us to remember such information as the names of the Great Lakes by using the acronym HOMES to help us recall Lake Huron, Lake Ontario, Lake Michigan, Lake Erie, and Lake Superior.

The interplay between survey questions and respondents' memories is what affects retrieval. This can be:

- the way in which a survey question is worded and the way in which the memories are encoded (e.g., the question asks about "trash pickup" and the survey respondent calls it "garbage collection"),

- the degree to which the question provides retrieval cues (e.g., think about trips to the grocery store you most often visit) and the quality of those cues, and

- the passage of time since the event in question and the survey.

"Retrieval refers to the process of bringing information help in long-term storage to an active state, in which it can be used" (Tourangeau et al., 2000, p. 77). We continue a discussion of retrieval cues and their use in survey questions in Chapter 5.

Judgement

Tourangeau et al. (2000) divide *judgement* into three distinct types: judgement for factual questions, judgement about dates and durations, and judgement about frequencies. When respondents answer factual questions, they must determine how accurate their retrieval is before rendering a judgment and constructing or selecting a response (given an open- or closed-ended question). They must determine whether their retrieval was complete or whether it needs to be supplemented by inferences. In addition, people have particular difficulty remembering exact dates and frequencies of relatively mundane events. For example, if a survey question asks, "How many times in the last 12 months did you visit a doctor's office?" a respondent might experience something like the following thought process that demonstrates the interplay between retrieval and judgement and how inference becomes part of the equation:

I remember going to the doctor in late winter when I first had the problem and then again sometime during the summer when it appeared again. I think I had two appointments then, maybe a couple of weeks apart? Yes, I remember having to ask for extra time off work for those, especially for the one when I had x-rays. That took a few hours. I didn't actually see the doctor that day, though. Does that one count? Oh wait, a few weeks after the x-rays, I saw the doctor for results and to change medications, so that's three appointments in summer. Now, have I remembered them all? Hmmm . . . I probably had a follow-up appointment sometime in the fall after those summer appointments. Yes, that's probably it. I don't remember exactly when, but my doctor usually asks for a follow-up visit after I've seen her for a problem, so I probably did have at least one more appointment. Oh! I just remembered! I did call the office once, right before the holidays, I think, when the problem flared up again. I didn't actually go in that time, but the doctor called me back and we talked on the phone. I wonder if that counts as a "visit." It probably does. I mean, what's the difference? They probably want to know how many times I've talked with a doctor about a medical problem and a phone call should count, right? I think it does . . .

Judgement is closely related to and in fact dependent on retrieval.

Response

Response requires selecting and reporting an answer to a survey question. Responding to a survey question involves groups of processes around "mapping" the answer to available response options (as with a multiple-choice type question) and "editing" the answer to meet certain criteria. Response can be particularly complicated. It's not quite as simple as a respondent thinking, *I think I visited the doctor 6 times in the last year. Let me see where "6" is in these options.* Many things can potentially go wrong in the response process, especially if the question itself is problematic. Perhaps, as in the previous example of a respondent's thought process, it is not clear as to what "counts" as a visit to a doctor's office. Perhaps the response options contain overlapping frequencies, such as 0 visits, 1–3 visits, 3–6 visits, 6–9 visits.

Other problems occur as the respondent "edits" the answer in the context of the response options. When the options presented (in this case, a "frequency scale") include relatively low frequencies (e.g., 0 visits, 1–2 visits, 3–4 visits, 5 or more visits) or relatively high frequencies (e.g., 0 visits, 1–4 visits, 5–8 visits, 9 or more visits), it may cause respondents to rethink their judgements in the context of what is offered and decide to respond differently. For the low-frequency response scale, a respondent's thought process might go something like this:

> *Hmmm, I think I visited the doctor 6 times in the last year. Wait, 5 or more visits is the top answer here? They must be looking for people who are really sick. I'm not that sick. I'm probably more in the middle. Maybe I won't count the x-ray visit and the phone call. That would make 4 actual visits. That's in the middle of their scale. Yeah, that's probably where I would fall.*

For the high-frequency scale, this same respondent might indeed count the x-ray visit and the phone call because the estimate of 6 visits falls in the middle of the response options. Part of the reason for this is that respondents use the options provided to infer what the researcher is looking for. Humans tend to compare themselves to others, and the options provided may signal to respondents that these are actual frequencies for typical or "average" people. If they feel "average," they may indeed select response options in or near the middle of the scale to reflect this, even if those options do not match the estimates of occurrences of the behavior derived before considering the options offered.

Respondents' efforts to comprehend survey questions, retrieve information, render judgments, and choose responses do not necessarily happen in a sequential or independent manner. Instead, these cognitive processes operate simultaneously and overlap one another. The processes of retrieval and even judgement, for example, likely begin *before* respondents have finished reading and comprehending a question. As we look to explore the complexities and considerations around composing response options as part of the survey design process, what comprehension, retrieval, judgement, and response bring to bear on the question answering process will emerge.

Schwarz and Oyserman (2001) outline key lessons learned about self-reports of behavior from numerous studies that emerged from the CASM movement in the 1980s and 1990s. Although some of these lessons are specific to questions about behavior, they can also be applied to other types of questions and, at the very least, make us more aware of respondents' experiences when they are asked questions. In the list that follows, the four components outlined earlier—comprehension, retrieval, judgement, and response—are reflected along with additional details about what may actually happen in the minds of survey respondents. Schwarz and Oyserman (2001) introduce the question-answering process by sharing researchers' expectations when respondents read our questions.

> [We] . . . implicitly hope that participants will (1) understand the question, (2) identify the behavior of interest, and (3) retrieve relevant instances of the behavior from memory. When the question inquires about the actual frequency of the behavior, researchers further hope that participants (4) correctly identify the relevant reference period (e.g., "last month"), (5) search this reference period to retrieve all relevant instances of the behavior, (6) correctly date the recalled instances to determine whether they fall within the reference period, and (7) correctly add up all instances of the behavior to arrive at a frequency report. Once participants have determined the frequency of their behavior, they are (8) often required to map this frequency onto the response alternatives provided by the researcher. Finally, participants are expected to (9) candidly provide the result of their recall effort to the interviewer. Implicit in these—rarely articulated—hopes is the assumption that people *know* what they do and *can* report on their behavior with candor . . . and accuracy. (p. 129)

Just reading this list of expectations seems exhausting; imagine how our respondents might feel when we ask them a litany of questions in a survey! Furthermore, imagine if those questions are difficult to understand or have ambiguous language, if the response options we provide do not match their experiences, or if our questions otherwise make it challenging for them to answer accurately. Consider the mental energy it might take to answer a poorly written and constructed question, such as the one in Figure 3.1.

The bad news, according to Schwarz and Oyserman (2001), is that "cognitive research suggests that respondents are rarely able to live up to the researchers' hopes" (p. 129). Poorly constructed questions account for just some of the conditions that cause respondents to be less engaged in surveys, less willing to devote time and attention to comprehending and answering questions well, and less willing to persist and complete surveys.

Although many of the previous steps were intended by Schwarz and Oyserman to apply specifically to particular types of questions—those about behavior that include a **reference period** (e.g., in the last month, over the last year, in a typical week) and multiple-choice response options that are usually frequencies

Chris Lysy, Fresh Spectrum

(see Figure 3.2)—a similar set of steps can be envisioned for other types of questions. When asked about attitudes, for example, respondents must still use elements of memory and judgement to arrive at an answer (see Figure 3.3). They must search their minds and memories for impressions of what is being asked, and they may rely on stereotypes, general attitudes or feelings about the topic, and their own specific beliefs and experiences.

FIGURE 3.1   ●   Example of a Poorly Worded Question

Do you believe that it is possible or impossible that astronomers may someday discover life forms other than those that exist on Earth on other planets either within or outside of our solar system, or perhaps even our galaxy?

- O I believe it is possible.
- O I believe it is impossible.
- O I am unsure of whether I believe it is possible or impossible.

One possible alternative: Break this question into separate questions (depending on purpose of the question and what it is supposed to measure)

Do you believe astronomers may someday discover life forms on other planets?

- O YES
- O NO

If you answered YES, where do you believe these life forms may be found?

	YES	NO
On other planets inside our solar system?	O	O
On other planets outside our solar system?	O	O
On other planets outside our galaxy?	O	O

FIGURE 3.2   ●   A Question About Behavior

Over the last 6 months, about how many times did you purchase food (either dine-in or take-out) from what would be considered a "fast-food" restaurant (e.g., McDonald's, Burger King, Wendy's)?

- O 1 to 3 times
- O 4 to 6 times
- O 7 to 9 times
- O 10 or more times
- O I did not purchase food from a fast-food restaurant during this period.

FIGURE 3.3 ● A Question About an Attitude or Opinion

Should elementary students be able to use personal cell phones in school? Why or why not?

Respondent Willingness and Ability to Participate in a Survey

It is vital for researchers to understand respondents' willingness and ability to participate in a survey *before* crafting our questions. Respondent willingness and ability to respond to a survey is influenced by a number of factors, including the nature of the question.

Factors Related to Willingness

Respondents must be willing to answer questions accurately. Bradburn, Sudman, and Wansick (2004) give us excellent insight into the issue of willingness as they view the survey process as a conversation between researcher and respondent in which the two are strangers.

> Unlike witnesses in court, survey respondents are under no compulsion to answer questions. They must be persuaded to participate in the [survey], and their interest (or at least patience) must be maintained throughout. If questions are demeaning, embarrassing, or upsetting, respondents may terminate the interview or falsify their answers. Unlike the job applicant or the patient answering a doctor's questions, respondents have nothing tangible to gain. . . . Their only reward is some measure of psychic gratification—such as the opportunity to state their opinions or relate their experiences . . . , the chance to contribute to public or scientific knowledge, or even the positive feeling that they have helped the [researcher]. The willingness of the public to participate in surveys has been declining in recent years for many reasons, one of which is the tremendous number of poor and misleading surveys that are conducted. It is therefore doubly important for the survey researcher to make sure that the questionnaire is of the highest quality. (pp. 8–9)

Generally speaking, respondents will be most willing to answer well-composed questions that offer appropriate response options (i.e., options that align well with the question stem), thus making the question easy to answer. The type of question and nature of the question may also influence respondent willingness to answer survey questions.

Question types. Respondents may be more or less willing to respond to particular questions types. For example, some respondents may be reluctant to respond to open-ended questions, those that do not provide specific response options but rather ask respondents to write a sentence (or more) in response to a question. Some people enjoy writing detailed answers to questions because they like to reflect on their experiences or perspectives, they appreciate the researcher's interest in their opinions and want to share, or they have a desire to help the researcher understand the phenomenon of interest. However, many survey respondents prefer to be able to easily locate the response option that best fits their perspective (i.e., in a closed-ended question such as multiple choice), mark their answer, and move on quickly. Chapter 4 features a thorough review and discussion of question types and specific advice for composing open-ended survey items.

DESIGN DETAILS
QUESTIONS OR ITEMS?

Survey questions are also commonly referred to as "items." Some researchers prefer the term *item* because not all survey questions appear in the form of a question. Some "questions" are actually statements to which a respondent is expected to react by choosing among a set of response options (for example, those all-too-familiar "agree-disagree" scales). We tend to use *question* more often in this text but consider the terms interchangeable.

Nature of the question. Questions of a sensitive nature will also impact respondent willingness and motivation to answer. There are few universal rules about what constitutes sensitive or threatening questions; this is highly culture and context dependent and will continue to evolve over time. For some respondents, questions about income may feel sensitive or threatening, whereas other respondents may be perfectly comfortable being forthcoming with this type of information. Some may willingly offer their opinions on such topics as gun control, the death penalty, or reproductive rights, whereas others consider these too deeply personal to address in a survey. For some, asking about attitudes toward company management or organizational programs or policies may feel threatening (especially if the survey originates from inside the organization), whereas others will readily and honestly answer these questions. It is perfectly acceptable to ask a question about age in some cultures, whereas in others it would be considered a taboo topic. Some would be willing to offer their exact age, whereas others will only be willing to reveal this by choosing a 5- or 10-year interval from a number of response options.

Questions of a sensitive or threatening nature often result in nonresponse. If given the opportunity to skip a sensitive or threatening question, many respondents will do just that. Especially in online surveys, respondents are faced with certain choices, depending on how a sensitive or threatening question is presented. Of course, whether or not a question requires an answer for the survey to proceed, a respondent must choose whether to comply and provide an answer (be it an accurate or inaccurate one) or to skip the question altogether. If the question includes a "prefer not to answer" or some variant of that option, common sense tells us that a respondent may be more likely to continue the survey. If a sensitive question is required with no "prefer not to answer" response option and respondents *cannot* continue the survey without providing an answer, they may refuse to answer, thus ending the survey and denying the researcher access to the remainder of the respondent's information and a completed survey. Or respondents may edit their answer in such a way as to make themselves "look good" to the researcher behind the survey (or to the in-person or telephone interviewer in those administration modes), thus providing inaccurate and lower-quality data and contributing to survey error. This phenomenon of editing answers to survey questions is called **social desirability bias** and is described in greater detail in Chapter 6.

For the purpose of question design, a researcher must make key decisions about the nature of each survey item. Will the item potentially be considered sensitive or threatening to some or even all respondents? How necessary is an accurate answer to this item for the research study? For example, in market research, companies can learn a tremendous amount about their customer bases through surveys. Respondents may be willing and able to provide detailed perspectives on their purchase habits, shopping experiences, product opinions, and more, *even* when they refuse to answer questions about personal income.

Factors Related to Ability

As we saw earlier, answering survey questions is a much more complex task than most researchers have considered. It behooves us to invest sufficient time and effort into learning about and understanding what happens in the minds of respondents as they participate in surveys, and take this into deep consideration as we undertake a survey design process. Researchers from the CASM movement brought significant attention to the interrelated cognitive tasks survey respondents must complete in order to effectively answer questions. Schwarz (2007) describes respondent tasks in the context of **response effects**, variations in response that can be caused by the ways in which questions are posed to respondents.

> Respondents first need to interpret the question to understand what is meant and to determine which information they ought to provide. . . . Once a "private" judgment is formed in respondents' minds, they have to communicate it to the researcher. To do so, they may need to format their judgment to fit the response alternatives provided as part of the question. Moreover, respondents may wish to edit their response before they communicate it, due to influences of social desirability and situational adequacy. Performance of each of these tasks is highly context dependent and often profoundly shaped by the research instrument. The resulting contextual influences are usually referred to as "response effects" in the survey literature. (p. 278)

The comprehensibility of a question and respondent memory are two of the key factors related to respondent ability to accurately answer survey questions.

Memory. The fallibility and malleability of human memory has been tremendous fodder for brain researchers in recent decades. Researcher thinking about how memory works has changed over time as research methods and tools have matured and increased in sophistication. However, even Payne acknowledged the role of memory in survey research as early as 1951, decades before the CASM movement was underway in the 1980s. "The researcher can go astray by assuming that people are more aware of the commonplace than they actually are," he cautions (Payne, 1951, p. 29). A number of prominent CASM-era survey researchers (Norman Bradburn, Norbert

Schwarz, Seymour Sudman, and Roger Tourangeau, to name a few) have contributed significantly to the literature base and general understanding of key aspects of human memory and their implications for question construction.

The study of memory is also as important as ever in criminal law, due to the significant role it plays in legal proceedings. It is from this field in part that memory researchers now understand that *memories change* each time they are recalled and that recall is not accurately depicted by simplistic metaphors such as retrieving a file from a file drawer. What people are able to retrieve from memory is not, as once thought, an exact "copy" of an event that occurred with all relevant details in perfect order, no matter how vivid the memory may feel to the person. Simons and Chabris (2011) found that many Americans (63% of their survey sample in fact) believe that "human memory works like a video camera, accurately recording the events we see and hear so that we can review and inspect them later" whereas all 16 experts surveyed (professors with 10 or more years of memory research) disagreed (p. 5). To remember is in fact a much more complex proposition than most of us understand and is highly susceptible to the ravages of time and experience that substantially interfere with accuracy. Consider this recent explanation for the fallibility of human memory:

> What we remember is constructed from whatever remains in memory following any forgetting or interference from new experiences that may have occurred across the interval between storing and retrieving a particular experience . . . Because the contents of our memories for experiences involve the active manipulation (during encoding), integration with pre-existing information (during consolidation), and reconstruction (during retrieval) of that information, memory is, by definition, fallible at best and unreliable at worst.

> This fallibility of memory includes not only the omission of details from the original experience, but extends to errors of commission including the creation of *memory illusions*. (Howe & Knott, 2015, p. 634; emphasis in original)

This construction and reconstruction process leaves people with memories that are splintered, with specific details and experiences out of order, missing, and sometimes just plain false. It is important for us to understand that remembering is actually an act of *reconstruction*. People do not necessarily recall a memory directly or completely. Instead, they rebuild it through remembering key parts and filling in with inferences from general knowledge of the world and of themselves. They summarize and group bits and pieces and fill in where needed in order to feel as if the memory is consistent and "complete." Most of the time, they are not even aware of which parts of a given memory are "true" and which have been filled in with inferences. For example, as a respondent is attempting to reconstruct a memory, she might think,

I usually wear a sweater and khaki pants to a restaurant, so I was probably wearing a sweater and khaki pants the night we had a great meal at that new place downtown. Or, *I usually go to the gas station twice a week, so I probably went to the gas station eight times in the month of March.*

The passage of time is a well-known factor in memory deterioration. The more time that passes after an event, the more likely it is that people experience additional, similar events. These later events can and do interfere with the ability to retrieve details of the initial event. For example, an individual might visit a grocery store several times per month or even more often. Perhaps sometimes he purchases fresh produce, and other times he does not. It would likely be quite difficult for him to recall whether he purchased produce during the shopping trip he took six or seven weeks ago, because he would have shopped several additional times in the interim, and these similar events blur together. People tend to remember the *patterns* of such events as grocery store visits (e.g., starting at one end of the store and working through the aisles, or always picking up perishable items last) rather than individual visits and the ways in which they differ.

Surveys commonly ask about respondents' behaviors and events in their lives, so it makes sense that much of what concerns survey researchers has to do with understanding how **autobiographical memory** works. Autobiographical memory is how people store and retrieve the events, people, and places in their lives, as well as general knowledge of the world. Memory tends to be episodic in nature, meaning that people associate memories with certain time periods in their lives, such as when they were in high school, lived in New York, or worked at the hardware store, as opposed to memories being stored by years. Of course, a person may well remember that she lived in New York from 1992 to 1997 but may not remember as easily exactly which summer it was that she took that cruise in the Caribbean. As mentioned earlier, the passage of time affects memories as well. People can remember specific events and people from high school when they are recent graduates, but less so if they have just attended their 30th or 40th reunion. Emotions play a large role in memory retrieval as well. Events associated with strong emotions are more easily retrieved than others. The memory of a childhood surgery or broken bone is more easily retrieved than the memory of having a common cold during the same time frame. Memories associated with very strong emotions (e.g., graduations, weddings, births, deaths, job changes) tend to remain longer and in greater detail.

The greater the role that memory plays in answering a survey question, the less accurate respondents' answers are likely to be. Therefore, it will always be difficult for us to know just how accurate respondents' answers are. That said, in the absence of direct observation, survey researchers must rely on human memory as prime material for our datasets. When it comes to memory, Payne (1951) cautions, "the point to keep in mind here is that recall may differ from fact, and therefore should not be taken as fact" (p. 29). Fortunately, we do have strategies for question design that help respondents answer as accurately as they are able.

Comprehensibility. When questions are easy to understand and answer, respondents are better able to provide accurate answers. "If questions are difficult to understand (because of their linguistic complexity, for instance), respondents may not be willing or able to invest the additional effort required to overcome these difficulties, and thus may not provide meaningful answers" (Lenzner, 2012, p. 2). Consider the somewhat linguistically complex question in Figure 3.4, from a subscription service. We can surmise that the survey designer wanted to use as few words as possible, in hopes that

---

FIGURE 3.4 ● Real-World Questions: *Problem With Comprehensibility*

What is the most important factor to you when customizing your monthly box by choosing a sample or featured box?

One possible alternative: Chunk information for better comprehensibility

Each month you have the option of customizing your monthly box by either choosing one sample or choosing the featured box. What is the most important factor to you when customizing your monthly box?

---

a question shorter in length would be more comprehensible to respondents. However, this is not successful. Using more words to chunk the information can often increase comprehensibility, as can be seen in the suggested alternative.

Using complex and difficult to comprehend questions can lead to respondents providing nonsubstantive or "**satisficing**" answers, responses that satisfy the requirements of the question but do not help us understand the phenomenon of interest. Satisficing is when respondents give us minimally acceptable answers, rather than optimal ones that more accurately depict their thoughts or behaviors. Krosnick (2000) describes this phenomenon as when "some respondents do just enough to satisfy the survey request, but no more" (p. 4).

> Satisficing response strategies include saying "don't know" instead of reporting an opinion, selecting the first answer option that seems reasonable, or selecting the midpoint response option. All of these strategies are problematic in surveys, as they increase measurement error and produce lower-quality data. (Lenzner, 2012, p. 4)

Hence, "designing questions to minimize the cognitive effort required to process them is an important strategy for reducing comprehension difficulties and thus response error" (Lenzner, 2012, p. 3). We cannot overstate the importance of comprehensibility in survey design but also recognize its inherent challenges in the survey design process. As Czaja and Blair (2005) forewarn, "Ambiguity is the ghost most difficult to exorcise from survey questions" (p. 83). As a concept, comprehensibility crosscuts a number of other topics; hence, we continue to flesh it out in greater detail in both a later section of this chapter on cognitive tasks respondents undertake to answer questions and again in Chapter 4 on question design.

> *Ambiguity is the ghost most difficult to exorcise from survey questions.*
>
> *—Czaja & Blair*

In doing research for this text, we discovered a potentially useful online tool for assessing the comprehensibility of survey questions. The QUAID (Question Understanding Aid) tool developed by the Institute for Intelligent Systems at the University of Memphis (available at http://quaid.cohmetrix.com) helps researchers improve the wording and sentence structure of survey questions by offering specific feedback on questions entered on the site. We took the question from Figure 3.1 and entered

FIGURE 3.5 ● QUAID Tool Feedback

QUAID Tool

How To Use The Tool

Unfamiliar Technical

Term

Vague or Imprecise

Relative Term

Vague or Ambiguous

Noun-phrase

Complex Syntax

Working Memory

Overload

Home

Question:

Do you believe that it is possible or impossible that astronomers may someday discover life forms other than those that exist on Earth on

Context:

Answer:

Enter answer here...

Submit

1. Unfamiliar technical terms: astronomers, someday, planets, solar, galaxy
The following term may be unfamiliar to some respondents: astronomers, someday, planets, solar, galaxy, in sentence 1 in the Question.

2. Working Memory Overload
Sentence 1 in the Question imposes a heavy load on the working memory of the respondent: (3 ors).

Source: University of Memphis Institute for Intelligent Systems, n.d.

it into the QUAID tool (see Figure 3.5) and received the feedback that some of the words—*astronomers, someday, planets, solar,* and *galaxy*—might not be familiar to some respondents and that the presence of three "ors" in the question may tax their working memory. This feedback at the very least gives us a place to start when we want to consider redesigning some first-draft survey questions. However, this tool should not be considered a substitute for the valuable insights that can be gained through human feedback from peers, topic experts, or most importantly, potential respondents (see Chapter 7 on pretesting strategies)!

Language. The use of appropriate language is obviously and directly related to the comprehensibility of a survey question. In keeping with respondent-centered design, survey content should reflect the language of desired respondents as much as possible (rather than that of the researcher, where different). This means not only translating the survey into another language if that is needed (more on that shortly) but also diligently and carefully considering the actual words chosen for the survey and all survey materials (e.g., reminders), so that they reflect phrasing commonly used by desired respondents. Throughout this text we discuss reasons that word and wording choices must be carefully made; thinking about wording in the context of respondent culture is central to doing so. Engaging with those familiar with the language used by desired respondents, whether they are called informants, guides, or liaisons, is critical to ensuring that survey questions are worded appropriately, which is discussed further in Chapter 7. The following story comes from a blog about a large-scale survey that helped researchers understand a significant social problem through the eyes of respondents by shifting the language used in a set of questions.

STORIES FROM THE FIELD
USING RESPONDENTS' LANGUAGE HELPS RESEARCHERS UNDERSTAND AN AMERICAN CRISIS

In an article on the website FiveThirtyEight (best known for blog articles on polls and surveys) titled "How We Undercounted Evictions by Asking the Wrong Questions," author Andrew Flowers describes how eviction is a huge problem in America that disproportionately affects our poorest citizens but, until recently, was a poorly understood concept. There was a lack of good data to help researchers understand the phenomenon of housing instability that also contributes to other significant problems this vulnerable population faces. That changed with the Milwaukee Area Renters Study (MARS), which "may be the first rigorous, detailed look at eviction in a major city" (Flowers, 2016). In addition to other strategies, such as careful training of interviewers, targeted to access the hardest-to-reach respondents, the survey designers changed the way in which they asked the questions, in order to better align with respondents' conception of the key indicator being measured—eviction. Although the question "Have you ever been evicted?" seems perfectly reasonable and straightforward, it proves problematic for the particular respondent population who view "eviction" as a very formal procedure that includes the presence of law enforcement officials, among others. By taking the time to learn about their respondents, researchers began to understand that "informal evictions" or "off the books" evictions account for nearly half of all forced moves, and many respondents don't

actually view these as "evictions" (Flowers, 2016). In understanding the language that respondents use to describe forced moves and other aspects of housing and living, researchers developed a new bank of questions to capture the data they needed to gain a deeper understanding of evictions.

> Instead of just asking, "Have you ever been evicted?" the MARS survey posed a roster of questions about a tenant's housing history—when and where they had lived and why they left. This "moving module" was the centerpiece of the MARS study. . . . Small wording details made a big difference. Rather than "Where do you live?" people were asked, "Where do you spend most nights?"

The change in question wording has such powerful implications that some of the MARS questions have been added to the U.S. Census Bureau's biennial American Housing Survey (Flowers, 2016). Armed with new knowledge, policymakers are then better positioned to address housing instability as one of the many problems linked to poverty.

"Conducting good survey research is hard. Conducting good survey research on people with low incomes—who tend to be transient, hard to reach and often hesitant to greet strangers knocking on their doors—is even harder" (Flowers, 2016).

—Andrew Flowers

It is vital to recognize that language is cultural and even political. Lydia X. Z. Brown (2016), a blogger and law school student who describes herself as "autistic and multiply otherwise neurodivergent and disabled, queer, asexual-spectrum, genderqueer/non-binary and sometimes read as feminine, and transracially and trans-nationally adopted east asian person of color from China (into a white adoptive family)" shares on her blog *Autistic Hoya*, "It is self-evident that the language we use to express all sorts of ideas, opinions, and emotions, as well as to describe ourselves and others, is simultaneously reflective of existing attitudes and influential to developing attitudes." Using appropriate language can help avoid misunderstandings and ensure offending respondents is avoided. Further, carefully considered wording can actually support equity. In its public Statement on Cultural Competence in Evaluation, the American Evaluation Association (2011) includes "recognize and eliminate bias in language" as an essential practice for culturally competent evaluation work, noting that language can do the following:

- Respectfully and effectively convey important differences in the worldviews of key stakeholders

- Challenge stereotypes and patterns of marginalization or subordination

- Accurately reflect how individuals view their own group memberships and create nuanced understandings that move beyond simple classifications

- Promote full participation when evaluation activities are conducted in participants' primary or preferred languages; this includes consideration of culturally specific communication styles and mannerisms

Consider the following abelist terms (those that discriminate against those with disabilities) discussed on the *Autistic Hoya* blog: *dumb, lame, nuts, wheelchair-bound.* The blog offers much better alternatives, including simply *person with a disability*. Note that this phrasing, sometimes called people-first language, is different from *disabled person*—using disabled as an adjective implies that the personhood of someone with a disability requires a qualifier. Even far more commonplace words—often used in colloquialisms—can be limiting. *Walk of life*, *listening session*, and *mission and vision* all contain terms that potentially exclude those who cannot walk, hear, or see. Of course, people with disabilities are just one marginalized group that researchers should consider when crafting surveys.

When it comes to translating surveys into additional languages, Frierson, Hood, Hughes, and Thomas (2010) provide specific guidance to support retention of both the content and semantics of a survey. Most importantly, they recommend that researchers do not rely on a single direction translation (from the researcher's language into the respondents' language(s)). Instead, a combination of methods should be used: forward/backward translation, multiple forward translation, and/or translation by committee. We find it useful, at the very least, to engage native speakers of the language, and ideally those who are familiar with both the subject matter and survey methodology. Regardless, in the pursuit of **culturally responsive** research (discussed in the next section), researchers should never consider the translation of a survey itself, with no other consultation of those familiar with (or part of) the respondents' culture, sufficient.

Context and Culture

Gone are the old-fashioned assumptions that if done right, applied research can be entirely objective. Instead, researchers increasingly acknowledge and attend to context and culture as data collection tools are designed, data collected, and analysis completed.

Survey Context

There are many potential components of the context in which a survey is conducted: for example, political, environmental, organizational, and cultural. We think of context as broadly as possible, encompassing all of the systems or environs in which a survey is administered. Designing a survey with an empathic approach to understanding respondents requires that researchers understand the context in which they are conducting that survey and in which respondents will answer that survey. These two contexts may or may not overlap. For example, very often researchers are operating and designing surveys within an academic context. In contrast, desired respondents may be from a specific organization or geographic region and may be wholly unconnected to academia.

Researchers can be situated internally or externally to the organization being studied (or whose stakeholders make up the researcher's desired respondent pool). When a researcher is *internal* to the organization, such that surveys are clearly being conducted by the organization itself, respondents may think differently about how they answer survey questions and may have increased or different concerns about anonymity or confidentiality than they may when researchers are *external* to the organization. Researchers who are external, such as those contracted independently to conduct program evaluations, still need to consider how their positions will be perceived by respondents. Do respondents have any familiarity with the researchers? If not, why might they be compelled to respond? How can researchers reach respondents to explain who they are, their relationship to the organization, and why respondents should complete the survey? These are considerations that may inform the way survey invitations or introductions are composed.

Not only must researchers be fully aware of their own context, they must also thoroughly consider respondent context. It might be very important to know, for example, that there has been a recent change in leadership or policy in an organization, which can influence survey responses. A worker's union going through contract negotiations, or on the verge of striking, could greatly influence how respondents answer questions about job satisfaction, as would the recent receipt of holiday bonuses or additional paid vacation.

Distinguishing Researcher and Respondent Culture

Just as the broader contexts in which researchers and survey respondents operate vary, the culture(s) influencing researchers and survey respondents also often differs. Sensitivity and responsiveness to respondent culture requires awareness of the differences between researcher and respondent culture, at minimum. A researcher's own cultural leanings and experience can influence not only what data are collected but also how respondents engage with a survey. As the reader may remember from Chapter 1 as well as earlier in this chapter, a survey is a sort of conversation—a social exchange—between researcher and respondent in which each must seek to understand the other. Many definitions of culturally competent research begin with researchers understanding their own position, perceptions, and biases. Understanding (or seeking to understand) the culture and context of the desired respondents is also an important aspect of empathizing with those respondents.

Cultural Competence and Responsiveness

One very important aspect of context is culture. Given that we can no longer assume that survey research is entirely objective or neutral, it follows that researchers should pursue survey development in a culturally competent or responsive manner. Cultural competence is about the ability to work across cultures. It's about conducting research in a manner that is respectful and responsive to all people, allowing us to understand, relate to, and learn from those involved. Cultural responsiveness extends the concept of competence, calling for researchers to adapt and respond appropriately to a given culture and context, effectively customizing their efforts. Professional organizations including the American Evaluation Association (AEA) have issued public statements calling for researchers to develop and act with cultural competence. AEA's (2011) statement, which certainly could apply to researchers working outside of evaluation, begins:

> The diversity of cultures within the United States guarantees that virtually all evaluators [and we contend, applied researchers of all varieties] will work outside familiar cultural contexts at some time in their careers. Cultural competence in evaluation theory and practice is critical for the profession and for the greater good of society.

The American Psychological Association and American Sociological Association (and likely other similar organizations) also call out cultural competence in their codes of ethics for research. We have attempted to weave considerations related to context and culture in survey research throughout this text, and this section highlights some of the key aspects related to question development. Though most of our examples are related to organizational culture, we acknowledge that there are many other aspects of culture, which itself is quite fluid and complex.

Power Dynamics

It is impossible to talk about the context of both researcher and respondent without explicitly calling out power dynamics. The AEA (2011) statement mentioned earlier also states:

> Culture is not neutral. Cultural groupings are ascribed differential status and power, with some holding privilege that they may not be aware of and some being relegated to the status of "other." For example, language dialect and

DESIGN DETAILS
CULTURALLY RESPONSIVE EVALUATION

Culturally responsive evaluation (CRE) is a framework from the world of program evaluation that can be applied to survey design.

> Culturally Responsive Evaluation is a holistic framework for centering evaluation in culture. It rejects culture-free evaluation and recognizes that culturally defined values and beliefs lie at the heart of any evaluation effort. Evaluation must be designed and carried out in a way that is culturally responsive to these values and beliefs, many of which may be context specific. (Hood, Hopson, & Kirkhart, 2015, pp. 282–283)

CRE asks researchers to act with cultural competence in all stages of research, including preparing for and framing the research and designing the study and instrumentation. Of course, applying a culturally responsive evaluation framework to survey research doesn't give us strict detailed guidance for all surveys. Rather, it requires that researchers consider and stay vigilant about the context surrounding a given research effort and to continually question how culture may influence our work.

> The design of a [culturally responsive] evaluation is responsive to context; it is not dictated by the CRE approach itself. CRE designs are congruent with the questions to be answered/learnings desired, the evidence that is valued by stakeholders, and the cultural values represented in the setting. (Hood et al., 2015, p. 293)

accent can be used to determine the status, privilege, and access to resources of groups. Similarly, in some contexts, racialized "others" are framed against the implicit standard of "whiteness" and can become marginalized even when they are the numerical majority. Cultural privilege can create and perpetuate inequities in power and foster disparate treatment in resource distribution and access.

Through the very act of collecting and analyzing information from and about others, researchers hold power and privilege. A given researcher may also hold additional privilege and power or be perceived as having such privilege and power. For example, a respondent is likely to perceive an academic researcher (especially one who uses a title or postnominal letters such as PhD) as having expertise and authority, whether the researcher has knowledge of a topic or not. Respondents from nonprofit organizations also tend to perceive surveys administered by funding agencies as coming from those with particular privilege and power, given their typical funding relationships.

Furthermore, researchers capture information about the privilege and power of others, often through cultural categories (e.g., through a question about educational level or employment status). The AEA (2011) statement goes on to note:

> Culturally competent evaluators work to avoid reinforcing cultural stereotypes and prejudice in their work. For example, evaluators often work with data

organized by cultural categories. The choices evaluators make in working with these data can affect prejudice and discrimination attached to such categories.

We began to discuss this in the earlier section on language and provide additional advice, at least as it relates to capturing demographic information, in Chapter 6.

Preparing for Cultural Responsiveness

Learning about respondents (as was detailed in the empathy phase of design thinking in Chapter 1) is a critical part of preparation for designing a culturally responsive survey tool. This can look like simply asking potential respondents about themselves, or can mean traveling great distances to live with and among the proposed respondent population. Although complete cultural immersion is rarely necessary for most survey efforts, it's also possible that even this will not suffice in certain circumstances. Consider the following instructive example from a pair of survey researchers who describe their survey effort as only "partially successful" (Bowen & Tillman, 2015, p. 28). Merle Bowen, serving as principal investigator for a research project, traveled to Brazil to live with and study the people who would eventually become her survey respondents. Her aim was to garner their support and assistance with survey administration and data collection and conduct focus groups with leaders in the communities being studied—*quilombos*, former fugitive slave communities—in order to design culturally responsive surveys. Bowen and Tillman (2015) openly acknowledge the numerous challenges they faced during this study despite their best attempt to be culturally responsive:

> Although we made every effort to be respectful of and sensitive to cultural norms and language, we encountered obstacles during assessment development, data collection, and data analysis. Some challenges were not exclusive to indigenous communities in international settings; rather they are commonly encountered in contexts when researching or evaluating programs with diverse language and ethnic communities. (p. 28)

The study authors caution that "considerable preliminary fieldwork is critical to carefully contextualize marginalized communities and to increase the researchers' sensitivity to cultural norms and nuances" (p. 37). They also offer the following advice for survey researchers:

- Documenting the process of attempts to be culturally responsive at multiple phases in evaluation and research becomes increasingly important.

- Using a culturally responsive data collection instrument is not sufficient; the administration of the survey plays an equally important role in being culturally responsive.

- Culturally responsive inquirers need to acknowledge and address the potential tension between conventional methods of quantitative instrument development, data collection, and analysis, and the desire to be CRE centered. (p. 37–38)

Finally, the authors recommend (as do we!) piloting surveys and giving "serious attention to the quality of survey design" (p. 37).

It would take an entire text to explore the evolving and important topic of culturally responsive survey design as fully as we would like to. We offer a number of further related readings under Extended Learning, and encourage survey researchers to watch for the latest literature on culturally competent and responsive research practice.

 ## Discussion Questions

- How might you sum up the cognitive tasks respondents must complete in order to answer a question? What might be your best strategies for minimizing cognitive load?

- What political or cultural context factors can you identify in your organization that could impact survey design?

- How should survey researchers balance the need for particular types of information with a desire to be culturally responsive? When might a researcher have to choose one over the other?

 ## Design Drills

1. Research Scenario, Part 3 (additional parts are found in other chapters): You are tasked with capturing information that will help assess the effectiveness of a new and ongoing program to support low-income senior citizens. The program is based at public libraries in several small towns and cities across a large region. Your research team has determined that asking participating senior citizens about their behaviors and thoughts related to the program will provide important data for the project. Assuming a survey is appropriate, craft a research question (or a couple of research questions) and a purpose statement for the survey. How will this help you make further decisions about survey design and administration?

2. Consider this somewhat linguistically complex real-world question from a cosmetics subscription service: *We'd love to know about some of the places where you shop for non-beauty purchases. What are the 2–3 retailers or brands whom you shop with the most for apparel and/or accessories?* How might the question be redesigned for greater comprehensibility?

3. Your survey: How might you plan for your survey design process and the instrument you create to be culturally responsive? What specific steps might you take with your potential respondents, given your knowledge and understanding of them, to ensure cultural responsiveness?

 ## Extended Learning

For more on the cognitive processes involved in answering survey questions:

- Schwarz, N., & Oyserman, D. (2001). Asking questions about behavior: Cognition, communication, and questionnaire construction. *American Journal of Evaluation, 22*(2), 127–160.

For more on culturally responsive research practices:

- Bowen, M. L., & Tillman, A. S. (2015). Developing culturally responsive surveys: Lessons in development, implementation, and analysis from Brazil's African descent communities. *American Journal of Evaluation, 36*(1), 25–41. This is an interesting and useful example of developing and administering a survey internationally and with a culturally responsive focus.

- Frierson, H. T., Hood, S., Hughes, G. B., & Thomas, V. G. (2010). A guide to conducting culturally responsive evaluations. In J. Frechtling (Ed.), *The 2010 user-friendly handbook for project evaluation* (pp. 75–96). Arlington, VA: National Science Foundation.

- Hood, S., Hopson, R., & Kirkhart, K. (2015). Culturally responsive evaluation. In K. E. Newcomer, H. P. Hatry, & J. S. Wholey (Eds.), *Handbook of practical program evaluation* (4th ed.) San Francisco: Wiley. Culturally responsive evaluation is described thoroughly in Chapter 12.

HOW to Develop Survey Questions and Response Options

Even the most well-conceived research questions will not be answered well with poorly designed survey (or interview, focus group) questions. The most thoroughly designed sampling and data analysis procedures will be a waste of time, energy, money, and other resources in the wake of questions that are poorly understood, misinterpreted, or skipped entirely by respondents.

The second part of this text introduces the heart of the survey design process: developing quality survey questions and response options. This is the prototyping phase of our design thinking approach. As interesting as it is to plan, consider what is possible, and get to know our potential respondents (all covered in Part I), this is where we think the fun truly begins with regard to survey design. Quality questions can be sourced from preexisting surveys, generated with respondents, or crafted "from scratch." The three chapters in this section are critical companions, particularly Chapters 4 and 5, which cover question sourcing/drafting and response options, respectively.

Purposeful Survey Design

1. Planning and predrafting
   a. Determining and articulating survey purpose
   b. Understanding what surveys can measure
   c. Understanding survey respondents

2. **Developing questions**
   a. **Sourcing questions**
   b. **Crafting question stems and response options**

3. Finalizing
   a. Pretesting
   b. Preparing for administration, analysis, and use

Chapter 4, "Sourcing and Crafting Questions," introduces how researchers can generate and develop questions, including how potential respondents can be engaged in that process and how researchers can use existing instruments. This chapter introduces open- and closed-ended questions and covers a range of question types commonly used for surveys. Specific aspects of text and language that can be problematic and potentially influence response are also addressed.

Chapter 5, "Constructing Response Options," focuses on crafting response options with special attention to rating scales. Included is discussion of the number of options to offer, whether to include a midpoint (i.e., whether to have an even or odd number of scale points), and labeling options.

Chapter 6, "Special Purpose and Sensitive Questions," covers just some of the special and sensitive questions a survey researcher may need to use, and considerations for how best to do so. Included are questions with special purposes such as filter and quality control questions, as well as questions on demographics such as race/ethnicity and gender identification.

4

Sourcing and
Crafting Questions

If you do not ask the right questions, you do not get the right answers.

—Edward Hodnett, 20th-century poet and writer

Designing effective questions requires a well-rounded understanding of all the possibilities for writing questions from scratch and for sourcing questions from other surveys or through other methods, such as focus groups. This chapter covers both critical background information about the anatomy and physiology of questions, question types, and more, as well as strategies for sourcing questions. A solid understanding of this material will be of great benefit in drafting questions.

Sourcing Survey Questions

There are a number of ways to find, develop, or adapt survey questions. Researchers may start with a blank slate and brainstorm to develop question drafts. However, ideally, researchers do not develop survey questions in a vacuum. Instead, we can engage the help of experts or those in the target population of respondents in drafting questions. Entire surveys or questions can also be adopted or adapted from existing tools, minding copyright, intellectual property, and related issues, of course! We briefly discuss some of these strategies for sourcing questions in this section.

Brainstorming

Brainstorming is often the first step in survey question drafting and is one of the easier ways to develop a bank of potential survey questions. This is especially true if researchers are not looking to use or cannot find appropriate existing measures with questions that could be adopted or adapted. Brainstorming is also an important strategy when access to desired respondents is limited or timelines are short, such that it is difficult to engage potential respondents in developing questions. We urge researchers to engage others in brainstorming, whenever possible, even if very informally. Research colleagues and those familiar with the research subject can provide inspiration for potential questions, as well as serve as a sounding board or "devil's advocate," identifying possible weaknesses or challenges in early question ideas. Chapter 1 introduced brainstorming as one phase of design thinking in which survey designers can start with a series of "How might we" questions to catalyze the brainstorming session.

Engaging Potential Respondents or Informants

Members of the potential respondent pool, those who are familiar with the desired respondents, or informants who have subject-matter expertise can help greatly in developing questions. Although informal conversations may be helpful, more formal interviews or focus groups can provide input well worth the additional time and resources they require. Either can provide especially critical guidance for survey development if the researcher is not a member or otherwise highly familiar with the desired respondents' culture(s) and experience(s).

Fowler (2014) discusses the value of focus groups to the question development process. In focus groups used for survey design, researchers typically invite small groups (usually about 6 to 10 people at a time) to engage in a moderated discussion of the survey topic or construct in hopes of learning more about it as well as eliciting input from participants on issues that should be included in survey questions. Focus group participants, especially if they are either members of the respondent population or closely connected to the topic of study, can provide greater understanding of a topic and lead researchers to explore aspects of a topic that might otherwise be overlooked. Their insights can help us understand the topic as they do and offer the language they use to describe the topic and associated conditions that can inform question development. Focus group composition is usually determined by the topic, though mirroring the target population for the survey is often ideal. Researchers must take care, especially when working with sensitive topics, that the composition of the focus group will result in people feeling comfortable and willing to openly discuss the topic with others in the room (for more information on how focus groups are used in survey development, see Rea and Parker [2014]). Focus groups can also be used later in the survey design process, specifically for pretesting survey questions, once a draft is developed (see Chapter 7 for more on pretesting).

Individual interviews are particularly effective in soliciting input from informants with subject-matter expertise, unless it is possible to gather a small group of such informants for more of a group brainstorming session or focus group. Informants may be able to share insights related to the subject matter more readily than potential respondents and may also be able to help anticipate potential challenges regarding particular questions. In some cases, it is easier or more appropriate to conduct individual interviews with a small group of potential respondents. For example, when the subject matter is particularly sensitive, or when the target population is quite diverse, and a more private conversation is warranted, individual interviews may be preferable to focus groups.

Focus groups and interviews are also commonly used in the pretesting phase once a survey draft has been created. More information about this is included in the description of the testing phase of design thinking that follows as well as in Chapter 7, where we explore how to finalize surveys in greater detail.

Using or Adapting Existing Measures

Most research builds on prior research, aiming to confirm, extend, or refute earlier results. Just as researchers use (and cite) the theoretical underpinnings of any new research effort, researchers can and should explore existing surveys or measures before creating their own. Use or adaptation of existing tools or questions is particularly valuable under the following circumstances:

- When the research subject has been well studied by others (i.e., when there is a large and/or diverse body of research about it already)

- Where existing tools are accessible and available for use or adaptation

- Where a research effort will benefit from previously conducted validation and reliability tests (e.g., in a replication study or where expectations related to the credibility of the results demand extant reliability and **validity** of tools used)

This is best done, or at least begun, early in the survey design process—once research goals are clarified, a survey is selected as the tool of choice, and constructs to be measured are articulated. An Internet search or basic literature review will likely yield a wealth of information about whether a topic has already been well explored by others. This also gives survey researchers insight into which topics are likely to turn up articles, databases or catalogues of available instruments, information about who to contact or how to access the instruments (some are free, but many do have costs associated with their use), or even the existing instruments themselves. As researchers explore existing surveys and questions, it is especially important to learn about the population for which any existing survey or questions were designed. Likewise, if the survey or questions have been validated through previous research, be sure to inquire as to which population of respondents was included in validation analyses. Often, existing tools and questions were developed for, and validated with, majority populations only (or even convenience samples of university students) and may therefore not actually be valid or appropriate for use with the population of interest.

As research is increasingly published openly, and research tools such as surveys are shared more openly alongside those results, it should become easier to benefit from the efforts of others. However, it is important to ensure the process used to develop any survey was as rigorous as necessary. Researchers should expect that not all existing surveys are freely available for use or adaptation. It is important to check any copyright or other intellectual property restrictions and to reach out to tool developers to request permission, even if no restrictions are immediately obvious. Regardless of how openly tools are shared, it is an ethical mandate that researchers seek permission to use and adapt surveys prior to doing so and that resources used are cited in an appropriate manner (just as other materials would be in any research effort). Often, conversations with survey designers can also result in great advice about what to do differently as a result of previous use of the survey, or cautionary tales about particularly challenging questions. The following story illustrates how a survey was designed using a combination of locally designed questions as well as intentional and careful selection of questions from an existing measure.

STORIES FROM THE FIELD
AN ARTS EDUCATION SURVEY ADAPTED FROM EXISTING TOOLS

In 2015, the Research Department at the Oregon Community Foundation wanted to learn about the arts education provided by nonprofit organizations throughout the state of Oregon to provide context for efforts to improve arts education access and quality in Oregon. Years of budget cuts have resulted in decreased arts education offerings available through schools. In many communities, nonprofit organizations have stepped up to fill the gap, providing an increasing amount of arts education, sometimes in partnership with schools. Although information was available in the recent past about the arts education provided through schools and school districts, similar information was not available about the arts education programming provided by nonprofit organizations.

After considering other methods that could be used to gather such information (e.g., community asset mapping), the research team determined that a survey was the best possible tool, especially considering that information was desired from as large a group of respondent organizations as possible, across a large geographical area. However, rather than starting to build a survey from scratch, researchers began with a review of recent efforts to capture similar information in other cities and states. Researchers not only reviewed existing tools, they spoke with the people who had developed and/or used those tools to learn about what worked well about them and what they wished they'd done differently. They also requested and received permission to use questions from the various tools from their owners. As a result of reviewing these tools and gathering this advice, researchers were far better positioned to develop a survey tool that would meet the needs of this research project. The survey used was a combination of questions developed in-house, as well as those from other existing tools. In a few cases, existing questions were adapted based on advice provided by others and to ensure they would be relevant to the desired respondents in Oregon.

—Kimberly Firth Leonard

The Anatomy and Physiology of Survey Questions

In medicine, *anatomy* refers to the *structure* of body parts, whereas *physiology* refers to the *functions* and *relationships* of those parts. We think of the anatomy of a survey question as the parts of the question that make up its structure. Simply put, this includes the **question stem** (i.e., the question or statement itself) along with any response options that may accompany that stem. A question stem with no response options is an open-ended question (sometimes referred to as an "unstructured" question), and a question stem with a set of response options is a closed-ended (or "structured") question.

The physiology of a survey question is a combination of 1) the function of the question stem and any response options (in other words, their individual purposes and how they work to form a complete survey question) and 2) the relationships *between* the question stem and response options (in other words, how they work *together*). This physiology—the function and relationship of the question parts—has significant implications for survey response, a major focus of this and the next two chapters.

The main impetus for employing a purposeful survey design process that incorporates design thinking is concern for response effects. Response effects are changes or differences in survey responses that occur due to various aspects of survey design or administration. Although response effects can arise from any part of the survey design and administration process, we focus on those effects that result from the design of survey questions themselves. As we reiterate throughout this text, the design choices we make as researchers about what to ask and how to ask are key to a successful survey effort.

Composing Question Stems

Much of our text is devoted to survey question design through the lens of understanding *how* respondents answer survey questions and the various influences of question features and context on responses. No survey research text is complete without at least a brief discussion of a foundational work (or perhaps *the* foundational work) on how question wording influences responses. In 1941, Donald Rugg published *Experiments in Wording Questions: II* in the highly acclaimed *Public Opinion Quarterly*. The 90-year old *POQ* is a tremendous resource for survey researchers. Rugg's now-famous World War II–era experiment had to do with varying the wording in survey questions (see Figure 4.1) for different cross sections of a sample of the U.S. population.

FIGURE 4.1 ● Two Variations of a Question From Rugg (1941)

- Do you think the United States should **allow** public speeches against democracy?
- Do you think the United States should **forbid** public speeches against democracy?

The difference is around one word choice: *allow* versus *forbid*. In theory, if one answers yes to the question using the word *allow*, that person would also answer no to the second question using the word *forbid* because "to forbid" is essentially the opposite of "to allow." In fact, and what makes this a most interesting and oft-cited case, Rugg (1941) found "a very striking difference in response to the two forms of the question" (p. 92). Rugg not only found response differences among certain subgroups of the population as one might expect, but the phenomenon itself—people responding very differently to the two questions—was consistent across subgroups. Rugg (1941) surmised that "evidently the 'forbid' phrasing makes the implied threat to civil liberties more apparent, and fewer people are willing to advocate suppression of antidemocratic speeches when the issue is presented in this way" (p. 92). Many similar, more recent studies have also been conducted testing two versions of a question. In one such study, Goetz (2008) tested two forms of a question with the terms *affordable housing* versus *lifecycle housing* and found that more respondents supported *lifecycle housing* and more expressed strong opposition to *affordable housing* even though both terms refer to low-cost, publicly assisted or subsidized housing.

As we learned in Chapter 3, respondents must be able to understand a question before they are able to answer it. The best survey questions are written in language that respondents can easily understand and worded in ways that make sense to them. Questions must be *syntactically* correct (i.e., employ correct grammar and usage) and also *semantically* valid (i.e., make sense). In other words, respondents need to interpret words and phrases in the way in which the researcher intends them to be understood. A well-known example by noted linguist Noam Chomsky that demonstrates a syntactically correct but not semantically valid sentence is this: "Colorless green ideas sleep furiously." This sentence is perfectly grammatical but makes no sense. In addition to ensuring questions make sense to respondents, the most effective questions also limit cognitive load—the amount of mental effort respondents must exert in order to answer the question—and limit the burden on working memory.

Reference Periods

Respondents rely on context from the question stem (as well as from any response options offered) in order to respond to a question. Sometimes, this context includes a reference period that is part of the question stem. Reference periods are the specific time frames survey researchers ask about in individual questions. Survey questions often feature reference periods such as *in the last month* or *in the last year* as they ask respondents to recall instances of certain behaviors, feelings, or events. The choice of *which* period of time to investigate can have significant implications for how respondents interpret the question. For example, if asked how many times they have felt sad *in the last year*, respondents may infer that researchers are interested only in very memorable events that caused significant or extreme sadness such as the death of a loved one. If, however, the reference period is *in the last week*, respondents may remember and include instances of sadness such as watching a sad movie (see, for example, Igou, Bless, & Schwarz, 2002; Winkielman, Knäuper, & Schwarz, 1998).

Choosing a reference period for any given question is a contest of opposing forces. Both shorter and longer reference periods possess inherent advantages and shortcomings. Because memories fade with time, respondents may have an easier time searching within shorter time periods (a few days or weeks). However, if respondents rarely experience the feeling or behavior of interest, the reference period must be long enough to result in useful responses. For example, most respondents are likely to have shopped at a grocery store within the last month but may not have shopped at a hardware store within that time period. Longer reference periods may include more instances of the feeling or behavior of interest, but responses are more subject to memory deterioration and underestimation. Conversely, shorter reference periods are subject to overestimation (Tourangeau et al., 2000). Imagine a respondent being asked how many times he has eaten carrots in the last 12 months. Unless he eats them on a *very* regular and consistent schedule, or doesn't consume them at all, he will likely be unable to accurately recall all instances of eating carrots over the period of a year. Ultimately, survey researchers should consider how shorter or longer reference periods might help achieve the purpose of the question and determine which are appropriate given the relative frequency of the behavior or event. For example, use a shorter reference period for more common occurrences, such as a question about purchasing milk, and a longer reference period for less common ones, such as a question about purchasing a car battery.

Reference periods can also be prone to ambiguity. For example, if a respondent is taking a survey on March 15, 2017, and is asked a question with the reference period "in the last 12 months," how might that be interpreted? Is "the last 12 months" the entirety of the last calendar year (i.e., all of 2016)? Or does "the last 12 months" span from March 16, 2016, to March 15, 2017? Would considering roughly March 2016 through roughly February 2017 suffice, because that is the last 12 complete months? Adding to the difficulty, respondents can rarely remember abstract dates from months prior unless they included significant events such as holidays, anniversaries, or special events. This has played out in large-scale surveys such as the American Community Survey (ACS), a household survey conducted by the United States Census Bureau. After being asked a question about salary earned, respondents were asked, "Did you receive any additional tips, bonuses, or commissions DURING THE PAST 12 MONTHS?" (Hinsdale, McFarlane, Weger, Schoua-Glusberg, & Kerwin, 2009, p. 61). During cognitive interviews about this group of questions, interviewers determined that respondents interpreted that reference period inconsistently, based on the variations in their responses. Some used estimation strategies to add up weekly or monthly income for what they thought was the reference period; some reported for only part of the reference period; and others simply thought of the prior calendar year as a whole and reported for that (p. 64). As with any survey question, pretesting the question with potential respondents can help determine which reference periods may elicit the types of responses desired (more on pretesting in Chapter 7).

Avoiding Problematic Wording and Question Types

One of our goals in writing this text was to offer advice for survey designers framed in positive language. In other words, we set out to help the reader know what *to do* in the process of designing survey questions, as opposed to what *not to do*. We did not want to simply reiterate a list of "don't do this" and "don't do that" rules common to many survey texts. However, in the following sections, out of necessity, the "to dos" come in the form of things to *avoid* such as certain words and phrases and their placement in questions, as well as problematic ways of asking questions. In each section, we offer explanations and examples to point the reader in a positive direction and offer ideas of what *to do* even when it is difficult to directly state the rule in a positive manner.

Problematic Text Features

The words we choose to compose survey questions matter deeply and can have profound impacts on our resulting datasets. Even the choice of one word versus another, as in the Rugg (1941) and Goetz (2008) studies described earlier, can produce significant response effects. Lenzner, Kaczmirek, and Lenzner (2010) identified 12 specific text features survey designers should avoid when composing questions. These particular features have been shown to increase cognitive load, tax working memory, and otherwise contribute to difficulties with question comprehension. This can result in respondents not completing surveys (i.e., nonresponse) or engaging in "satisficing" behaviors. Respondents satisfice when they answer a question too quickly without much thought, overuse "don't know" or "neutral" response options when these are offered, or choose the first minorly acceptable or reasonable answer they see, resulting in poor-quality data. The following is Lenzner et al.'s (2010) list of text features to avoid, along with explanations and examples of how to avoid using them that we have added to elucidate each point:

- *Acronyms* (Abbreviations formed from the first letters of a name or term. E.g., use *United States Postal Service* instead of *USPS*.)

- *Low-frequency terms* (Words and terms less often encountered in "everyday" language. E.g., use *wealthy* instead of *affluent*; use *angry* instead of *irate*.)

- *Vague quantification terms* (Words and phrases used to communicate uncertain or approximate amounts. E.g., wherever possible, use exact numbers or a range of numbers instead of terms such as *frequently, seldom, many*, or *few*. We discuss vague quantifiers in greater detail in Chapter 5.)

- *Left-embedded syntactic structures* (This happens when respondents encounter several phrases, adjectives, adverbs, and prepositions *before* they get to the critical part of the question stem. This type of syntax requires them to begin interpreting and holding information in working memory before they read the actual *question*. E.g., use "The boy who hit the home run had wanted to play baseball of his life" instead of "The boy who had wanted to play baseball all of his life hit the home run.")

- *Ambiguous syntactic structures* (This happens when the structure of the sentence or phrase is open to more than one interpretation. E.g., use clear and explicit language that generally leads to only one interpretation: "Can you name famous newscasters *other* than Dan Rather?" or "Can you name newscasters *more famous* than Dan Rather?" instead of "Can you name more famous newscasters than Dan Rather?" The latter question can be interpreted in either of the two suggested ways.)

- *Dense noun phrases* (Simply put, noun phrases are nouns and any other words that modify them, such as adjectives, adverbs, or articles. Dense noun phrases occur when many adjectives, adverbs, and articles are attached to a single noun. The following is an example of a noun followed by progressively denser noun phrases: "Muscles; your four muscles; your four shoulder muscles; your four strong shoulder muscles; the biggest of your four strong shoulder muscles; the biggest of your four strong shoulder muscles on each side; the biggest of your four strong shoulder muscles connected by tendons on each side" [Swierzbin, 2014]. E.g., use only as many noun modifiers as necessary to convey meaning. Use "your primary vehicle" rather than "the vehicle used every day considered to be your primary mode of transportation.")

- *Quantitative mental calculations* (This is the adding respondents must do in their heads when we ask questions about behaviors or events and use specific reference periods. E.g., Limit the "mental mathematics" respondents must do to answer a question. Use "About how many hours per weekday (Monday–Friday) do you spend watching television" instead of "About how many hours per month do you watch television on weekdays?" In the former, respondents only need do the math for one day, versus adding up 7 days' worth of watching to come up with the total for the week.)

- *Hypothetical questions* (These questions ask about assumed situations as opposed to current facts. They are often "What if" questions. E.g., if hypothetical questions are necessary, keep them brief and clear. Use "If we added a staff break room to the floor, would you use it?" instead of "If we added a space where workers could sit and talk, use a refrigerator or coffee machine, and spend time with coworkers during breaks, would you go there?")

- *Numerous logical operators* (Logical operators are connecting words such as *and*, *but*, *or*, and *if*. Too many in one question taxes working memory. E.g., separate questions and explanations into clear, brief statements. Use "*Family members* include parents, children, and any others living in your home or staying with you. *Medical facility* includes any place you visit to receive health care. How many times in the last 6 months have you or any family members visited a medical facility?" instead of "How many times in the last 6 months have you or any of your family members [including parents, children, and any others living in your home or staying with you] visited a health care or other medical facility?")

- *Nominalizations* (Nominalizations are verbs or adjectives that have been changed into nouns or noun phrases[1] such as "the expansion of" from "to expand." E.g., use "Should developers continue to expand the shopping center?" instead of "Should developers move forward with the expansion of the shopping center?")

---

[1]An excellent list of examples of nominalizations and an explanation of why they matter can be found at the Purdue Online Writing Lab (OWL). See "Sentence Clarity: Nominalizations and Subject Position" at https://owl.english.purdue.edu/owl/resource/1002/01.

- *Passive constructions* (This happens when the object of the action in a sentence becomes the subject. E.g., use "Developers expanded the shopping center" instead of "The shopping center was expanded by developers.")

- *Bridging inferences* (This happens especially when respondents must make inferences about an introductory sentence in order to answer the question that follows. E.g., ensure introductory sentences do not contain information that must be comprehended in order for respondents to answer the question. In a follow-up study, Lenzner, Kaczmirek, and Galesic (2011) found that "bridging inferences may only undermine question comprehension if the introductory sentence contains implicit information which is crucial for understanding and answering the question" (p. 370).

Although understanding all of these text features can be challenging, we think it is well worth the investment of time to read and reread these explanations and examples to ensure quality question design.

Ambiguous Wording

Ambiguous wording makes questions very difficult for respondents to answer accurately. Many studies on question wording (Lenzner et al., 2010, for example) have shown that words and phrases open to multiple interpretations or difficult to understand are associated with respondents taking longer to answer, skipping questions, choosing "don't know" or neutral responses more often, and otherwise providing nonsubstantive answers. Survey researchers must have a keen eye for identifying words and phrases whose meanings or interpretations are easily taken for granted but are in effect open to multiple interpretations or meanings. Consider the question in Figure 4.2 from a well-known office supplies retailer.

FIGURE 4.2 ● Real-World Questions: *Question Stem With an Ambiguous Term*

Did you encounter any issues during your experience with [store name]?

    O YES   O NO

Although a respondent might interpret the word *issues* as "problems" or "concerns," exactly what the retailer is attempting to measure is not clear. Is this company interested in major or minor "issues"? Do they want to know if the pen and pencil aisle was a bit messy and the shopper spent a few more minutes than he would have liked searching for his preferred brand? Whether or not the item he was looking for was in stock? Or is the retailer interested in a potentially more significant complaint, such as a cashier being rude, overcharging, or giving out the wrong change? Ambiguous wording can typically be avoided by returning to the survey purpose and identifying exactly what is to be measured (e.g., constructs) before composing questions. If the purpose of the survey includes gathering data about customer experience, the retailer would need to identify exactly *which* parts of the experience are important to understand (e.g., cleanliness of the store, availability of products, friendliness of cashier) and compose a series of questions to tease these out. If they want to know if a customer has encountered a problem that other questions did not identify, then the question could include the word *problem* (see Figure 4.3) along with an explanation of what is meant by the term or examples of the types of experiences they are looking for.

FIGURE 4.3 ● A Suggested Alternative: *Use a Clearer Word and Offer Assistance With Interpretation*

A problem is anything major or minor that negatively impacts a shopper's experience. Did you encounter any problems during your experience with [store name]?

O YES   O NO

Ambiguous terms can easily hide in questions that sound perfectly reasonable. Consider the question in Figure 4.4 from a prominent organization in survey research and polling.

FIGURE 4.4 ● Real-World Questions: *Question Stem With an Ambiguous Term*

How many years have you been employed in your current job?

O 1–2 years
O 3–4 years
O 5–9 years
O 10–15 years
O More than 15 years

How might a respondent interpret "current job" if she has held several positions within the same company? What if those positions were varying levels within the same general category such as department manager, assistant manager, manager, and store manager? Is the question asking how many years she has been a manager with the company or how many years she has in her current position as *store manager*? Knowing the purpose of the question is necessary to suggest less ambiguous alternatives. One suggestion is to add a brief description such as "We want to know only about your current job position or title" to clarify what information the researcher desires.

Using parameters around potentially ambiguous words. In Chapter 1, we offered examples of potentially confusing words such as *family*, *farmer*, and *athlete*, illustrating potential problems respondents might have as they try to interpret them and determine what "counts" in each case. Adding language that places parameters around these types of words (i.e., clarifying what does and does not count as a *family* for the purpose of a particular study) is one strategy that can go a long way toward encouraging accurate responses and collecting high-quality data. For example, if a survey asks questions about the respondent's family, an explanation such as "for the purpose of this survey, please think of 'family' as anyone related to you who is currently living in your home" will help respondents understand what researchers are looking for.

In Chapter 3, we introduced the QUAID tool, an online program that provides feedback on question wording and sentence structure. This tool detects and offers feedback on several text features (including potentially ambiguous words) that can interfere with comprehensibility, including the following:

- Unfamiliar technical terms

- Vague or imprecise relative terms

- Vague or ambiguous noun phrases

- Complex syntax

- Working memory overload (QUAID Tool, n.d.)

The QUAID output alerts the researcher to the presence of these problems, letting the researcher know where parameters or explanatory language could increase comprehensibility. The tool can be helpful during the brainstorming and prototyping phases of question design, especially when used prior to any pretesting strategies (for more on finalizing questions and pretesting, see Chapter 7).

Double-Barreled Questions

Questions must ask respondents only one thing at a time. One of the most common survey design mistakes is to compose double- or even triple-barreled questions. Consider the examples in Figures 4.5 and 4.6 from a school district customer service survey and a retail store survey.

FIGURE 4.5 ● Real-World Questions: *A Triple-Barreled Question Stem*

Has the district been responsive to your customer service needs with timely, informative, and accurate information?

○ YES   ○ Sometimes   ○ NO

FIGURE 4.6 ●   Real-World Questions: *A Double-Barreled Question Stem*

Rate how knowledgeable and helpful we were in assisting you.

   ○ 1-poor   ○ 2   ○ 3   ○ 4   ○ 5-excellent

In the first example (Figure 4.5), if a respondent was a district community member and received timely information that turned out to be inaccurate or received accurate information but had to wait an inordinate amount of time for it (two plausible scenarios), how might the respondent answer this question? In the second example (Figure 4.6), if a respondent encountered a store clerk who was extremely friendly and helpful but did not demonstrate knowledge of the products of interest, how might the respondent answer this question?

It is easy to make this mistake given our desire to limit the number of questions included in a given survey. Often, a double- or triple-barreled question can be easily divided into two or three questions. Although this adds to the number of questions asked, it may not add to the time it takes to answer the questions. Two or three questions that are easier to comprehend are far less bothersome than one question respondents don't know how to answer. Sometimes, it is even feasible to develop a single question with multiple parts (see Figures 4.7 and 4.8).

FIGURE 4.7 ●   A Suggested Alternative: *Divide Question Stem Into Three Separate Parts*

Has the district been responsive to your customer service needs with information that is

a. Timely?	○ YES	○ Sometimes	○ NO
b. Informative?	○ YES	○ Sometimes	○ NO
c. Accurate?	○ YES	○ Sometimes	○ NO

FIGURE 4.8 ●   A Suggested Alternative: *Divide Question Stem Into Two Separate Questions*

Please rate how <u>knowledgeable</u> we were in assisting you.

   ○ 1-poor   ○ 2   ○ 3   ○ 4   ○ 5-excellent

Please rate how <u>helpful</u> we were in assisting you.

   ○ 1-poor   ○ 2   ○ 3   ○ 4   ○ 5-excellent

Although it may seem as if double-barreled questions are easy to avoid, it's quite possible to compose a straightforward-sounding question without realizing that it actually asks more than one thing. Consider for example, "How often do you and your family take walks?" If the respondent is an avid walker but never goes on walks with family members, this may be difficult to answer, even though *never* may appear as a response option. Respondents want to please the researcher and provide accurate information. One way to steer clear of double-barreled questions is to read a question stem carefully and look for the possibility that one part of the question may be true whereas another part is false, leaving a respondent for whom this is the case no way to accurately answer. Avoid composing double-barreled questions by ensuring that each survey question asks respondents just one "thing" at a time.

Leading and Loaded Questions

Survey questions can also intentionally or unintentionally lead respondents to provide certain answers. Asking "How much did you enjoy the movie" uses language that implies that respondents did indeed *enjoy* the movie. Even if one of the response options is negative (e.g., "I did not enjoy the movie"), the question itself sets the respondent up to provide a more positive response, whether that is accurate or not. When question wording includes a reason for a respondent's opinion on a particular topic (as in the examples in Figure 4.9), that reason can load the question. This is especially true when the reason is socially desirable, such as saving lives or combating obesity.

FIGURE 4.9 ● Examples of Loaded Questions

- Do you agree with federal laws on seatbelt use to save lives?
- Do you agree that sugary sodas should be banned in schools in order to combat childhood obesity in America?

Presuppositions, or facts tacitly assumed to be true, can be especially dangerous in survey questions. Details found in the wording of a question will often be presumed true by respondents, even when they are not. Consider this illustrative example of how a detail in the question can lead respondents to create false memories:

> *Leading questions* . . . can cause addressees to misremember the event as if the presupposition were true. A question like *How fast was the car going when it went through the yield sign?* can cause subjects to report the presence of a yield sign on a follow-up memory test, even if no such sign was part of the traffic event that subjects witnessed. (Tourangeau et al., 2000, p. 42)

Many words and phrases are politically loaded and can both reflect different perspectives and significantly influence question responses. Consider these pairs:

- Pro-choice vs. pro-abortion

- Pro-life vs. anti-abortion

- Freedom fighters vs. anti-government guerillas

- War vs. armed conflict

- Taxes vs. revenues (Clark & Schober, 1992, p. 29)

FIGURE 4.10 ● Real-World Questions: *Loaded Questions*

- Are you in favor of comprehensive tax reform that keeps income taxes low while eliminating some deductions?

- Are you concerned about rising inflation undercutting your savings, devaluing your home, and increasing your cost of living?

- Do you believe medical malpractice reform to stop frivolous lawsuits and ever-increasing insurance premiums should be a priority of healthcare reform legislation?

Sometimes leading and loaded questions can be easy to spot. The questions in Figure 4.10 appeared in a survey from an explicitly political group commonly associated with a particular party and therefore policy position.

However, sometimes loaded questions are not that easy to identify. To avoid unintentionally including such a question, careful pretesting strategies (see Chapter 7) can be employed to gather insight on how potential respondents might interpret not only the questions themselves but the individual words or phrases within them. Whether a question is leading or loaded can be tricky to tease out. The difference between the two is much less important than the ability to detect the presence of either one in any given question and to know when it is appropriate to use them strategically and purposefully. According to Clark and Schober (1992), "It is futile to search for truly neutral questions. They don't exist" (p. 30).

> *It is futile to search for truly neutral questions. They don't exist.*
>
> *– Clark & Schober*

All that said, a leading or loaded question may have a place in a well-designed survey under certain conditions. Some advocate the deliberate use of loaded questions to increase the likelihood that respondents will report on certain sensitive behaviors. An example of this includes adding wording to the introduction of the question (or question stem) to the effect that "it's OK if you do this" or "many people do this," giving respondents the message and comfort of thinking they are not alone or made to feel badly about engaging in potentially socially undesirable behaviors for questions that might have a level of sensitivity (see Chapter 6 for more on sensitive questions and social desirability). This obviously requires deep understanding of the survey subject matter and the desired respondents well enough to know that such strategies would be more helpful than harmful to the research effort.

Open-Ended Questions

Open-ended or unstructured questions offer no response options, relying on the respondent to provide an answer. Open-ended questions come with their own set of considerations and implications, and many survey designers struggle with if, when, why, how, and even where to use open-ended questions in any given survey. Answers to open-ended questions can range from a single word or number (e.g., "What is your age?") to a paragraph or even multiple-paragraph response (e.g., "How do you feel about the organization's new management policies?"). Open-ended questions feel very natural. After all, we spend much of our lives in conversation with each other asking open-ended questions. They are also relatively easy to compose and feature the prom-ise of collecting rich, nuanced, and detailed data. "Open questions produce fuller and deeper responses reflecting differences in opinions and attitudes that are missed by the constraints of pre-coded categories" (Bradburn & Sudman, 1988, p. 147). Open-ended questions also present a unique opportunity for the researcher to discover new and perhaps unexpected responses in comparison to more rigid, closed-ended questions.

However, open-ended questions require more time and effort on the part of respon-dents, something a researcher must carefully consider especially when determining *how many* open-ended questions are used in a single survey instrument. Too many open-ended questions, and we risk item nonresponse when respondents skip these questions, fail to provide meaningful answers, or fail to complete the remainder of the survey (a good argument for making these questions optional wherever possible). Respondents may also answer the question minimally, with little effort expended, resulting in less useful information than desired (Krosnick, 1999). Finally, open-ended questions also come with implications for data analysis, not the least of which is the need for the types of coding strategies that characterize qualitative analysis. This can very easily become an overwhelming proposition with massive amounts of text-based answers (i.e., qualitative data). Some online survey platforms and indeed some researchers are not well equipped to analyze qualitative data.

DESIGN DETAILS
OPEN-ENDED VERSUS CLOSED-ENDED QUESTIONS

Open-ended questions are not necessarily supe-rior or inferior to closed-ended questions, but it is important to note that comparative stud-ies on questions presented in both formats have consistently yielded different results (see, for example, Schuman, Ludwig, & Krosnick, 1986; Schuman & Presser, 1979; Schuman & Scott, 1987). That is, the two questions—one open-ended and one closed-ended—will often result in different

responses and can lead researchers to make dif-ferent interpretations of those results. Consider a scenario (see Figure 4.11) in which a survey fea-tures a closed-ended question about job satisfac-tion in the workplace.

When asked about the most important fac-tors that contribute to their current level of job satisfaction, employees might choose "compen-sation" if offered as one of the response options

FIGURE 4.11   ●   Comparison of a Closed- and Open-Ended Question

Closed-ended question:

From this list, please choose the three most important factors that contribute to your level of satisfaction with your job.

- ☐ supervisor
- ☐ coworkers
- ☐ compensation
- ☐ hours
- ☐ nature of the work
- ☐ location of the business
- ☐ fringe benefits

Open-ended question:

What are the three most important factors that contribute to your level of satisfaction with your job?

in a closed-ended question. However, they may not offer "compensation" as part of an open-ended question response. Respondents to the open-ended version who do not list "compensation" in their answers either may not consider that the researchers are interested in compensation, or they may not think of it as a factor in their level of satisfaction. Unfortunately, researchers would not know this without conducting a comparative study using *both* forms of the job satisfaction question, and they would likely reach different conclusions using different versions of the question. Consider this scenario from the Pew Research Center (n.d.-b), a public opinion polling fact tank:

In a poll conducted after the presidential election in 2008, people responded very differently to two versions of this question: "What one issue mattered most to you in deciding how you voted for president?" One was closed-ended and the other open-ended. In the closed-ended version, respondents were provided five options (and could volunteer an option not on the list). When explicitly offered the economy as a response, more than half

of respondents (58%) chose this answer; only 35% of those who responded to the open-ended version volunteered the economy. Moreover, among those asked the closed-ended version, fewer than one-in-ten (8%) provided a response other than the five they were read; by contrast fully 43% of those asked the open-ended version provided a response not listed in the closed-ended version of the question. All of the other issues were chosen at least slightly more often when explicitly offered in the closed-ended version than in the open-ended version.

Open-ended questions generally require more mental effort from respondents than do closed-ended questions that offer a specific set of response options. Open-ended questions demand greater attention to both formulating and encoding answers in writing. In addition to this increased level of cognitive load, some respondents may feel self-conscious about their writing ability or even embarrassed about sharing their writing with researchers and, thus, may hold back on offering too much in response to these questions.

Why Use Open-Ended Questions?

Open-ended questions can be used for many purposes:

1. When researchers believe that there will be too wide a range of potential responses to construct a reasonable list of response options for a closed-ended question.

2. When researchers are unsure about an appropriate set of response options for a particular closed-ended question. In a pretesting phase of a survey, an open-ended question can be used to identify the most common responses in order to construct a closed-ended question for the final instrument.

3. When researchers want to capture rich, detailed, and nuanced understanding of respondents' thoughts, feelings, opinions, attitudes, or experiences. This only works *if* (and this is a big IF!) respondents are able and willing to share these with us (see Chapter 3 on respondent ability and willingness to participate in survey research).

4. When researchers want respondents to answer using their own "voice," their own word choices and terminology and language that is comfortable for them.

How to Compose Open-Ended Questions

The best open-ended questions are simple and highly specific, letting respondents know exactly what we hope to learn from them without having to stumble through an overwhelmingly long or complicated question stem. Open-ended questions, like any question, should be written for comprehensibility, using language familiar to respondents. Survey designers can employ several strategies to encourage the best responses possible. The strategies we include here are aligned with our respondent-centered design and support the development of empathy for respondents. They help us put ourselves in their shoes and ask "what might cause me to want to make an effort to answer this question well?"

> The best open-ended questions are simple and highly specific, letting respondents know exactly what we hope to learn from them.

Tell them why. Providing introductory language that describes *why* the question is being asked or tells the respondent why this information is important to the research effort (Smyth, Dillman, Christian, & Mcbride, 2009) can encourage respondents to give longer, richer, and more detailed answers. Reja, Manfreda, Hlebec, and Vehovar (2003) advise,

> Especially in the case of attitudinal questions, the researcher has to be very explicit in trying to get more specific answers, since many respondents answer in very broad terms. This is a particular problem in all self-administered questionnaires where there is no interviewer who could probe and motivate respondents to give more specific answers. (p. 174)

Here is an example of some encouraging introductory language we found in the invitation to a survey on cars and auto repair: *On a few occasions, we will ask you to type your answers. <u>Please don't skip them</u>; we read every one of them and are really curious to know what you think.* Researchers can emotionalize the appeal for information by emphasizing to them how the information will be used to improve programs, products, systems, policies, or practices—in other words, how these efforts will help people. This can be especially powerful if the people helped are also part of the respondent population (e.g., others who are parents, car owners, or runners).

Put fears to rest. Introductory language can also serve to allay any anxiety respondents may have regarding their writing style (e.g., their grammar or spelling) by letting them know at the outset this will not be of concern to the researcher.

Communicate expectations. Researchers can directly ask respondents to give detailed answers, letting them know the level of detail or approximate length of answers expected. Examples can be helpful at times but need to be balanced with the desire to keep the survey language brief and straightforward.

Break longer or complex questions into separate parts. Respondents will often fail to answer one or more parts of a complex question that asks several things at once. Rather than ask one multipart question, ask a series of simple, direct questions (see Figure 4.12).

FIGURE 4.12 ● Converting a Multipart Question to Separate Questions

A multipart question:

1. Describe your general reaction to the movie. Which was your favorite part, and why? Which part did you like least, and why?

Separate questions:

1. Describe your general reaction to the movie.
2. Which was your favorite part?
   a. Why?
3. Which part did you like least?
   a. Why?

When to Use Open-Ended Questions

Open-ended questions are typically used sparingly in surveys, but there are several reasons researchers may choose to include them, including when

- more detailed, nuanced answers are useful;

- answers in respondents' own words are needed;

- exact numbers are needed (e.g., how many cars a respondent owns);

- the range of possibilities is virtually infinite (e.g., how many sexual partners a respondent has had);

- researchers suspect that providing response options may overly influence answers; and when

- the survey is in a pretesting phase and an open-ended question is needed to determine the general range of responses it will generate in order to inform the eventual design of a closed-ended question.

Additionally, not all questions about behavior need a set of response options, and some may be better asked as open-ended questions. For example, offering a set of responses for sensitive questions like, "How many sexual partners have you had in the last year?" may encourage respondents to "edit" their answers for reasons of social desirability (see Chapter 6 for more on social desirability). It may happen this way: respondents read the question, search their memories, and come up with a number they believe is accurate. However, they also believe that they are "average" in comparison to other respondents. So, upon reading a closed-ended question that contains a set of response options, they decide to select a middle option *regardless* of the number they came up with, assuming that the researchers who designed the survey offered response options that capture a range that is typical for respondents like them. We discuss how response options influence answers in greater detail in Chapter 5.

If it is reasonable and feasible to do so, we advise ending a survey with what we call an "invitational open-ended question." This can be as simple as asking, "Is there anything else you would like to share about {topic}?" Despite our best efforts to empathize with and understand respondents, the balance of power inevitably remains with the researcher. Pettit (2016) reminds us of the unique relationship of survey researcher and respondent and advises,

> For the entire survey, you, the researcher, have been in charge. You have dictated every topic and every answer. You have bossed people around. Now it's time to give power to the people. Give people space to expand on their answers, give answers to questions you didn't ask. (p. 7)

Allowing respondents to have a voice in this way returns some of the power that researchers hold to our respondents and may in fact result in learning even more than expected.

Closed-Ended Questions

Closed-ended or structured questions are composed of two parts, the question stem and a set of researcher-generated response options. Closed-ended questions are omnipresent in survey research due to their efficiency and reliability. They are easy to analyze and provide a tidy, uniform dataset. Closed-ended questions allow the researcher to make broad comparisons among respondents with ease. The response options that accompany closed-ended questions can stimulate respondents' thinking and remind them of alternatives that may not have come to mind if the question were posed as an open-ended one (see Figure 4.11 for a comparison of a closed- and open-ended question). For example, if asked in an open-ended question format about the most pressing challenge public school districts face today, respondents might come up with a whole range of possibilities, such as too many mandates, too little funding, class sizes, or student achievement. The issue of poverty may or may not come up. If asked as a closed-ended question that includes *poverty* as one of the response options, respondents may select *poverty* even if they would not have listed it as a response to an open-ended question. The downside of the availability of response options is that some respondents may guess or answer randomly, rather than devoting time to a more thoughtful response. "Closed-ended questions, in a sense, compel respondents to choose a 'closest representation' of their actual response in the form of a specific fixed answer" (Rea & Parker, 2014, p. 34). It is critical that a researcher carefully balance the pros and cons of open- and closed-ended questions in constructing an effective survey.

Closed-ended questions appear deceptively easy to write. However, most of the poor questions we have encountered are closed-ended questions, often with problematic response options. A number of things can go awry, but the two most common mistakes we've seen are response options that are not exhaustive and mutually exclusive. For closed-ended questions to be effective, response options must be both *exhaustive*—they must fully cover the range of expected responses—and *mutually exclusive*—they must not overlap (i.e., they must not encourage or compel a respondent to select more than one). Figure 4.13 features a question with insufficient response options. The list does not represent the entire range of possible responses and so is not *exhaustive*. Figure 4.14 features a question with overlapping response options, leaving potential respondents *two* correct choices for their answer to the question; thus, the response options are not *mutually exclusive*. Problems we have routinely uncovered include incomplete sets of response options and ambiguous or unclear categories, among many others.

> Closed-ended questions, in a sense, compel respondents to choose a "closest representation" of their actual response in the form of a specific fixed answer.
>
> –Rae & Parker

FIGURE 4.13 ● Real-World Questions: *Insufficient Response Options*

How often do you visit the {department name} website?

- ○ This is my first time
- ○ About once a year or less
- ○ About once a month
- ○ About once a week
- ○ About every day

How might a respondent answer if he visits twice a week? Three or four times per year? These options, among others, are missing. This set of response options is not exhaustive (we revisit this question and offer a possible alternative in Chapter 5).

FIGURE 4.14 ● Real-World Questions: *Overlapping Response Options*

How long have you owned your product?

○ Less than 1 year
○ 1–3 years
○ 3–5 years
○ More than 5 years

How might a respondent answer if she has owned the product for 3 years? 5 years? These answers appear in two response options each and are thus not mutually exclusive.

Types of Closed-Ended Questions

The most common types of closed-ended questions are outlined in this section. Each type includes a question stem and is characterized by the number or format of response categories and the number of possible responses (i.e., whether respondents are expected to choose one category or more than one).

DESIGN DETAILS
COMMON TYPES OF CLOSED-ENDED QUESTIONS

All closed-ended questions start with a question stem and include a finite set of response options.

- Multiple choice

- Check all that apply

- Rating scale

- Ranking scale

- Semantic differential scale

Multiple choice. These questions (see Figure 4.15) feature two or more response options. When only two options are present (as in yes/no or true/false questions) we refer to them as **dichotomous questions**. Respondents are generally expected to choose one category only for multiple-choice questions, unless directions specify a different number. Respondents can be directed to choose *exactly* a certain number of responses or *up to* a certain number. Each has specific implications for data analysis.

FIGURE 4.15 ● *Multiple Choice* Questions

A dichotomous question:

Do you own or rent your home?

- ○ Own
- ○ Rent

Multiple-choice questions with specific instructions for responding:

What device do you use most often to compose email? (Choose only one)

- ○ Desktop computer
- ○ Laptop computer
- ○ Tablet computer
- ○ Cell phone

What are the three most important programs our agency offers? (Choose exactly three)

- ☐ Program A
- ☐ Program B
- ☐ Program C
- ☐ Program D
- ☐ Program E
- ☐ Program F

What are your favorite ice cream flavors? (Choose up to five)

- ☐ Chocolate
- ☐ Vanilla
- ☐ Pistachio
- ☐ Banana
- ☐ Rocky Road
- ☐ Butter Pecan
- ☐ Strawberry
- ☐ None of these

Check all that apply. These are a subset of multiple-choice questions in which respondents are asked to choose as many categories as they feel apply to the question stem (see Figure 4.16). These questions can be problematic in that some studies (e.g., Rasinski, Mingay, & Bradburn, 1994) have shown that respondents do not always read and consider all categories, especially if the list of categories is long. Whereas a checked box can indicate a respondent's endorsement of that particular item, an unchecked box leaves the researcher not knowing whether the item applies to the respondent, whether the respondent was unsure as to whether the item applied, or whether the

FIGURE 4.16 ● *Check All That Apply* Question

How did you hear about our product? Please check all that apply.

☐ Television

☐ Radio

☐ Newspaper

☐ Website

☐ Word of mouth

☐ Other

Dichotomous question alternative to check all that apply:

Do you own the following devices? Place an X on the line for YES or NO.

	YES	NO
Television	_____	_____
Smartphone	_____	_____
DVD player	_____	_____
Desktop computer	_____	_____
Laptop computer	_____	_____
Tablet computer	_____	_____
Stereo system	_____	_____

respondent even saw, read, or considered the item. An alternative to asking a "check all that apply" question is to ask about each list item separately as a dichotomous (i.e., yes or no) question. This alternative also makes for more straightforward analysis. However, there are implications for this as well, especially if there is a specific need to measure how many or in what combinations respondents choose list items.

Rating scale. These are a subset of multiple-choice questions with three or more response options on some sort of continuum with an inherent order (see Figure 4.17 for a poor rating scale question and Figure 4.18 for a good one). To design a good rating scale question, researchers must do the following:

- Carefully choose wording that aligns with the question stem

- Determine the appropriate number of response categories on the scale

- Craft either a **unipolar** (i.e., from the absence of something to the presence of something as in "not satisfied" to "satisfied") or **bipolar** (i.e., from one polar opposite to the other as in "dissatisfied" to "satisfied")

- Include a midpoint, neutral, don't know, or not applicable category as needed (one or more of these is often needed)

- Label the response options if needed (such as with numbers or words)

Rating scale questions have generated substantial discussion, controversy even, among researchers. There is very little definitive research on the best ways to construct rating scales and therefore little agreement among researchers on the many aspects of doing so. However, because the wording, number, and even the order of response

FIGURE 4.17 ● *Rating Questions* With Misaligned Response Options

Please indicate how useful the following content will be to your work going forward:

	Strongly disagree	Disagree	Agree	Strongly agree	N/A
The webinar on the topic	O	O	O	O	O
The research we shared	O	O	O	O	O
The document we sent	O	O	O	O	O

On a scale of 1–10 please rate how our website performed on the following:

The specific product you were looking for was available for purchase on our website:

Poor   Excellent

1	2	3	4	5	6	7	8	9	10
O	O	O	O	O	O	O	O	O	O

FIGURE 4.18 ● *Rating Scale* Questions With Properly Aligned Response Options

How useful did you find our product?

- O Very useful
- O Somewhat useful
- O Not at all useful

I believe that cursive handwriting should be taught in U.S. elementary schools.

- O Strongly disagree
- O Disagree
- O Neither agree nor disagree
- O Agree
- O Strongly agree

On a scale of 1–10 where 1 = very poor and 10 = outstanding, please rate our customer service:

1	2	3	4	5	6	7	8	9	10
O	O	O	O	O	O	O	O	O	O

options can significantly influence responses, and because each of these decisions carries with it specific advantages and disadvantages, we have devoted much of Chapter 5 to the research and resulting advice on constructing rating scales.

Ranking scale. Yet another subset of multiple-choice questions, ranking questions ask respondents to choose a specific number of response options *in order* (e.g., from greatest/most to least) on a certain dimension, such as preference, importance, or intensity (see Figure 4.19). Varieties of ranking questions ask respondents to rank all available options, or only some (e.g., rank your top three choices). Respondents can also be asked to rank a certain number of both top and bottom choices (e.g., rank the four most important and four least important). Limiting the number of options a respondent is asked to select is especially helpful if the list of available options is long. Respondents typically have an easier time identifying choices that are the best fit for them at the ends of a scale (e.g., most and least preferred) as compared to those in between. Ranking scales are also especially useful when the expectation is that respondents feel generally favorably about all options.

FIGURE 4.19 ● *Ranking Scale* **Questions**

Rank each of these colors in order from your most favorite (1) to your least favorite (7):

_____ blue

_____ red

_____ green

_____ purple

_____ pink

_____ brown

_____ yellow

Of the following places, rank only the three (3) most exciting vacation spots (even if you have never traveled there):

_____ New York City

_____ Orlando, Florida

_____ Paris, France

_____ San Diego, California

_____ Rome, Italy

_____ Sydney, Australia

_____ London, England

_____ Honolulu, Hawaii

Although ranking questions allow respondents to help us understand how they see response options in relation to each other, these questions do not allow us to understand the strength or intensity of respondents' feelings. For example, in Figure 4.19, a respondent may choose Paris, France, as her first preferred vacation spot, and Orlando, Florida, and New York City as choices 2 and 3. The respondent may, in fact, absolutely *love* traveling to all three places and may have found it difficult to rank them as she did. Or it is possible that the respondent finds Paris, France, *very* exciting and the other two much less so. The point is that we cannot know this from a response to one ranking scale item.

Semantic differential scale. This type of question, or more accurately *series of questions*, usually features a list of adjectives (or short adjective phrases) respondents might use to describe something (e.g., a concept, event, or product) along with their polar opposites (e.g., small-large; hot-cold) and plotted at the ends of a numeric rating scale (see Figure 4.20). The numeric scale most often includes seven options between the poles, though sometimes only five options are used. The scale can also be drawn as a simple horizontal line with no numeric labeling, allowing the respondent to mark approximately where on the line (between the two polls) she feels her answer belongs. This presents unique challenges for analysis and interpretation because respondents would be able to make their marks anywhere on the line.

A single item on a semantic differential scale is essentially a bipolar rating scale item. The group of items that make up the semantic differential scale is a composite measure designed to give the researcher a sort of image of how respondents perceive the thing being measured. An advantage of using this type of survey question is that it allows respondents to report their feelings about a topic or construct in degrees, thus providing for a fairly wide range of responses that can give us a detailed understanding of a concept.

FIGURE 4.20 ● *Semantic Differential Scale*

I found this hotel:

DIRTY	O	O	O	O	O	O	O	CLEAN
UNFRIENDLY	O	O	O	O	O	O	O	WELCOMING
UNCOMFORTABLE	O	O	O	O	O	O	O	COMFORTABLE
INADEQUATE	O	O	O	O	O	O	O	ADEQUATE
EXPENSIVE	O	O	O	O	O	O	O	INEXPENSIVE

Discussion Questions

- How might you go about determining whether to search for an existing survey tool or design a survey from scratch?

- How might you know when to engage potential respondents in the question drafting (or prototyping) phase of survey design?

- What are some possible specific scenarios when open-ended questions might be needed?

 Design Drills

1. Research Scenario, Part 4 (additional parts are found in other chapters): You are developing a survey that will ask low-income senior citizens about their behaviors and thoughts related to a program delivered at local libraries. The program is intended to help senior citizens feel more engaged with their communities and to be more social, given concerns about seniors becoming too isolated.

   a. What question types might you employ in drafting your survey? What else might you need to know to determine what question types you should use, or to otherwise begin drafting questions?

   b. Walk through the design thinking process for this survey. What might you do at each stage? How might each stage impact the questions you draft?

   c. Draft five questions for the survey, using at least three types of questions. You'll use this draft in a future chapter's exercises.

2. Consider a current highly politically charged or controversial topic in the news today. How might you construct a set of questions to measure respondents' attitudes about this topic? What strategies would you use to build rapport with respondents and avoid using leading or loaded questions?

3. Your survey: Practice composing variations of each question type presented in the chapter, based on the research question and survey purpose you identified in previous chapters.

 Extended Learning

- Alreck, P. L., & Settle, R. B. (2004). *The survey research handbook* (3rd ed.). Chicagoasis: Irwin.

- Fowler, F. J. (2014). *Survey research methods* (5th ed.). Thousand Oaks, CA: Sage.

- Rea, L. M., & Parker, R. A. (2014). *Designing and conducting survey research: A comprehensive guide* (4th ed.). San Franciscoasis: Jossey-Bass.

5

Constructing
Response Options

If you do not know how to ask the right question, you discover nothing.

**—W. Edwards Deming, American engineer,
statistician, author, and management consultant**

Taken together, all the decisions that factor into question design, including construction of response options and rating scales, can be overwhelming. Nearly a century's worth of research into this topic has yet to produce definitive instruction, likely for the same reason this text provides more guidance than prescription throughout. The right approach, wording, and order of response options depend a great deal on context. Survey designers must couple a solid understanding of the question answering process from the respondent's point of view with the extensive existing research in order to design effective survey questions with appropriate response options. Doing so can help ensure that survey questions will measure what we want them to measure and will result in rich, nuanced, usable data.

In particular, response options cannot be left to chance or simple intuition, and researchers must devote careful attention to developing them. The following question offered by Schwarz and Oyserman (2001) is a helpful "check" as we craft response options: "Does the scale convey information that is likely to influence respondents' interpretation of the question in unintended ways?" (p. 133). Though written about frequency scales in particular, this question can be applied to all types of response options. It is also a reminder that response options sometimes provide critical clues for respondents to use in making sense of survey questions and inferring researchers' interests.

Determining Appropriate Response Options

To answer a survey question accurately, respondents must read all parts of the question stem and response options and then select their responses according to any instructions the survey designer provides (e.g., check all that apply, select only one, choose up to three). Each part of the question can impact the nature and quality of the response. For example, **frequency scales** (sets of response options that indicate frequencies such as occasionally, rarely, never, once per week, yearly) seem easy to compose. However, the specific set of frequencies we choose can significantly influence survey response. Research indicates that respondents use clues from the available response options to make inferences, develop estimates, and even edit their answers as they respond to survey questions (see, for example, Courneya, Jones, Rhodes, & Blanchard, 2003; Gaskell, O'Muircheartaigh, & Wright, 1994; Meadows, Greene, Foster, & Beer, 2000; Schwarz, Hippler, Deutsch, & Strack, 1985). With this in mind, survey designers have a multitude of decisions to make even after determining how to word a closed-ended question stem. Too often they rely more on simple intuition than on nearly a century's worth of empirical research (Krosnick, 1997). Among these key decisions are the following:

- How many response options to offer

- Which response options to offer

- Whether to offer an even or odd number of response options

- When to include a "no opinion," "don't know," or an "other" option

- Whether to label some or all points on a rating scale with verbal or numeric labels

- How to order response options if no inherent order (e.g., numerical) exists

The following sections cover these decision points, as well as the various types of response options, including unipolar and bipolar scales, frequency scales, and Likert (and Likert-type) items. In addition, we discuss strategies such as decomposition and retrieval cues that can be employed to encourage thoughtful and accurate survey responses. However, before we jump too quickly into the details of how to compose response options, one key point we made in Chapter 4 bears repeating here and that is that any set of response options *must be* both exhaustive and mutually exclusive. In other words, in a question for which respondents are to select exactly one answer, they must be able to find one and only one possible answer.

How Many Response Options to Include

The number of response options to include is subject to great and ongoing debate. *There is no right or wrong answer to the question of exactly how many response options to offer for any given survey question.* In theory, the more response options (or scale points) to choose from, the more a respondent will be able to distinguish her attitude toward one thing versus another (e.g., does a respondent slightly agree, somewhat agree, mostly agree, or strongly agree with a given statement) or provide a more accurate assessment of how often he engages in a behavior (e.g., once per day, 2–3 times per week, several times per month). Given our desire to be empathetic to the respondent's task, giving more options rather than fewer would seem a good idea. After all, wouldn't respondents prefer a wide range of meaningful choices so that they can identify the one that most closely matches their feeling or experience? This "granularity," as it is sometimes called, may allow researchers "to make more subtle distinctions among individuals' attitudes toward the same object" (Krosnick, 1997), thus leading us to believe we have measured the phenomenon of interest with greater precision.

However, many other considerations influence how many response options or scale points to offer respondents. The downside of getting too granular is that the difference between various points can get messy, and the meaning of any specific point on a rating scale may be less precise. Respondents can become fatigued when faced with too many choices and find it more difficult to decide on the best answer for them, resulting in satisficing behavior. Imagine a respondent thinking, *I don't really know if I somewhat agree or mostly agree . . . oh well, I'll just pick the first one.* Such satisficing can result in measurement error if the choice made is not a true indication of the respondent's level of agreement. How well respondents can discriminate between individual scale points largely depends on what is being measured and how it is described in rating scale labels. Respondents may also perceive survey items with shorter scales (e.g., 3–5 points) as easier and quicker to answer, thereby motivating their response. However, they may find shorter scales insufficient for describing their attitudes, opinions, or behaviors (Preston & Colman, 2000). In these instances, whenever given the opportunity, we find that respondents write in their own responses or skip questions altogether when they find the opportunity to do so. Dichotomous questions (e.g., yes/no questions), although useful in some circumstances, generally limit our ability to describe a phenomenon of interest. Often, a question with a set of scaled response options is a better choice. For example, rather than asking respondents *if* they use a grocery delivery service, we can ask *how often* they use this service, offering response options from zero on up. This allows us much greater depth of understanding of the respondent's experience without increasing respondent burden with additional questions.

Researchers have conducted numerous studies on scale length, and although there is no absolute determination of a "best" number of scale points, many if not most researchers (e.g., Krosnick, 1997; Lozano, Garcia-Cueto, & Muñiz, 2008; Tourangeau et al., 2000; Weijters, Cabooter, & Schillewaert, 2010) as well as a number of early 20th-century researchers (Symonds, 1924, likely the first to suggest a specific number) settled on recommending either 5- or 7-point scales (Malhotra, Krosnick, & Thomas, 2009) or a range of 4- to 7-point scales, thus including the two options (4- or 6-point) of using an even number of scale points; some claim that up to 9 points is also more than acceptable (e.g., Cox, 1980). Most agree that little is to be gained from rating scales with more than 7 to 9 points. That said, one study (Pearse, 2011) demonstrates the utility of a 21-point scale in which respondents meaningfully used all 21 options. This resulted in sufficient variability and caused the researcher to conclude that "researchers should pay more attention to the scale granularity that they use when designing a questionnaire, rather than simply applying conventional wisdom" (Pearse, 2011, p. 169). We concur and add that it is more important to carefully consider the research question, survey purpose, and measurement goals to determine an appropriate scale and level of granularity for each item. No matter how many options are offered, they must each be meaningful for respondents, *and* respondents must easily be able to discriminate among each option. This may mean different response scale lengths for different survey questions, and even different response scale lengths for different respondent populations (Viswanathan, Sudman, & Johnson, 2004).

The Odds or Evens (Midpoint) Debate

Another perennial debate among survey researchers is whether to include a midpoint response option, typically resulting in an odd number of choices. As with any question design decision, there are several considerations. In some instances, we may not want to give respondents the option of answering using a middle category. In other words, we want them to definitively choose sides. The thinking around this "forced choice" scenario is that without a midpoint, respondents will give their "truest" feelings or attitudes. Some researchers feel that very few people are actually neutral or feel genuinely indifferent about topics and that most, if pressed to do so, would be able to express even a slight leaning one way or another. These researchers fear (and rightly so) that when given a neutral option, more respondents will select it than should do so. This could be due to satisficing, lack of certainty or genuine opinion on the topic, social desirability and other biases, or avoidance of the mental effort required to select another response.

One of the most important concerns survey designers face is the potential overuse of a neutral or midpoint, which yields less precise, less usable data. For example, if asked to respond to this statement: *The 1847 Sonderbund War was the most important factor in Switzerland's transition to a federal state* and given a 5-point scale of *strongly disagree; disagree; neither agree nor disagree; agree; and strongly agree*, how might a respondent choose? If a respondent doesn't know anything about the Sonderbund War, she might choose the midpoint option (*neither agree nor disagree*). If a respondent has heard of this war but doesn't remember the outcome or political implications, he might choose the midpoint option. If a respondent knows about this war and its outcome but is uncertain whether it was or was not "the most important factor" she might endorse the midpoint option. We could continue to present other scenarios. The problem is that when responses cluster at a midpoint, it often tells us very little (is it indifference, ambivalence, lack of information or knowledge, or something else?), and we cannot make the assumption that respondents necessarily have no opinion or, in this case, truly "neither agree nor disagree" with the statement. Sturgis, Roberts, and Smith (2014), for example, found that the majority of respondents who chose a neither/nor (as in "neither agree nor disagree") option were expressing what the researchers called a "face-saving don't know" versus a true neutral opinion on the question topic (p. 30). One interesting contribution of this study was that these "face-saving don't knows" appear "to derive from a desire to avoid social embarrassment among respondents who feel that they should have an opinion on important issues" (p. 34).

Midpoints are not all bad, however, and can offer some benefit to the researcher. "The size of the response to the middle category can give extra information about the intensity of attitudes—information that might be absent in a forced-choice situation"

(Sudman & Bradburn, 1982). The other side of the coin, though, is that without offering a midpoint, respondents who are truly neutral are forced to take a side they don't necessarily lean to.

Although different researchers fall on each side of the odds/evens debate, we find more who lean toward using an odd number of scale points (including a midpoint) when reasonable to do so, thus dismissing the theoretical or actual disadvantages of doing so (e.g., Bradburn, Sudman & Wansink, 2004; Sturgis, Roberts, & Smith, 2014; Sudman & Bradburn, 1982; Weijters, Cabooter, & Schillewaert, 2010; Weisberg, Krosnick, & Bowen, 1996). Problems arise, however, when survey designers want to heed this advice regardless of the nature of the construct being measured. Not all constructs lend themselves to an odd number of scale points with a midpoint, and we often find response option labels "retrofitted" to match a preconceived number of scale points, as in Figure 5.1, a question from a professional association postconference survey.

In general, survey designers use a midpoint especially when they are confident that respondents could *legitimately* have a neutral opinion (or no opinion) on the domain of interest, or when forcing respondents to one side or the other may result in measurement error (because forced choice would reduce the accuracy of their responses). One caution and additional consideration of a midpoint is that respondents naturally make inferences about other respondents (or even the researchers) based on the set of response options presented. Respondents may infer that the midpoint option in a behavioral question represents an "average" or "typical" respondent, leading respondents to tailor their own answers comparing themselves to what they perceive as the "average" value (Tourangeau et al., 2000). For example, if presented with the question, *About how many hours per week do you spend interacting with online social media?* and the following response options: *a. 1 hour per week or less, b. 2–3 hours per week, c. 4–5 hours per week, d. 6–7 hours per week, e. 8 or more hours per week*, respondents may

FIGURE 5.1 ● Real-World Questions: *Meaningless Midpoint*

Overall, to what extent did you find the onsite guide to be a valuable resource for conference participation?*

O Very helpful
O Somewhat helpful
O Neither helpful nor unhelpful
O Not at all helpful
O Did not use

*As is often the case, this question features multiple design flaws: 1) a meaningless midpoint, as explained earlier (something that is "not helpful" is the same as "unhelpful"; "helpfulness" as a construct is unipolar—from zero degrees of helpfulness or unhelpful, to a high degree of helpfulness); 2) a mismatch between the question stem "to what extent did you find the onsite guide to be a valuable resource . . ." and the response options that do not answer that stem (i.e., asking how "valuable" but answering with degrees of "helpfulness"); and 3) an imbalance of positive ("very helpful," "somewhat helpful") and negative ("not at all helpful") response options.

Chris Lysy, Fresh Spectrum

(incorrectly) assume that the researchers have reason to believe that 4–5 hours per week is "average" or "typical" and intentionally constructed the response options with this in mind. Respondents may base their answers on how they see themselves as compared to an average user, as opposed to searching their memories for what might be a more accurate response.

Balancing response options. Regardless of whether a response scale includes an odd or even number of responses, we recommend ensuring that response options for any given question feature a balance between positive and negative options (see Figure 5.2). An odd number of options can include a midpoint that is considered neutral, neither positive nor negative.

FIGURE 5.2 ● An Unbalanced and Balanced Set of Response Options

An unbalanced set of response options		**A balanced set of response options**	
Please rate the program:		Please rate the program:	
○ Outstanding	(positive)	○ Outstanding	(positive)
○ Excellent	(positive)	○ Excellent	(positive)
○ Very good	(positive)	○ Very good	(positive)
○ Fair	(negative)	○ Fair	(negative)
○ Poor	(negative)	○ Poor	(negative)
		○ Terrible	(negative)

FIGURE 5.3 ● Real-World Questions: *Unbalanced Scale Options*

Based on this flight, please rate the airline on the following:

	Excellent	Very good	Good	Fair	Poor	N/A
Overall experience with this flight	O	O	O	O	O	O
Value for fare paid	O	O	O	O	O	O

How likely are you to:

	Definitely will	Probably will	May or may not	Probably will not	Definitely will not
Recommend this airline to others	O	O	O	O	O
Purchase a ticket on this airline in the future	O	O	O	O	O

As the reader can see in Figure 5.3, it is all too easy to get tripped up composing rating scale questions with an imbalance of positive and negative response options. In a survey from a major airline, two consecutive sets of questions illustrate this; the first features unbalanced scale options, and the second features a balanced set of options.

In the first question, there are three positive response options—excellent, very good, and good—and two negative options—fair and poor. That said, some would argue that *fair* isn't necessarily negative but closer to a neutral response. A suggested alternative set of response options that would work well for this set of questions is this: Excellent, Very Good, Average, Poor, Terrible. This response scale features two positive options (excellent and very good), one neutral option (average), and two negative options (poor and terrible).

Unipolar and Bipolar Response Scales

Rating scales can be either unipolar or bipolar. Unipolar scales contain levels of a specific construct (e.g., understanding) ranging from the absence of the construct (e.g., no understanding) to a high degree of the construct (e.g., great understanding; see Figure 5.4). Bipolar rating scales measure a construct from one polar opposite to the other (e.g., dissatisfaction to satisfaction; see Figure 5.5). Bipolar rating scales tend to feature midpoints and therefore tend to have an odd number of response options. However, there is some support for using an even number of scale points with a bipolar construct. Yorke (2001) argues, "A decision has to be made at the outset whether a forced-choice scale or a scale with a mid-point is more appropriate for the problem" (p. 179). See the odds/evens debate earlier in this chapter for more on this decision.

Some constructs lend themselves more readily to either a unipolar or bipolar scale. Unipolar constructs have a natural zero point and theoretically cannot go below zero. For example, *effectiveness* has a natural "zero" point. Something that is "not effective" has no degree of effectiveness. Therefore, a unipolar scale, likely with no midpoint, is needed. Bipolar rating scales, although more common, can actually be trickier to craft.

FIGURE 5.4 ● Example of a Survey Question With a Unipolar Rating Scale

Please rate your level of understanding of quantum physics:

○ I have no understanding of quantum physics

○ I have a little bit of understanding of quantum physics

○ I have a fair amount of understanding of quantum physics

○ I have a great deal of understanding of quantum physics

FIGURE 5.5 ● Example of a Survey Question With a Bipolar Rating Scale

Please rate your overall satisfaction with our services:

○ Very dissatisfied

○ Somewhat dissatisfied

○ Neither satisfied nor dissatisfied

○ Somewhat satisfied

○ Very satisfied

Identifying appropriately opposite terms can be difficult for some constructs. They also require that respondents understand that the poles are indeed opposite in meaning.

It is all too easy to get tripped up creating rating scales, and even the best researchers and organizations make mistakes. Figure 5.6 includes a set of questions from a midsized nonprofit organization. It appears that the survey designers wanted to use a bipolar scale to measure the level of frequency with which customers use their resources or services. *Frequency* has a natural zero point, however, that could be expressed as "not at all." *Infrequently* is still *more* than zero, not less, making a bipolar scale the wrong choice for this construct. Because a bipolar scale often includes a midpoint, the survey designer again "retrofitted" one in, and it does not make sense in this context. Additionally, *Not sure* does not come *between* frequent and infrequent usage of services and resources; therefore, if used, it should appear as the last response option (or even separated a bit from the rest of the scale), not technically part of the rating scale. Finally, *less frequently* implies a comparison that is not clear in this context. Less frequently than *what*?

In Figure 5.7, a question from the same nonprofit, the survey designer made a similar mistake, using a bipolar rating scale with a construct that calls for a unipolar scale. The construct of familiarity lends itself to a unipolar rating scale, because *not familiar* equates to having no level of (or zero) familiarity, even if the word *unfamiliar* is used instead. Using the phrase *less familiar* implies comparison to something that is not made clear in the question, much like the use of the phrase *less frequently* in the previous example. A respondent cannot have a "neutral" position on familiarity, because familiarity is neither positive nor negative. Respondents are either unfamiliar with or familiar with something in various degrees.

FIGURE 5.6 ● Real-World Questions: *Poorly Constructed Bipolar Scale*

I and/or my organization have used the following {organization name} services and resources within the last 5 years:

	Frequently	Somewhat frequently	Not sure	Less frequently	Infrequently
Keynote speeches	O	O	O	O	O
Tools/workbooks	O	O	O	O	O
Infographic posters	O	O	O	O	O

A suggested alternative: Revise question stem and use unipolar response options with an added "not sure" option (at the end)

How often would you say you or your organization used {organization name} services and resources in the last 5 years?

	Very frequently	Somewhat frequently	Infrequently	Not at all	Not sure
Keynote speeches	O	O	O	O	O
Tools/workbooks	O	O	O	O	O
Infographic posters	O	O	O	O	O

FIGURE 5.7 ● Real-World Questions: *Poorly Constructed Bipolar Scale*

How familiar are you with {organization name} services and resources?

	Very familiar	Somewhat familiar	Neutral	Less familiar	Not familiar
In-person professional development	O	O	O	O	O
Virtual workshops/webinars	O	O	O	O	O

A suggested alternative: Use unipolar response options

How familiar are you with {organization name} services and resources?

	Very familiar	Somewhat familiar	Not familiar
In-person professional development	O	O	O
Virtual workshops/webinars	O	O	O

Using a "Don't Know" Option

It is important to anticipate that respondents may not know the answer to every question, regardless of how well we have empathized with and developed understanding of our desired respondents. Survey designers must decide whether and when to offer respondents the option of answering "don't know" to certain questions. At times, "don't know" provides meaningful data, letting us know that respondents truly do not know the answer to a question that we ask. It can also mean that respondents are choosing not to answer for other reasons, such as a concern for privacy if questions are of a sensitive or threatening nature. Some researchers feel as if the endorsement of a "don't know" option means that the respondent "is unwilling to do the work required to give an answer" (Fowler, 2014, p. 83). This can also point to potential problems with a given question. If a substantial portion of respondents answer "don't know," that can reveal that a question is inappropriate for a given population. Fortunately, this is something that can be uncovered during a pretesting phase (discussed further in Chapter 7).

For most questions about attitudes or opinions, using a filter question can eliminate the need for a "don't know" option. The filter question asks if the respondent knows enough or is interested enough about the topic to have formed an opinion. If the respondent answers positively, the next question becomes available. If the respondent answers negatively, one or more of the following questions can be skipped, leaving the researcher with data on opinion questions only from those who have declared having enough knowledge to answer meaningfully. See Figure 5.8 for an example. It is important to note that using this strategy can lengthen a survey considerably, especially if its purpose is to uncover attitudes about a wide range of topics (for more on filter questions, see Chapter 6).

Offering a "don't know" option may also imply to respondents that we are looking only for "informed judgements" (Clark & Schrober, 1992, p. 32) and expecting that they will answer the question only if they know enough about what is being asked to give such an answer. In the absence of a "don't know" option, the implication is that they are to give an answer regardless of their depth of knowledge. Similarly, having a "no opinion" option on a question about attitudes can discourage respondents from doing the mental work it takes to express an opinion. But it can also help to prevent "meaningless answers" when respondents actually know little about what is being asked (Weisberg et al., 1996, p. 89). If we are relatively certain that a large majority of our respondents will indeed know enough about what they are being asked to have an opinion and would be willing to share it, we can feel safe in omitting this option.

FIGURE 5.8 ●   Using a Filter Question Instead of a "Don't Know" Option

1. Do you feel as if you have enough information on the war in Syria to have formed an opinion on U.S. involvement in it?

   ○ YES

   ○ NO

If you answered YES, please proceed to question 2. If you answered NO, please skip to question 3.

Frequency Scales

Ordered sets of response options called frequency scales can be used to provide options for "how often" or "how many times" a respondent engaged in a behavior, felt an emotion, or had a particular experience. Schwarz, Strack, Müller, and Chassein (1988) tested a survey question about how often respondents felt "really annoyed." They presented groups with different sets of response options and found that "the range of the response alternatives induced respondents to consider different behavioral instances to be the target of the question" (p. 107). It turned out that the way in which respondents interpreted "really annoyed" depended on whether the researchers offered low or high frequencies as response options. Similarly, Meadows et al. (2000) found that when respondents were presented with "medium frequency" response options, they "reported significantly fewer target events than those presented with high frequency" options (p. 389). Continuing the example shared in Chapter 4 in which respondents are asked about feelings of sadness, if our question is "How often do you feel sad?" and response options include low frequencies such as 1 to 2 times per year up through once every month, respondents may interpret episodes of sadness as "major" sadness, such as the loss of a loved one. When the frequency scale includes higher frequencies, such as several times per week, or once per day or more, respondents may include "minor" episodes of sadness, such as when watching a movie (see Figure 5.9).

FIGURE 5.9 ● Interpreting a Question Stem in the Context of a Frequency Scale

Respondents will likely interpret "sadness" differently in these two questions:

Version 1: How often do you feel sad?

- ○ About once per year
- ○ A few times per year
- ○ At least once per month
- ○ At least once per week

Version 2: How often do you feel sad?

- ○ About once per month
- ○ A few times per month
- ○ At least once per week
- ○ Several times per week
- ○ At least once per day

As discussed in Chapter 4, adding parameters around concepts in the question stem, such as describing what is meant by "shopping" or letting participants know what counts as "attending a cultural event," may lessen the impact of problematic inferences respondents may make. Survey designers can include examples of what we are looking for or add descriptive words to provide more information for the respondent (e.g., significant sadness vs. sadness). These retrieval cues assist respondents in recalling or retrieving instances of the feeling or behavior in question and determining whether they fit the question's intent. However, this also comes with the risk of limiting what respondents might think fits the researcher's interests and can lead respondents to second-guess their initial impressions.

Dating recalled events. Chances are, you have been to a doctor in the last year. Off the top of your head, do you remember the date? Probably not. You may have also visited a hardware store. Do you remember that date? Most likely, the answer is no. How about the date of your wedding or the birth of your child? Chances are, you do remember these. In general, people are not well suited to remembering dates for more mundane events and are only good at remembering ones particularly important to them. Surveys, however, ask about the more mundane all the time. Although we do not often directly ask, "On what date in the last year did you see a doctor?" on a survey, researchers do use questions such as "How many times in the last year did you see a doctor?" This requires respondents to remember those dates (or approximations of them) in order to map them onto the available response options. Human memory also fades with time, making mundane events even more challenging to recall with accuracy the further they are in the past.

Likert Items and Likert-Type Items

Likert is perhaps the most misunderstood, misused, and even mispronounced term in survey research. Rensis Likert (pronounced "Lick-ert," not "Lie-kurt") was a mid-20th-century American social psychologist, primarily known for developing the 5-point **Likert scale**, a **psychometric scale** (i.e., a carefully crafted combination of questions devised using the science of scaling) that allows a researcher to measure respondents' attitudes about particular topics (see Figure 5.10). A Likert scale is a cluster of survey items related to each other that probes a particular construct of interest with a very specific set of consistent response options (*strongly disagree, disagree, neither disagree nor agree, agree, strongly agree*). The details of scaling science and the intricacies of the misconceptions around the use of the term *Likert* are well beyond the scope of this text, but we offer an example and brief explanation in an attempt to avoid confusion.

First and foremost, even though a single question may be in the form of a statement accompanied by a response scale whose options consist of Strongly agree to Strongly disagree, this is not a Likert scale. It is still a single question or item. Some researchers feel that even to label a survey question a "Likert item" it must adhere to certain conditions.

A Likert item looks much like one of the items in Figure 5.11—a statement with which a respondent must agree or disagree with the response options as presented (and often numbered 1–5). It contains a midpoint (*Neither agree nor disagree*) option. The five response options are symmetrical—that is, they would include an equal number of positive and negative options—and it is bipolar, meaning that the ends represent polar opposites as in *strongly agree* and *strongly disagree*. If one or more of these conditions is varied (e.g., using a 4-, 7-, or 9-point response scale, or using labels other than around "agreement"), the item would more accurately be called **Likert type** (or "Likert like") (see Figure 5.12). Some experts allow for a Likert-type item to feature a 6-point (or other number) response scale and no midpoint (e.g., *strongly disagree, moderately disagree, mildly disagree, mildly agree, moderately agree,* and *strongly agree*) (DeVellis, 2017, p. 127).

FIGURE 5.10 ●   Example Format of a Likert Scale

Please rate the degree to which you agree or disagree with each statement.

	Strongly Disagree	Disagree	Neither Agree nor Disagree	Agree	Strongly Agree
High-quality public education is one of the most important issues facing Americans today.	1	2	3	4	5
Every American deserves access to a free and appropriate public education.	1	2	3	4	5
America currently has the best public school system in the world.	1	2	3	4	5

FIGURE 5.11 ●   A Likert Item

Please rate the degree to which you agree or disagree with the statement.

	Strongly Disagree	Disagree	Neither Agree nor Disagree	Agree	Strongly Agree
Diet affects weight loss more than exercise.	1	2	3	4	5

FIGURE 5.12 ●   A Likert-Type Item

Please rate your level of satisfaction with:

	Dissatisfied	Somewhat Satisfied	Satisfied	Very Satisfied
The customer service you received.	1	2	3	4

The less an item resembles one from a true Likert scale, the less it should be referred to as a Likert-type item. However, many continue to use the terms *Likert item* or *Likert-type item* to refer to any survey question that includes an ordered set of response options (e.g., *very often, often, sometimes, rarely, never*). Others use the term *Likert scale* simply to refer to the set of response options. We generally prefer to steer clear of using the terms *Likert item* or *Likert-type item* so as to avoid entering into one of the many and common spirited debates found on listserv discussion boards, social media, blogs, or any other place social scientists and survey researchers tend to discuss these labels. Instead, we prefer to describe a question as "a closed-ended question with a rating scale" or "a closed-ended question with an agree-disagree scale."

Strategies for Designing Response Options

Researchers can use a number of strategies to improve or ensure the quality of response options. This section includes those we find most helpful to address:

- Matching response options to question stems

- Offering enough response options

- Labeling response options

- Ordering response options

- Decomposition

- Retrieval cues

Matching Response Options to Question Stems

Response options *must* match the question being asked. Part of what prompted the writing of this book was our constant frustration with mismatched question stems and response options, or in other words, incorrectly labeled rating scales. Some survey researchers think it is important to ask a series of questions (or provide a series of statements for respondents to react to) using the same rating scale, perhaps in an effort to mitigate respondents' cognitive load. This effort, though noble, can result in quite laughable question stem and response option sets (see Figure 5.13). These not

---

FIGURE 5.13 ● Real-World Questions: *Mismatched Question Stem and Response Options*

Overall, how satisfied were you with the product(s) you purchased today?

Very poor	Poor	Satisfactory	Good	Excellent
○	○	○	○	○

only appear on informal workplace surveys quickly dashed off and distributed to a department but also on large-scale surveys from national corporations and other large organizations.

Figure 5.14 shows a question from a survey from a $40 billion national retailer in which we presume the survey designer wanted to measure customers' perceptions of how their online store performed on a number of indicators such as product prices, visual appeal of the website, and ease of navigation. Each of these indicators easily lends itself to a rating scale with any number of degrees between a positive and negative response. The problem is that another indicator, the availability of a desired product, does not. Product availability is dichotomous, that is, the product was either available, or it wasn't. Rating product availability on a scale of 1–10 as a 3 or a 7 is meaningless.

FIGURE 5.14 ● Real-World Questions: *Mismatched Question Stem and Response Options*

On a scale of 1–10, please rate how {retailer name.com} performed in regard to the following:

	Poor									Excellent	Don't know
	1	2	3	4	5	6	7	8	9	10	
The specific product you were looking for was available for purchase on {retailer name.com}	O	O	O	O	O	O	O	O	O	O	O
The product prices on {retailer name.com}	O	O	O	O	O	O	O	O	O	O	O
The visual appeal of {retailer name.com}	O	O	O	O	O	O	O	O	O	O	O

Often, it appears that survey designers want to limit the question types they use and attempt to repurpose a response scale for multiple items. This may be where the previous retailer went awry, but the example in Figure 5.15, from a health care office, is even more obvious.

FIGURE 5.15 ● Real-World Questions: *Mismatched Question Stems and "Repurposed" Response Scale*

Was the {health care facility name} staff friendly, knowledgeable, and helpful?	Excellent	Good	Fair	Poor	N/A
Front desk/reception	O	O	O	O	O
Technologist	O	O	O	O	O
Medical assistant	O	O	O	O	O

(Continued)

FIGURE 5.15 ● (Continued)

	Excellent	Good	Fair	Poor	N/A
Were you able to make an appointment quickly and easily?	○	○	○	○	○
Were you greeted with a smile?	○	○	○	○	○
Upon arrival, was the registration quick and efficient?	○	○	○	○	○
How thoroughly was your procedure explained to you?	○	○	○	○	○
Do you feel your exam was performed professionally?	○	○	○	○	○
If you met with a physician, was she/he polite and informative?	○	○	○	○	○
How would you rate the comfort and cleanliness of our facility?	○	○	○	○	○
Overall, how would you rate the quality of care you received?	○	○	○	○	○
How would you rate your total visit time?	○	○	○	○	○

*We also wish to note that this particular set of questions includes other problems in its construction, and as such, we offer the reader the opportunity to redesign it in the exercises at the end of the chapter.

Mismatches are so common in surveys that people even call them out on social media as in Figure 5.16.

The problem of mismatched question stems and response options is easily remediated by simply labeling response options with language that matches what the question is asking (see Figure 5.17). This approach is also referred to as "direct labeling" (Fowler, 2014) or using **item-specific (IS)** rating scales. Some researchers are reluctant to use IS rating scales. They feel that offering a set of questions with the

FIGURE 5.16 ● Real-World Questions: *Tweet About a Mismatched Question Stem and Rating Scale Options*

Derek Bruff @derekbruff · Feb 20
"Rate the TA's overall contribution." Scale: Strongly disagree to strongly agree.
#courseevals #surveydesign

↩   ⟲ 1   ★   •••

same response options—such as using the common "agree-disagree" (or "AD") rating scale—is easier on respondents. Although this may be true in some ways, there is some empirical support for choosing IS rating scales. Saris, Revilla, Krosnick, and Shaeffer (2010) conducted a study of questions using IS versus AD rating scales, and "results attest to the superiority of questions with IS response options" (p. 61).

We had the opportunity to talk with evaluator E. Jane Davidson on when Likert-type survey items can potentially be problematic and how to create survey questions that are more evaluative.

FIGURE 5.17 ● Examples of Matching Question Stem and Rating Scale Language (Item-Specific Rating Scales)

How helpful was our staff?

- O Not at all helpful
- O Somewhat helpful
- O Very helpful

Please rate the performance of our staff.

- O Terrible
- O Poor
- O Fair
- O Good
- O Very good
- O Excellent

How useful is the product?

- O Not at all useful
- O Somewhat useful
- O Very useful
- O Extremely useful

Please rate your level of satisfaction with the product.

- O Very dissatisfied
- O Somewhat dissatisfied
- O Neither satisfied nor dissatisfied
- O Somewhat satisfied
- O Very satisfied

MINI-INTERVIEW WITH E. JANE DAVIDSON
WHEN AVOIDING LIKERT-TYPE ITEMS MAY BE BEST

E. Jane Davidson is an internationally recognized evaluation thought leader, best known for developing evaluation rubrics as a methodology for drawing conclusions about quality and value. She has also made significant contributions in the areas of causal inference for qualitative and mixed methods, and in synthesis methodologies for evaluation.

As a thought leader in evaluation and smart data collection and analysis, you've been outspoken about how Likert-type response options are problematic when evaluating the quality or value of a program. Can you share more about why?

EJD: Real, genuine evaluation is evaluative. In other words, it doesn't just report descriptive evidence for others to interpret; it combines this evidence with appropriate definitions of *quality* and *value* and draws conclusions about the quality, value, and effectiveness of a program.

Likert scale response options usually provide purely descriptive information, which is difficult to interpret. Consider this example:

To what extent do you agree or disagree with the following?

The program was well designed. (strongly disagree, disagree, neutral, agree, strongly agree)

What does it mean if most respondents agree? How well designed was the course? What can be done with these results?

What does a more evaluative question look like?

EJD: If we build evaluative language into the question, and particularly the response options, the data are far easier to interpret for evaluative purposes. Here's a better way to ask the question above:

How would you rate the program? (poor, adequate, good, very good, excellent)

Better yet, when we have clear outcomes we're trying to measure, we can use that language in both the question stem and response options.

Is it possible to get helpful information about the overall value of a program from a survey?

EJD: Yes, BUT!! That's not the only evidence you should use to draw a conclusion about overall value, but by all means, tap into that as one source of evidence.

As for how to ask about overall value, the same concept applies here! Asking respondents how they would rate the value of a program overall is best included in surveys *after* asking about specific outcomes (because that will help the respondent reflect on the overall value as you've defined it). Questions about this can be crafted about the value of the program for an individual or respondents' perspectives on the program's value for an organization or sector. Here's an example:

An important evaluation question about a set of leadership development programs I evaluated a while back was whether each of them was "worth it" in some overall sense. This was a relatively low budget evaluation relative to the size of the programs themselves, so the opportunity to do a really in-depth cost-benefit analysis didn't exist. Besides, many of the outcomes did not easily reduce themselves to some monetary benefit. Here are two questions we used to help gauge value for individuals:

How would you rate the program overall as a worthwhile use of your time? (A+, A, A−, B+, B, B−, C+, C, C−, D, F)

To what extent do you believe the benefits of the program outweigh the financial, time, opportunity, and other costs of attending? (Costs clearly outweigh benefits, Benefits of similar value to costs, Benefits clearly outweigh costs, Unable to estimate)

What are some key caveats/considerations for evaluators in writing better survey questions?

EJD: Survey responses should never be the only data used in an evaluation effort. Additional evidence is needed to triangulate responses. However, evaluators can write far more useful (and interesting) questions than we often see in surveys.

The extent to which response options need to be spelled out—or even just specifically worded—depends on what is being evaluated and how much the details matter. Sometimes a single question will suffice, and the constructs may not need to be tightly defined or specified in order for responses to a question to be useful. At other times, it may be very important to get a clear sense of what lies underneath respondents' thinking about quality (or whatever is being measured). If this gets too detailed or complicated, it may be that a survey isn't the best tool for the job anyway (e.g., interviews that would allow for probing for more detail would generate more useful information).

For more about Jane's thinking on this and other evaluation topics, see posts at the *Genuine Evaluation* blog, http://GenuineEvaluation.com; check out her Real Evaluation website, http://RealEvaluation.com; or read one of her great texts, such as *Actionable Evaluation Basics: Getting Succinct Answers to the Most Important Questions* (2012, Real Evaluation; also available in Spanish and French) or *Evaluation Methodology Basics: The Nuts and Bolts of Sound Evaluation* (2005, Sage).

Offering Enough Response Options

Survey designers must ensure that response options reflect the entire range of possible responses; in other words, as discussed earlier, response options must be *exhaustive*. Problems arise when respondents are not offered options that accurately represent their attitudes or experiences. Once again, consider the question in Figure 5.18 from a federal executive department charged with collecting and analyzing data.

FIGURE 5.18 ● Real-World Questions: *Insufficient Response Options*

How often do you visit the {department name} website?

- ○ This is my first time
- ○ Once a year or less
- ○ About once a month
- ○ About once a week
- ○ About every day

Clearly there are not enough response options here. The survey designer may have wanted to limit the options a respondent needed to consider. Indeed, trying to cram in all of the possible options may make for too many choices, resulting in a heavy cognitive load for respondents who must 1) read the various options, 2) consider their own behavior, *and* 3) map their responses onto those available options. Figure 5.19 is an example of how this question might appear if a more comprehensive list of choices were offered.

FIGURE 5.19 ● Real-World Questions: *Too Many Response Options*

How often do you visit the {department name} website?

○ This is my first time
○ Once a year or less
○ About twice a year
○ About 3–5 times per year
○ About 6–8 times per year
○ About 9–11 times per year
○ About once a month
○ About 2–3 times per month
○ About once a week
○ About twice a week
○ About 3–5 times per week
○ About every day

Figure 5.20 illustrates an example of what a "happy medium" might look like for this particular question.

FIGURE 5.20 ● A Suggested Alternative: Revise Both Stem and Response Options to Capture *All* Potential Experiences

About how many times per year do you visit our website?

○ This is my first time
○ About 1 time per year or less often
○ About 2–4 times per year
○ About 5–7 times per year
○ About 8–10 times per year
○ About 11 or more times per year

For some questions, ensuring sufficient response options without overburdening the respondent or potentially missing responses can be alleviated by using a "catch-all" response such as "other." This can be done with or without the option of having respondents explain their answer. Figure 5.21 is one example of when "other" is an appropriate response option.

FIGURE 5.21 ● Using "Other" as a Catch-All

What is your favorite dessert?

- O Pie
- O Cake
- O Cookies
- O Ice cream
- O Fruit
- O OTHER

Labeling Response Options

Yet another key decision survey designers must make is whether to apply verbal labels (i.e., words or phrases) to all rating scale points, label only the endpoints (or "anchors"), or label the endpoints along with one or more middle points. Although it may seem as if numeric values are more precise than verbal labels, numbers are not what we typically use to communicate our thoughts, opinions, or attitudes in daily conversations (Krosnick, 1997). This may lead us in the direction of wanting to verbally label all scale points, but in practice, we find that especially with more than 4 to 5 points, this becomes burdensome and can easily result in labels that are meaningless as we point out in earlier examples. No matter how rating scales are labeled, it is important to remember that "respondents have difficulty using scales and pay attention even to incidental features of the response scales in interpreting the scale points" (Tourangeau, Couper, & Conrad, 2007, p. 92).

Numeric labels, though carrying no specific meaning individually, do at the very least carry the assumption of equal intervals between scale points, something that can only be loosely inferred from verbal labels. In Figure 5.22, given the example with mostly numeric labels, it is easy to infer that the intervals between 2 and 3 or between 7 and 8 are equal. In the second example with all verbal labels, we would be less confident that respondents will infer the intervals between *excellent* and *very good* or between *fair* and *poor* as necessarily equal.

FIGURE 5.22 ● Numeric Versus Verbal Labels

How would you rate your Internet service provider?

Poor   Excellent

1	2	3	4	5	6	7	8	9	10
O	O	O	O	O	O	O	O	O	O

How would you rate your Internet service provider?

Poor	Fair	Good	Very good	Excellent
O	O	O	O	O

Considering the levels of cognitive demand our respondents will experience when answering survey questions, it might seem less burdensome to use a numeric scale with endpoint labels only. This would eliminate the need for respondents to read and interpret five or more words or phrases, an especially challenging task if the phrases are linguistically complex. However, though it is certainly much easier for survey designers to verbally label just two endpoints and perhaps a midpoint on a 5- or even 7-point scale, this may not be the best course of action for our respondents. Respondents with an **extreme response style (ERS)** tend to choose the endpoints with more frequency when these are the *only* scale points that carry verbal labels: "End labeling evoked more ERS than full labeling, . . . because end labeling draws attention to the two extreme categories, which are thus clearer in meaning to respondents than the categories in between" (Moors, Kieruj, & Vermunt, 2014, p. 391). Numerous studies have shown the benefits of applying verbal labels to all scale points (see, for example, Conti & Pudney, 2011; Weijters et al., 2010; Weng, 2004; Wouters, Maesschalck, Peeters, & Roosen, 2013) with regard to obtaining the richest data possible.

Words and numbers are not the only labeling options available. One study we examined looked at respondents' motivations for preferring different types of rating scale labels and features, including icons such as stars and "thumbs up." The authors found that "the most relevant motivations for positive preferences are informativeness, speed and ease use, and ease of comprehension" (Cena & Vernero, 2015). Labeling all scale points potentially reduces error, especially when a survey or group of items on a survey includes a balance of items of which some are expected to be endorsed at the high end of the rating scale and others expected to be endorsed at the low end (Weijters et al., 2010) (see Figure 5.23).

Vague quantifiers. Words such as *many, most, sometimes, frequently,* and *several* are ubiquitous in surveys but can easily trip up respondents. As with all language in surveys, respondents must make sense of these terms, interpreting them as researchers intend and determining where to map their responses. Respondent interpretation of such terms is highly dependent on the specific content of the question asked as well as the characteristics of respondents (Tourangeau et al., 2000). "The translation of the response options back to numerical values is a complex undertaking. If designers want numerical information about frequencies or amounts, then it may be best for them to ask for it directly" (Tourangeau et al., 2000, p. 50).

FIGURE 5.23 ● Items Expected to Be Endorsed at the High and Low Ends of a Rating Scale

	Strongly disagree	Disagree	Neither agree nor disagree	Agree	Strongly agree
I would recommend this course to others	O	O	O	O	O
Most of the course content was review for me	O	O	O	O	O

For example, if a respondent eats eggs for breakfast twice a week, that respondent might regard this as "sometimes" eating eggs, whereas another respondent may label this as "frequently" eating eggs. It is easy to see how someone can struggle to choose an appropriate vague quantifier, especially if an exact quantity or frequency is known. "This is nicely illustrated in Woody Allen's *Annie Hall* [a movie from 1977]. Both Annie and Alvie Singer report that they have sex three times a week, but she characterizes this as 'constantly' whereas his description is 'hardly ever'" (Schaeffer & Presser, 2003, p. 74). In yet another good example, Courneya et al. (2003) compared five different response scales with undergraduate students who were identified as regular and non-regular exercisers. They found that 42% of nonregular exercisers—those who reported exercising 15 or fewer times in the past 30 days—"characterized their exercise frequency as 'occasionally,'" but 19% of the regular exercisers (15 or more times in 30 days) *also* characterized their frequency this way. Similarly, "63% of regular exercisers and 11% of nonregular exercisers characterized their exercise frequency as 'often'" (p. 617).

Using the most specific and precise language, including numbers whenever feasible, is preferable to using vague quantifiers. However, there are instances when a certain level of precision may not be necessary or when it would be too difficult for respondents to be precise in their estimated responses. In this case it may not even matter if all respondents interpret *frequently* (or other vague quantifiers) in the same way. It matters only that *they* considered their behavior as frequent. When vague quantifiers are necessary, ensuring that response options appear in their natural order (i.e., from least to most, or most to least) can be critical, especially in cases where two or more of the terms may be interpreted by respondents as being close in meaning (e.g., *some* and *a few*).

Ordering Response Options

Although the words and phrases we choose are certainly fundamental to constructing response options, people also "respond to the *ordinal* position of categories as well as to the descriptors" (Fowler, 2014, p. 89). Note that back in Figure 5.2 in the first of the two examples, the lowest possible response is "poor" whereas in the second example, the lowest possible response is "terrible"—one *below* "poor." Respondents may indeed select these options differently. Some respondents may approach the response options knowing that they want to assign the program the lowest rating possible (i.e., attending to ordinal position) regardless of the descriptor, whereas others may spend more time considering which descriptor most closely matches their feelings regardless of position on the rating scale.

Studies on response option order are numerous and their findings inconsistent (Weng & Cheng, 2000). Whereas Weng and Cheng (2000) found in one study that "response order is not a critical factor in affecting participant responses" (p. 922), Krosnick and Alwin (1987) found that order "effects were quite large in some cases" (p. 215), and Chan (1991) found evidence of a **primacy effect**—where the first item or items seen, read, or heard are best remembered or more influential than later items—on an attitudinal scale. According to Krosnick and Alwin (1987), order effects may be most evident with "respondents with less cognitive sophistication. . . . [and] Respondents with less formal education and more limited vocabularies were influenced more by our manipulation" (Krosnick & Alwin, 1987, p. 215).

Other respondent characteristics may play a role in response order effects as well, such as their motivation to read and consider all response options given before selecting an answer (Weng & Cheng, 2000). "The phenomenon was more likely to occur when examining all the options required much more cognitive demands on the participants than simply checking the first acceptable option without examining the rest" (Weng & Cheng, 2000, p. 911). In addition to endorsing the first options or those that appear nearest the first on an agreement/disagreement (AD) rating scale, order effects can be found in a question that asks respondents to rank one or more options among many. Krosnick and Alwin (1987) conducted experiments with ranking scales, asking respondents to choose three most important qualities among a list of 13 options. They found that "placing an item among the first three on the list increased the likelihood that it would be chosen as one of the three most important qualities" (p. 215). In general, respondents tend to lean toward the positive end of the scale (i.e., **positivity bias**) and also tend to avoid selecting scale end-points (i.e., **response contraction**). Although discussions of these two concepts—positivity bias and response contraction—are beyond the scope of this text, rich explanations and examples can be found in Tourangeau et al. (2000).

Specific advice for ordering response options. We can offer three specific pieces of advice for ordering response options:

1. To mitigate any possible order effects with a set of response options for which there is no inherent order (i.e., a simple multiple choice–type question), it is best to randomize the order of response options and then randomly assign respondents to different versions of the question. Of course, this strategy does involve additional planning on the part of the researcher regarding constructing multiple versions of a survey instrument.

2. If a numeric scale is used, it should read from least to greatest, either left to right or top to bottom depending on whether the rating scale is presented horizontally or vertically.

3. Rating scales should generally start with least desirable to most desirable responses to mitigate the primacy effect, even if small.

Decomposition

Many survey questions ask respondents to provide factual information about events such as the number of visits made to a hardware store or hospital, or the number of times they have purchased alcoholic beverages or clothing. Decomposition is a popular strategy in which more complex questions are broken down into smaller "chunks" by asking multiple questions about subcategories of the event of interest into "two or more mutually exclusive, less cognitively taxing subquestions . . . [providing] cues along a relevant dimension, such as time, place, person, context, or content" (Schaeffer & Dykema, 2011, p. 926). For example, instead of asking respondents how often they have "gone shopping" during a certain reference period, the question may be "decomposed" into several more specific questions that ask about shopping at department stores, home stores, discount stores, or grocery stores. It is the researcher's hope that including these retrieval cues—in this example, naming the different types of stores—will assist the respondent in remembering instances of shopping that might otherwise be forgotten. There is more speculation than empirical evidence of decomposition's effectiveness and significant concern that it results in overreporting. Decomposition is also a strategy probably best used when the reference period is shorter (Belli, Schwarz, Singer, & Talerico, 2000), when the number of events or behaviors in question is large, or when the behaviors or events are particularly memorable or infrequent.

Decomposition can also be especially useful in easing cognitive load. When we ask a question about satisfaction with a product purchase, for example, we are in essence asking two things: the *direction* of respondents' opinion (*whether* they were satisfied or dissatisfied) and the *intensity* of their opinion (*how* satisfied or dissatisfied they were). One way to mitigate the cognitive load of one question asking two things is to break or *decompose* the question into two separate questions (Dillman et al. 2014, p. 161). Figure 5.24 shows how we might accomplish this.

FIGURE 5.24 ● Decomposing a Bipolar Rating Scale Question

Undecomposed question:

Overall, how satisfied are you with today's purchase?

    ○   ○   ○   ○   ○

Very satisfied Somewhat satisfied Neither satisfied Somewhat dissatisfied Very dissatisfied
                             nor dissatisfied

Decomposed question:

Overall, are you satisfied, dissatisfied, or neutral about today's purchase?

    ○   ○   ○

Satisfied   Neutral   Dissatisfied

Overall are you slightly, somewhat, or very satisfied/dissatisfied?

    ○   ○   ○

Slightly   Somewhat   Very

Although Malhotra et al. (2009) found that this decomposition strategy does show promise, survey researchers must balance it with how potential respondents will perceive the length and difficulty of the survey.

Retrieval Cues

Retrieval cues may appear in survey questions as definitions or examples of what is being asked (see Figure 5.25), assisting survey respondents in a number of ways. This section includes advice for using these cues in question design not covered previously

FIGURE 5.25 ● Survey Question Featuring a Definition and Examples as Retrieval Cues

> How many times in the last 12 months did you participate in an individual sport competition? Individual sports are those played alone, without teammates. Examples include bowling, boxing, cycling, golf, skiing, swimming, running, and wrestling.

in this chapter or Chapter 3, where retrieval cues were discussed in the context of respondent memory.

Although there is always some degree of danger of respondents overreporting behaviors with the use of retrieval cues, they can be used effectively to aid recall, especially under a specific set of circumstances. Tourangeau, Conrad, Couper, and Ye (2014) conducted a series of studies asking respondents about food consumption and offering definitions of food groups (e.g., dairy, poultry) and examples of those foods to respondents in some of their experimental conditions. Their conclusions from the group of studies include the following:

- It may be better to give a lot of examples . . . or to give examples that cover the full category range.

- The best examples are those that are likely to be relevant and likely to be overlooked.

- Words may be better cues than pictures.

- Definitions for familiar categories are not useful and do not reduce the impact of examples. (p. 124)

The authors further note that "examples seem to improve the accuracy of the answers when they remind respondents to include items they might otherwise have left out, because they either had forgotten them or were unsure whether to include them" (Tourangeau et al., 2014, p. 100).

 Discussion Questions

- As a survey respondent, have you ever been annoyed by a poorly written question? If so, what bothered you about it? How might its problems have been avoided?

- Knowing that the research on survey response is not conclusive in all areas (for example, how many response options to include in a question), how do you balance what you know from the research with the decisions you have to make regarding the specific constructs you have to measure? What else informs your design decisions?

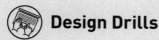 **Design Drills**

1. Identify question design flaws in this set of questions from a health care facility and redesign them:

   Real-World Questions: Mismatched Question Stems and "Repurposed" Response Scale

Was the {health care facility name} staff friendly, knowledgeable, and helpful?	Excellent	Good	Fair	Poor	N/A
Front desk/reception	○	○	○	○	○
Technologist	○	○	○	○	○
Medical assistant	○	○	○	○	○
Were you able to make an appointment quickly and easily?	○	○	○	○	○
Were you greeted with a smile?	○	○	○	○	○
Upon arrival, was the registration quick and efficient?	○	○	○	○	○
How thoroughly was your procedure explained to you?	○	○	○	○	○
Do you feel your exam was performed professionally?	○	○	○	○	○
If you met with a physician, was she/he polite and informative?	○	○	○	○	○
How would you rate the comfort and cleanliness of our facility?	○	○	○	○	○
Overall, how would you rate the quality of care you received?	○	○	○	○	○
How would you rate your total visit time?	○	○	○	○	○

2. Research Scenario, Part 5 (additional parts are found in other chapters): You are developing a survey that will ask low-income senior citizens about their behaviors and thoughts related to a program delivered at local libraries. The program is intended to help senior citizens feel more engaged with their communities and to be more social, given concerns about seniors becoming too isolated.

   a. Revisit the five questions you crafted after reading Chapter 4 and revise response options as needed.

   b. What retrieval cues have you already included? What retrieval cues might be added?

   c. Provide justification for your response option choices for each question. For example, how did you determine the appropriate number of response options, the best word choices, and whether scales would be unipolar or bipolar?

3. Find an existing survey question that would benefit from decomposition and craft a new set of questions with appropriate response options that could replace the original survey question.

Extended Learning

- Alreck, P. L., & Settle, R. B. (2004). *The survey research handbook* (3rd ed.). Chicago: Irwin.

- DeVellis, R. F. (2017). *Scale development* (4th ed.). Thousand Oaks, CA: Sage.

- Krosnick, J. A., & Fabrigar, L. R. (1997). Designing rating scales for effective measurement in surveys. In L. Lyberg, P. Biemer, M. Collins, E. de Leeuw, C. Dippo, N. Schwarz, & D. Trewin (Eds.), *Survey measurement and process quality*. New York: John Wiley.

- Likert, R. (1932). A technique for the measurement of attitudes. *Archives of Psychology, 22*(140), 5–55. (The foundational article that introduced Likert measurement)

- Tourangeau, R., Rips, L. J., & Rasinski, K. (2000). *The psychology of survey response*. New York: Cambridge University Press.

6

Special Purpose and Sensitive Questions

"Who are you?"

"No one of consequence."

"I must know."

"Get used to disappointment."

—William Goldman, *The Princess Bride*

When designing surveys with questions that may feel personal, sensitive, intrusive, or even threatening to respondents, we must return to our respondent-centered, purposeful survey design process and spend plenty of time in the empathizing phase of design thinking. As the chapter-opening quote illustrates, if we come on too strong or ask the wrong questions of our respondents at the wrong time, we risk their refusal to answer and end up learning little, if anything. To ensure questions are appropriate and will net the most useful data possible, researchers must also always keep in mind the specific cultures and contexts in which they are working and in which their desired respondents are living.

Before delving deeply into more common types of sensitive questions (e.g. demographic questions), we explore two types of questions—filter questions and quality control questions—that serve special purposes in surveys and therefore also warrant particular attention.

Two key pieces of advice we have discussed more deeply elsewhere become all the more relevant when working with special purpose and sensitive questions. Therefore, when including these types of questions in a survey, remember to

- let respondents know why the information is needed to encourage honesty and accuracy (see more about this in Chapter 4), and

- engage respondents in question design and testing prior to survey administration (see more about this in Chapter 7).

Questions With Special Purposes

Although all survey questions are designed to measure respondents' attributes, behaviors, abilities, or thoughts, certain question types also have additional functions as part of a survey instrument and require additional attention.

Filter Questions

Filter questions (also called contingency or screening questions) can be used for a variety of purposes. In Chapter 5, we briefly introduced the use of a filter question to avoid the need for a *don't know* response option. Here, we explain in greater detail and add additional purposes for filter questions, including to

- screen respondents for eligibility to complete the survey;

- direct respondents to different questions or sets of questions, depending on their answers to the filter question;

- solicit additional information about particular responses; and

- avoid the use of a *don't know* response option.

Screen respondents for eligibility to complete the survey. A survey may be administered to a large group of respondents, some of whom do not meet the criteria the researcher needs for the sample. For example, if a survey needs to reach only homeowners in a neighborhood who own two or more cars, and was sent to all residents of the neighborhood, a filter question about car ownership may be included. The answer to that question would determine if a particular respondent will complete the survey. There are also instances when a researcher needs to fill a certain quota of respondents from particular demographic subcategories, and once the quota is reached in any particular subcategory, no additional respondents from that subcategory are eligible to complete the survey.

Direct respondents to different questions or sets of questions, depending on their answers to the filter question. These questions are used to route respondents through the survey and avoid asking them questions that do not apply to them, effectively keeping the survey as short as possible for a given respondent. For example, a survey might ask if respondents rent or own a home. Depending on the answer to this question, respondents are then directed to one of two different sets of follow-up questions.

Solicit additional information about particular responses. If a researcher is interested in why respondents answer in a particular way, a filter question can be used to solicit follow-up information. This is as close as a survey gets to including the types of probing questions used in more qualitative research methods such as focus groups or interviews. For example, if a question asks respondents' opinions about a particular service and they answer negatively (e.g., *dissatisfied*), and the researcher wants to understand why, respondents can be directed to an additional question asking for detail about their opinions that is either open-ended or provides a list of possible reasons for their opinion.

Avoid the use of a don't know *response option.* By first asking if a respondent knows enough about or is interested in a topic enough to have formed an attitude, we can determine if that respondent should move forward with the survey to the attitude questions. This is sometimes preferable to simply adding a "don't know" option to each question. As we discussed in Chapter 5 when respondents choose "don't know," we often do not know if they indeed have no opinion or if they are in fact refusing to share that opinion.

Filter questions result in branching (also known as conditional branching, branch-logic, or skip logic). Most online survey platforms are equipped to help the researcher program for this, whereas instructions such as "if you answered YES to question 12, please skip to question 17" must be written into a paper survey. A trained telephone surveyor will have these instructions such that a respondent may not even be aware of any branching taking place. Figure 6.1 shows an example of a filter and follow-up question.

FIGURE 6.1 ● Example of a Filter and Follow-Up Question

1. Do you enjoy ice cream?

   ○ YES

   ○ NO

2. If you answered YES, which flavor do you like best? If you answered NO, please skip to question 3.

   ○ Chocolate

   ○ Vanilla

   ○ Strawberry

   ○ Butter pecan

   ○ Rocky road

   ○ Mint chocolate chip

   ○ Other (please write in): _____

Quality Control Questions

Have you ever participated in a survey and encountered a question like the one in Figure 6.2?

This is an example of a quality control question, designed to ensure that respondents are truly reading the questions and to ensure that the survey (usually an online survey) is not being completed by an automated program rather than a human. At times, such as in Figure 6.3, the purpose of a quality control question is explained to respondents.

FIGURE 6.2 ● Example of a Quality Control Question

For this question, please choose option 2.

   ○ 1

   ○ 2

   ○ 3

   ○ 4

FIGURE 6.3 ● Real-World Questions: *Quality Control Question Explained to Respondents*

This question is a little different. While most people carefully read and respond to the questions in our surveys a small number do not. To verify that you have read this question carefully, please select the fourth response from the list below.

   O Extremely important
   O Very important
   O Somewhat important
   O Not at all important
   O Don't know

At other times, the quality control question is designed to attempt to deceive respondents by using a fake word, as in Figure 6.4, a question from an online market research panel. The health problem they ask about, "holdequus syndrome," does not exist.

In Figure 6.4, the question is being used both for quality control and filtering purposes. The question is used to move the respondent (or not move the respondent) to a survey about health care, and because respondents are compensated for completing surveys, the panel must screen out those who would fabricate answers just to receive the rewards.

Another approach to a quality control question is to use negatively worded questions along with a number of positively worded ones to ensure that respondents are not simply answering questions randomly, answering them all exactly the same (e.g., always the third option), or otherwise without reading and considering them. For example, on a college course evaluation form, a series of questions may ask students to rate their instructors, the course material, and course activities with statements that ask students to strongly agree, agree, disagree, or strongly disagree. Although the hope is for ratings of "strongly agree," an additional statement for quality control

---

FIGURE 6.4 ● Real-World Questions: *Quality Control Question Designed to Deceive*

Have you, or someone for whom you provide care, been diagnosed with:
Holdequus Syndrome

   O I have been diagnosed with
   O I provide care for someone diagnosed with
   O Not applicable
   O Prefer not to answer

purposes might be one in which the hope is for a "strongly disagree" response, as in "This course was too difficult for me." This option is often better than the other quality control questions for at least two reasons. First, some researchers find quality control questions (such as the examples in Figures 6.2 and 6.4) disrespectful to respondents, potentially sending the message that they can't be trusted, and therefore caution against using them. Second, there is a greater concern about interrupting respondents' flow of thoughts and ideas around the topic at hand with the other types of quality control questions.

Sensitive Questions

Sensitive or threatening questions are those that feel intrusive or invasive to the respondent. They may ask respondents to disclose personal information or whether they have violated social norms or even laws (e.g., when respondents are asked about illicit drug use, criminal activity, or sexual behavior) to a third party (the researcher) (Tourangeau et al., 2000). Whether a question should be considered sensitive depends

STORIES FROM THE FIELD
SENSITIVE TOPICS ARE NOT ALWAYS OBVIOUS

As part of an evaluation of the benefits of out-of-school time (e.g., afterschool) programming funded by the Oregon Community Foundation (OCF) and partner The Ford Family Foundation, the research team at OCF set out to survey youth about their experiences and social-emotional development. Fortunately, there are many efforts underway to measure social-emotional learning concepts such as growth mind-set in youth through surveys. This includes well-established tools like the Developmental Assets Profile developed by the Search Institute, as well as newer tools such as the Youth Skills and Beliefs survey developed by the Youth Development Executives of King County and American Institutes for Research. These surveys often include items such as "How smart I am is something I can change" with a rating scale so that respondents can indicate the degree to which they agree with the statement (this is an adaptation of Carol Dweck's well-known growth mind-set measurement framework). At the outset this seems like a relatively answerable question. However, as we learned in discussing survey drafts with our evaluation advisory group, the concept of "smart" is loaded for students with physical, learning, or developmental disabilities—a population with a difficult history of being considered and labeled as less smart than their peers. As a result, we are taking extra care in how we use the results from our first survey effort (having not learned about this sensitivity until the design process was too far along) and will be considering alternatives for future survey efforts.

—Kimberly Firth Leonard

entirely on the respondents' perspective(s). A researcher could easily be unaware that a question is sensitive if she isn't aware of the respondents' perspective(s), context, or culture. For example, asking a respondent's age is not considered sensitive or threatening in some populations but is quite taboo with others. Something that seems innocuous at the outset may be a very loaded topic for a given set of respondents, as is illustrated in the preceding story.

Alreck and Settle (2004) identify 10 categories of questions that respondents may find threatening. These include questions regarding the following:

- Financial matters

- Mental or technical skill or ability

- Self-perceived shortcomings

- Social status

- Sexual identity or sexual behavior

- Alcohol consumption or illegal drug use

- Personal habits

- Emotional or psychological disturbance

- The aging process

- Death or dying (p. 170)

Of particular importance to the researcher is the fact that sensitive questions "tend to produce comparatively higher nonresponse rates or larger measurement error in responses than questions on other topics" (Tourangeau & Yan, 2007, p. 860). This is due to the fact that respondents may fear embarrassment or even repercussions for revealing certain information to researchers. The result is often social desirability bias, discussed in the following section.

Social Desirability Bias

Social desirability bias occurs when respondents edit their answers to questions to portray themselves in the best light, or at least better light to researchers. One of the best examples of questions prone to social desirability bias are those on a doctor's health status survey. How many people are completely truthful when answering questions about exercise habits or caffeine or alcohol consumption on these forms? Even when people *think* they are being completely honest, they tend to overestimate the amount of exercise they do and underestimate the amounts of caffeine and alcohol they consume. Research on social desirability bias has repeatedly found that respondents systematically overreport what are considered socially desirable behaviors and systematically underreport socially undesirable ones. These effects, however, are somewhat lessened with self-administered surveys as compared to in-person or telephone surveys that have respondents in direct contact with researchers (Touragneau et al., 2000). From a psychological perspective, the effects are due to the need for self-preservation, concern about personal risk, and avoidance of embarrassment and feelings of shame.

In some survey research situations, respondents may indicate that programs or specific interventions have resulted in positive changes whether or not this is accurate (as that is what they assume is the desired response). In other situations, respondents may indicate that their attitudes are consistent over time, because it is socially desirable to have consistent attitudes (just check any news outlet to find rampant public criticism of politicians who change their minds on the issues).

Social desirability bias is of greatest concern when survey questions are of a sensitive or threatening nature. Disclosing personal information such as sexual behavior, hygiene habits, criminal behavior, illicit drug or alcohol consumption, and even political preferences can be uncomfortable for many if not most people. Researcher promises of respondent anonymity do not necessarily mitigate social desirability effects. Although some assurances of confidentiality or anonymity can serve to increase responses, "elaborate assurances of confidentiality may defeat their purpose by heightening respondents' perceptions of the sensitivity or threat of the survey" (Singer, Von Thurn, & Miller, 1995). Overassurances may in fact *increase* respondents' suspicion and concern about who may have access to their data. It is also important to note that many of the studies on confidentiality and privacy of survey data were conducted in the 1990s, long before the ubiquity of online surveys and before concerns about personal data and privacy were endemic in the United States.

To mitigate the effects of social desirability bias, researchers can use closed-ended questions. "Fixed responses are less onerous to the respondent, who will find it easier simply to choose an appropriate response than to construct one" (Rea & Parker, 2014, p. 52). Further, researchers can intentionally design response options to account for a wider range of responses than might otherwise be constructed for nonsensitive questions. Remember that respondents are often influenced by the set of response options offered, believing that the range of options reflects the "average" or "typical" population. If this range is widened, it "implies that an accurate response is not outside the realm of social acceptability" (Rea & Parker, 2014, p. 51). This may encourage respondents to answer honestly, especially when they find their answer well with, in the limits of the options.

Using "forgiving wording" (Tourangeau et al., 2000, p. 288) can encourage respondents to be forthcoming in their responses to sensitive questions. Figure 6.5 is a question from the American National Election Studies Time Series Post-Election Questionnaire that employs this strategy of using an encouraging message to respondents in the question stem. Ultimately, researchers must weigh the importance of the sensitive information to the survey purpose with the risk of nonresponse. Oftentimes, we may think we need this information when, in fact, we can answer the research question(s) without it.

Demographic Questions

Demographic questions are omnipresent on surveys and may be collected for many reasons from understanding how people in different groups respond to attitude questions, to planning for how resources are allocated across populations, to

---

FIGURE 6.5 ● Real-World Questions: *Using Forgiving Language in a Sensitive Question*

In talking to people about elections, we often find that a lot of people were not able to vote because they weren't registered, they were sick, or they just didn't have time. Which of the following statements best describes you?

○ I did not vote (in the election this November).
○ I thought about voting this time, but didn't.
○ I usually vote, but didn't this time.
○ I am sure I voted.

Source: ANES (2016).

---

making key decisions on organizational policies. These questions most typically help the researcher describe the *characteristics* of a population or sample, that is, respondents' attributes such as age, gender, sexual orientation, race, ethnicity, occupation, education level, and religion. Demographic questions are also used to identify subgroups for use in the analysis of survey data. Depending on the research question(s), it may be meaningful to a researcher to compare how respondents of different genders, of different ages, or with different educational backgrounds respond to particular questions. Other types of questions can also serve as demographic questions, and these may be specific to the topic of the survey. For example, characteristics such as how long a respondent has been involved in a program, how often someone has used a service, or how many of something a respondent owns can also be used as demographic data.

For example, the Centers for Disease Control and Prevention (CDC; n.d.) asks demographic questions on its National Health Interview Survey, because "they provide a context for the health data collected in the survey, and because they help to explain interrelated trends in the survey data . . . [including] inequalities in health status and access to care." Polling groups such as Gallup also use demographic questions to understand what certain attributes bring to bear on people's attitudes or behavior. For example, they recently determined that "factors such as age, generation, gender, education level and tenure all relate to a worker's engagement" (Robison, 2015). Knowing this can help managers consider how their leadership styles and behaviors can potentially impact engagement among different groups.

Despite the common urge to capture all possible demographic information, it is important to limit the number and type of demographic questions included in a survey. *All* questions should be designed and included in a survey *only* if they serve a clear purpose and will provide useful information (in other words, if researchers can anticipate how they will be used to answer research questions). This includes demographic questions. Including only those necessary for the given research goals minimizes respondent burden and ensures that researchers aren't sitting on unused, but potentially sensitive, information.

DESIGN DETAILS
DEMOGRAPHIC VARIABLES

Alreck and Settle (2004) offer a list of what can potentially be measured with demographic questions.

Commonly Used Demographic Variables

A. Sex of respondent

B. Sex of family members

C. Age of respondent

D. Age of each head of household

E. Age of family members

F. Age of youngest child in the home

G. Education of respondent

H. Education of each head of household

I. Employment of respondent

J. Employment of each head of household

K. Occupation of respondent

L. Occupation of each head of household

M. Annual income of respondent

N. Annual income of each head of household

O. Annual family income

P. Racial or ethnic identity of respondent

Q. Race or ethnicity of each head of household

R. Religious preference of respondent

S. Religion of each head of household

T. Type of family dwelling

U. ZIP code or location of residence

V. Time of residence at present location

W. Self-designated social class membership

(p. 171)

Although this list is fairly comprehensive, a few notes are important: First, Alreck and Settle include "education of respondent" and "education of each head of household" (Items G and H). To be more precise, education is typically measured as *highest level of education*. Second, they include race and ethnicity (Item P) on the same line; however, these variables are distinctly different, as we highlight later. "Annual family income" (Item O) is a variable more appropriately termed "annual *household* income" because family status and household members are not necessarily the same. Third, regarding "religious preference of respondent" and "religion of each head of household" (Items R and S), it is important to note that *religious preference* and *religion* may in fact be quite different. We discuss the nuances of asking about religion later.

Demographic questions can be problematic when misused or misunderstood. They can compromise the anonymity of a survey, especially with smaller populations or samples. They can also make respondents feel uncomfortable about responding honestly and openly to other survey questions (especially if they feel their identity will be compromised through those demographic questions). For example, perhaps there is only one employee in the department of human resources with more than 15 years of service. If survey respondents are asked just two demographic questions—to identify their departments and to identify how many years of service they have had with the organization—a researcher can now easily identify the individual respondent.

Most (if not all) demographic questions carry a certain level of sensitivity or threat for some respondents, especially questions that ask about race or ethnicity, sexual preference, or income. Although some respondents may be perfectly comfortable sharing their age or income with researchers, others are not. Respondents can feel alienated or even offended if they don't find themselves represented in the response options of questions like these. If a "prefer not to answer" option is not offered, respondents may not be truthful or may ultimately give up on the survey if they feel strongly about not wanting to reveal this information. Therefore, any demographic questions can result in significant item nonresponse and survey nonresponse. Additionally, some demographic questions may take respondents a longer time to answer, especially if they must first consider whether to answer at all, thus adding to respondent burden.

Survey researchers must carefully consider not only *if* they need to include demographic questions but also *how* to ask them, where to place them in a survey, and how to create a positive rapport with respondents to encourage them to willingly give answers. Too many demographic questions can contribute to respondent fatigue, especially if placed at the beginning of a survey. That said, some demographic questions are easy to answer, and a few well-placed items can get respondents "warmed up" and ready to tackle other questions that demand more thoughtful attention and effort. In general, we want to get respondents engaged with the survey as quickly as possible; starting with the most relevant and interesting questions is an effective way to do so.

As with every aspect of survey design, a balance is necessary between capturing needed information and minimizing respondent discomfort and burden, and avoiding

DESIGN DETAILS
CHOOSING RESPECTFUL AND INCLUSIVE LANGUAGE FOR DEMOGRAPHIC QUESTIONS

We hope we have made clear the importance of language choices in survey questions and how questions must reflect the specific language, culture, and context of our respondents. When working with sensitive or potentially threatening questions, we must remember that respect and inclusion are of the utmost importance. After all, it's not just about the *research* but about the *people*.

To support this, here are a few additional important considerations when crafting sensitive questions:

- Terms and concepts related to various demographic attributes (e.g., gender, sexual preference, race, ethnicity) vary across communities and cultures and must be understood within the context of the specific community or culture being studied.

- Myths about people from certain cultures or communities abound, and careful research is needed to discern fact from myth.

- It is important to recognize that not all voices are represented within the very public and visible "movements" of diverse communities such as LBGTQ, African Americans, and Muslims.

- People who live at the intersections of these communities (e.g., Queer Latinx) are often subject to particularly challenging experiences and can be easily forgotten when we oversimplify these communities in our data collection.

Respectful research is designed with an openness to new learning, explicit steps to include respondents, and most importantly, a strong sense of gravitas.

nonresponse. Before including demographic questions, it is important for researchers to consider whether data will be disaggregated or results otherwise analyzed using the various subgroups captured (e.g., race/ethnicity or gender identification). If not, do we really need that information? We generally advise only including questions that have a clear purpose and are required in order to answer the research questions at hand.

Specific Categories of Demographic Questions

In the sections that follow, we offer the most specific and up-to-date information we have for asking about specific demographic details. Not only are these sensitive topics for which questions could be viewed as threatening to some respondent populations, the nuances of demographics are ever-changing. Although our vast collection of foundational literature on survey design from decades past still contains relevant advice for *other* areas of question design, we look only to the most recent sources for advice on how to ask about demographics, particularly age, race/ethnicity, gender, income, and sexual preference. For each of these areas there is not a single correct way to ask a question. It is critically important to revisit the research questions and survey purpose before making any question design decisions to ensure that questions are necessary and appropriately focused. Finally, we acknowledge the fact that we write from the perspective of researchers in the United States and understand that any advice we offer here with respect to how to design demographic questions may not hold true in other places or with other populations.

Asking about age. Asking about age is a relatively straightforward proposition, and there are only a few distinct ways researchers can pose a question, as seen in the examples in Figure 6.6. In general, respondents can be asked in an open- or closed-ended format to give their age, the year they were born (or their birthdate), or they can report their age in a range determined by the survey designer.

There is little empirical research that provides solid advice about questions related to age. Although asking about age can be a sensitive question for certain populations, in general, these questions tend to have a low item nonresponse rate and generally high accuracy rate (Healey & Gendall, 2007; Peterson, 1984). Regarding response rate, Healey and Gendall (2007) found that the "format of the age question makes relatively little difference to item non-response in self-completion surveys" (p. 720). Regarding accuracy, they advise asking participants to give their birthdate or year they were born, rather than asking their age (Healey & Gendall, 2007). This shifts the question from a two-step calculation question (What year was I born? How old does that make me?) to a simple retrieval question, thus reducing the cognitive load. It also avoids the problem of age-heaping whereby respondents offer their ages in multiples of 5 and 10 instead of offering their exact age resulting in overrepresentation at these points.

FIGURE 6.6 ● Asking About a Respondent's Age

How old are you? _____

What is your age? _____

Please select your age: (in an online survey, respondent is presented with a dropdown menu of choices)

What age did you reach at your last birthday? _____

In what year were you born? _____

Please select the year you were born: (in an online survey, respondent is presented with a dropdown menu of choices)

What is your date of birth? _____

What is your age range:

    ○ 18–25

    ○ 26–34

    ○ 35–44

    ○ 45–54

    ○ 55–64

    ○ 65 or older

If a researcher anticipates that respondents may be reluctant to report exact age, a series of age ranges can be used as response options (e.g., 26–35). The more creative example shown in Figure 6.7 asks respondents to report their ages in generational groups. It is worth noting that this particular question does not differentiate younger generations. We presume this information is not needed or that the researcher doesn't anticipate many respondents will be part of younger generations.

FIGURE 6.7 ● Real-World Questions: *Asking About Age in Generational Groups*

Generational Age Group

○ Born between 1922 and 1944

○ Born between 1945 and 1964

○ Born between 1965 and 1980

○ Born after 1981

The American Community Survey (ACS) asks respondents to fill in a blank box with their age and also fill in their date of birth. There are several reasons given by the ACS to ask about age, including identifying risk factors for vulnerable populations and to "monitor against age discrimination in government programs and in society" (U.S. Census Bureau, n.d.-a). Although a large-scale survey like the ACS may need the granularity of knowing each respondent's exact age, often with smaller-scale efforts a question using age ranges is sufficient.

Asking about race/ethnicity. Asking about race or ethnicity is a particularly sensitive and complex proposition. Although race and ethnicity are often combined in survey questions, they are not interchangeable. Each term is much more complex and has deeper connotations than we have room to address here, but we introduce some of the key considerations and include resources to learn more. Ethnicity refers to a person's ancestry, heritage, or culture, whereas race is a socially constructed category with no evidence of a biological or genetic basis. It is a highly charged concept that carries with it a long and difficult history of oppression and conquest. Consider the American Anthropological Association's Statement on Race:

> "Race" . . . evolved as a worldview, a body of prejudgments that distorts our ideas about human differences and group behavior . . . present-day inequalities between so-called "racial" groups are not consequences of their biological inheritance but products of historical and contemporary social, economic, educational, and political circumstances. (American Anthropological Association, 1998)

Currently, questions in the U.S. Census (n.d.-b) that ask about race and ethnicity do not distinguish between the two and include the following response options:

- White
- Black or African American
- American Indian and Alaska Native
- Asian
- Native Hawaiian and Other Pacific Islander
- Some other race

Definitions for each of these terms and potential response options can be found on the United States Census Bureau website (https://www.census.gov/topics/population/race/about.html). The most recent addition to the list came in 2010, when the option for respondents to check "Some other race" was added (U.S. Census, n.d.-b).

> The racial categories included in the census questionnaire generally reflect a social definition of race recognized in this country and not an attempt to define race biologically, anthropologically, or genetically. In addition, it is recognized that the categories of the race item include racial and national origin or sociocultural groups. People may choose to report more than one race to indicate their racial mixture, such as "American Indian" and "White." People who identify their origin as Hispanic, Latino, or Spanish may be of any race. (U.S. Census, n.d.-b)

Reasons for asking about race/ethnicity may vary for any given survey effort. The U.S. Census Bureau (n.d.-b) offers the following reasons for this type of demographic question:

> Information on race is required for many Federal programs and is critical in making policy decisions, particularly for civil rights. States use these data to meet legislative redistricting principles. Race data also are used to promote equal employment opportunities and to assess racial disparities in health and environmental risks.

As of the writing of this text, the Census Bureau is considering changes to the standard set of categories in preparation for the 2020 census, especially as pertains to collecting data about Hispanics. Many Hispanics "do not identify with the current racial categories" (Cohn, 2017). Many Hispanics choose "Some other race" instead of one of the standard options, resulting in a much greater usage of this last unofficial federal race category (Cohn, 2017). After a 2015 Pew research study in which 1.2 million U.S. households were contacted for a test census using separate or combined versions of race/ethnicity questions, the Census Bureau is now considering a combined version for the 2020 census. In this version, people would have the option of checking the box for Hispanic, Latino, or Spanish *and* also the option of checking a box for Mexican or Mexican American, Salvadoran, Puerto Rican, Dominican, Colombian, or Cuban. Other race/ethnicity categories would also feature options for their family's country of origin (Cohn, 2017).

Confusion around terms considered respectful for certain groups (e.g., Hispanic or Latino, White or Caucasian, Native American or First Nations) abounds, and preferences can change rapidly. Researchers must recognize that each term chosen carries with it both history (e.g., colonization, oppression, marginalization) and implicit or explicit assumptions (e.g., stereotypes) about the people identified by these terms. We stop short of making recommendations about which terms to use for which groups for this reason and strongly suggest that survey researchers do their own research for the most up-to-date reliable resources available coupled with asking potential respondents directly how they prefer to be addressed.

An additional consideration for the way in which we ask questions about race and ethnicity is that an increasing number of people in the United States identify as multiracial. The number of multiethnic or multiracial infants nearly tripled from 1980 to 2015 according to a Pew Research Center analysis of U.S. Census data (Livingston, 2017). Not surprisingly, this has "occurred hand-in-hand with the growth in marriages among spouses of different races or ethnicities" (Livingston, 2017), a number that has more than doubled in the last few decades. As racial and ethnic diversity continues to grow in the United States, survey researchers will have to consider not only *how* to design questions that reflect and respect respondents but also to think deeply about *if* and *why* measuring differences along racial and ethnic lines is important to the research.

Increasingly, we see survey researchers (especially those conducting surveys with large populations) opting to capture race and ethnicity information in a "select all that apply" format, using as many categories as are needed and feasible to ensure that any potential respondent can find one or more appropriate response. This has implications for analysis of the resulting data; those researchers who choose this approach also typically aim to disaggregate survey responses as much as is feasible.

Asking about gender identification and sexual preferences. If questions about gender or sexual preference are to be used in a survey, they *must* serve a specific purpose, and that purpose should be used to guide the design of the specific questions. There is no "right" way to ask these questions, and the response options offered for each closed-ended question will be informed by the reason for including the question. For example, on college applications (in a broad sense, a type of survey), the Consortium of Higher Education LGBT Resource Professionals (n.d.) recommends:

> Because a growing number of students are identifying outside of gender and sexual binaries, the questions on gender identity and sexual orientation should include nonbinary identity choices. Specifically, a gender identity question should include "genderqueer" and "agender" among the choices, and a sexual orientation question should include "asexual," "queer," and "pansexual" among the choices.

In general, when questions about gender or sexual orientation are used in a survey, they should be placed at the end of the demographics section and should, if at all possible, be self-administered, even if the rest of the instrument is administered in person or over the phone (The GenIUSS Group, 2014). The demographics section itself may appear at or near the beginning of a survey, or at or near the end, depending on the nature of the instrument. To foster a sense of inclusion and establish positive rapport as well as to mitigate nonresponse, we advise researchers to share with respondents the reasons for asking demographic questions along with an explanation of how resulting data will be used.

Asking about gender identification. Although it is still extremely common for surveys to ask a question about gender identification by simply offering two choices, woman or man, it is becoming increasingly common to see a "prefer not to answer" option as well. While the terms *gender* and *sex* are easily confused, they refer to who we are and our biological makeup, respectively. The terms *man* and *woman* are gender terms, while *female* and *male* describe sex. The inclusion of this or additional options, such as "transgender," "nonbinary," or "gender nonconforming," though exuding inclusivity, can also compromise anonymity, especially for surveys with a small sample, in which there may be very few individuals who select these options. Some researchers include an "other" option with or without a line for respondents to write on. The word *other* can carry a negative and disrespectful connotation in this instance and make people feel excluded rather than included. As such, we prefer not to use it. One way to allow for individual expression is to offer a "prefer to describe" option with a line for individuals to write on. The *most* inclusive way to ask the question about gender identity is

---

FIGURE 6.8 ● Real-World Questions: *Asking About Gender (Inappropriately)*

What is your sex?

- O Male
- O Female
- O Don't know

A suggested alternative: Allow respondents to self-identify an alternative to male or female or to opt out

What is your gender?

- O Male
- O Female
- O Prefer to describe: _____
- O Prefer not to answer

An additional suggested alternative: Ask an open-ended question

What term would you use to describe your gender identity? _____

to use an open-ended question, but several variations of closed-ended questions with appropriate response options can be designed as well (see Figure 6.8). Although an open-ended or more complex set of questions can result in more complicated analysis, we believe this is well worth doing so that all respondents are included and respected. One of the best ways to determine which categories to include is to ask members of the respondent population themselves and use the language they prefer. Greytak (2015) offers an example of how one word can carry different connotations for different groups: "For example, with youth populations, the identity label 'queer' might be fairly commonplace, whereas with older generations, this might still be predominantly considered a slur and its inclusion could put off respondents."

The previous examples illustrate two possibilities for asking a question about gender, depending on the research information needs, but the question can be formatted in other ways as well. For example, if the topic of the survey is health related, and more specificity is needed for data analysis, response options for transgender, or more specifically transgender F2M and transgender M2F, can be added to a closed-ended question.

The Human Rights Campaign (2016) offers specific advice for language that may precede the response options in questions about gender identification or sexual preference: "Our company does not discriminate on the basis of gender identity or expression. In order to track the effectiveness of our recruiting efforts and ensure we consider the needs of all our employees, please consider the following optional question."

Further, gender identity is increasingly being seen as far more complex than even just a few years ago. According to genderspectrum, a website devoted to helping create "gender sensitive and inclusive environments for all children and teens," gender identity is composed of three distinct dimensions and their "complex interrelationships":

- Body: our body, our experience of our own body, how society genders bodies, and how others interact with us based on our body.

- Identity: our deeply held, internal sense of self as male, female, a blend of both, or neither; who we internally know ourselves to be.

- Expression: how we present our gender in the world and how society, culture, community, and family perceive, interact with, and try to shape our gender. Gender expression is also related to gender roles and how society uses those roles to try to enforce conformity to current gender norms.

Each of these dimensions can vary greatly across a range of possibilities ("Dimensions of Gender," n.d.). These dimensions are represented and further described by the Human Rights Campaign in the following Design Details feature.

Asking about sexual orientation or preference. It is critical to understand that gender identity and sexual preference are not the same and that sexual orientations or preferences are not limited to hetero- or homosexuality. It is far less common to need to ask about sexual preference than gender identity. If it is deemed necessary to know respondents' sexual orientation, the Human Rights Campaign recommends asking in the format offered in Figure 6.9.

DESIGN DETAILS
UNDERSTANDING OPTIONS FOR ASKING ABOUT GENDER

Here, we offer definitions and clarity for some key terms and potentially unfamiliar terms.

Sexual orientation: An inherent or immutable enduring emotional, romantic, or sexual attraction to other people.

Gender identity: One's innermost concept of self as male, female, a blend of both, or neither—how individuals perceive themselves and what they call themselves. One's gender identity can be the same or different from their sex assigned at birth.

Gender expression: External appearance of one's gender identity, usually expressed through behavior, clothing, haircut, or voice, and which may or may not conform to socially defined behaviors and characteristics typically associated with being either masculine or feminine.

Transgender: An umbrella term for people whose gender identity and/or expression is different from cultural expectations based on the sex they were assigned at birth. Being transgender does not imply any specific sexual orientation. Therefore, transgender people may identify as straight, gay, lesbian, bisexual, etc. Other identities considered to fall under this umbrella can include non-binary, gender fluid, and genderqueer—as well as many more.

Gender transition: The process by which some people strive to more closely align their internal knowledge of gender with its outward appearance. Some people socially transition, whereby they might begin dressing, using names and pronouns, and/or be socially recognized as another gender. Others undergo physical transitions in which they modify their bodies through medical interventions. (Human Rights Campaign, 2017)

FIGURE 6.9 ● *Question About Sexual Orientation*

What is your sexual orientation?

    ☐ Straight/heterosexual
    ☐ Gay or lesbian
    ☐ Bisexual
    ☐ Prefer to self-describe _____
    ☐ Prefer not to say

Source: Human Rights Campaign, 2016.

If it is necessary to collect data on sexual orientation in greater detail, it is important to understand that this attribute, much like gender identity, is not as simple as it seems. It too is composed of three distinct dimensions, which could be asked about in separate questions if needed.

DESIGN DETAILS
RECOGNITION OF NONBINARY GENDER IDENTIFICATION IN THE UNITED STATES AND ABROAD

The United States is only recently beginning to recognize gender identifications beyond female and male in formal and legal ways. In 2016, Oregon allowed a resident to legally identify as nonbinary. Subsequently, Oregon's Department of Motor Vehicles, which initially refused the individual's request (Foden-Vencil, 2016), in 2017 added an option for residents who can now select gender options of M, F, or X (Wamsley, 2017). The District of Columbia also started offering nonbinary driver's licenses and identification cards in 2017 (Stein, 2017). The province of Ontario, Canada, offered its residents the same options earlier that year as well (Wamsley, 2017). Other countries including India, Pakistan, Australia, and Germany have also formally recognized a third gender (Foden-Vencil, 2016). And the United Kingdom now allows residents to use the "Mx" title on government and bank documents (Guy-Ryan, 2016). The notion of gender fluidity or gender as nonbinary is hardly new, however. In Indonesia, the concept is ancient, with some traditions dating from the 13th century, and some cultures identifying up to five gender categories (Guy-Ryan, 2016).

- Self-identification: how one identifies one's sexual orientation (gay, lesbian, bisexual, or heterosexual)
- Sexual behavior: the sex of sex partners (i.e., individuals of the same sex, different sex, or both sexes)
- Sexual attraction: the sex or gender of individuals that someone feels attracted to (Sexual Minority Assessment Research Team [SMART], 2009).

MINI-INTERVIEW WITH JARA DEAN-COFFEY
REFLECTING THE LANGUAGE OF YOUNG PEOPLE

Jara Dean-Coffey is a leading consultant in equitable evaluation who talked with us about her experience working with a nonprofit organization as it adapts a survey tool to reflect the language of the young people it serves.

First, tell us more about the organization and its work. What context is helpful in understanding its survey needs?

JDC: The RYSE Youth Center in Richmond, California, was developed in response to a request from young people who wanted and needed a safe place in their community following a series of violent incidents in the early 2000s, including a shooting death right outside the local high school. Richmond itself is an urban center without typical economic drivers of urban communities; it has all of the challenges and none of the money to address them. But adults responded to youth needs, and after several years of community forums and an extensive needs assessment, RYSE opened in 2008.

The mission of RYSE is to "create safe spaces grounded in social justice that build youth power for young people to love, learn, educate, heal

(Continued)

(Continued)

and transform lives and communities." Staff are largely from the community, and youth have always been involved in shaping the center; the organization has a deep commitment to young people and being responsive to their needs. The center now serves a diverse group of youth as young as 13, and young adults up to age 25, and provides programming in community health and wellness, education and career development, media arts and culture, youth justice and youth organizing, and leadership.

How was the youth survey initially developed?

JDC: Early on, a youth member survey was developed to attempt to understand the ways in which the values that RYSE lives to execute are showing up in programming, as well as changes in young people's sense of awareness, future orientation, connectedness to community, ability to negotiate relationships with peers—all relatively traditional measures of youth development and wellness. Most survey questions were initially carefully culled from preexisting reliable and valid instrument(s).

What challenges has RYSE experienced with the survey? How are you adapting the survey in response to those challenges, and to changing needs?

JDC: The survey is too long. We have done some intentional things to encourage response, including shifting to an online format (using tablets), incentivizing youth with $5 gift cards, and creating a sense of competition among staff to get students to respond. But we also hope to shorten the survey after completing strategic planning, which should help us to narrow the focus of the survey to those concepts in which RYSE is most interested.

It is also problematic that the tools that the original survey questions were drawn from were not likely tested for reliability and validity with this population, young people of diverse demographics, in an economically challenged community. This is something we're still working to address;

we hope to work on operationalizing the concepts in a way more relevant to this particular community in the future.

One of the most noticeable and ongoing challenges is in capturing demographics. First we had to decide whether to put the demographic questions at the beginning or the end. And we quickly realized that we would need to approach questions as "check all that apply," particularly for race/ethnicity. We have also used "none apply" as a response option that gives young people space to note that they don't fit into provided categories, but without having to check "other," which is problematic because it implies that there are ways to be worth naming and those that are not.

How did you know that you needed to make changes to the survey questions?

JDC: The connection between leadership at RYSE and the young people they serve is robust and authentic. Leaders were paying attention to how young people talked about themselves and could tell us when something was missing or not relevant any longer. I see our job in collecting data like this as being as responsive as possible, in as real-time as possible. We also looked at the data. We are careful to review responses and contextualize them with staff, not making assumptions about why responses look a particular way (or not).

Take gender identify as an example: it is especially challenging to capture in an authentic way. During a recent survey administration, staff noticed that more than half of students didn't identify with a particular gender or sex (they checked "none apply"). While an obvious challenge for data collection and analysis, RYSE views this positively for young people's identities—young people are less confined by traditional (biased) conceptions of gender identity. Changing these questions to ensure we're capturing how young people see themselves, with the current best language, is difficult. It may be we don't even have the right language for the way that young people view gender now. We strive to collect information in a way that honors who they are, and shift the burden to analysis, to prioritize getting the options right over how complicated it may make analysis later.

How have you engaged young people to help ensure the survey language remains relevant?

JDC: Fortunately, youth are deeply enough involved at RYSE, and staff are relatively young—not that far removed from the peer group served (some are former members)—that it is easy to ask young people to check on the survey to make sure questions still make sense. This is largely done informally but is done very intentionally, both as part of the pre-administration process and again when results are being reviewed, as part of the sense-making process.

For more on Jara's work, see The Luminare Group (https://www.theluminaregroup.com/) and Equitable Evaluation (https://www.equitableeval.org/project).

Asking about income. Although not always necessary, income data are especially important in certain areas of study such as "social stratification, inequality, and poverty" (Jansen, Verhoeven, Robert, & Dessens, 2013, p. 1358). Research in health, well-being, and even behaviors, such as volunteering and donating money, also relies on income data, especially as a predictor variable (Jansen et al., 2013). The American Community Survey asks questions about income to

> create statistics about income, assistance, earnings, and poverty status. Local, state, tribal, and federal agencies use our published income data to plan and fund programs that provide economic assistance for populations in need. Income data measure the economic well-being of the nation. In conjunction with poverty estimates, these data are often part of funding formulas that determine the distribution of food, health care, job training, housing, and other assistance. (U.S. Census Bureau, n.d.-b)

The ACS asks about income in the most detailed way, asking respondents to report income from individual sources separately, including the following:

- Wages, salary, commissions, bonuses, or tips from all jobs
- Self-employment income
- Interest, dividends, net rental income, royalty income, income from estates and trusts
- Social security or railroad retirement
- Supplemental Security income (SSI)
- Public assistance or welfare payments
- Retirement, survivor, or disability pensions
- Any other sources of income received regularly such as Veteran's Payments (VA), unemployment compensation, child support or alimony (U.S. Census Bureau, n.d.-b).

Respondents must then add up all individual sources of income to arrive at a total figure.

Most survey researchers will not need this degree of detail, if income data are needed at all, but this is a helpful reminder of potential sources of income. At times, all that is needed is an understanding of the *sufficiency* of income—whether it is a source of worry or stress for an individual or household—as opposed to needing to know the level of income. Being as specific as possible about what is needed will help ensure that survey responses can be properly analyzed. Here again lies a level of complexity that requires a researcher to revisit and carefully examine the research question(s) and articulated survey purpose. Income may be the appropriate variable for a survey question, but it is also closely related to issues of social class and socioeconomic status, and can be a source of confusion.

> Socioeconomic status (SES) encompasses not just income but also educational attainment, financial security, and subjective perceptions of social status and social class. Socioeconomic status can encompass quality of life attributes as well as the opportunities and privileges afforded to people within society. Poverty, specifically, is not a single factor but rather is characterized by multiple physical and psychosocial stressors. Further, SES is a consistent and reliable predictor of a vast array of outcomes across the life span, including physical and psychological health. Thus, SES is relevant to all realms of behavioral and social science, including research, practice, education and advocacy. (American Psychological Association, n.d.)

Income alone cannot serve as a proxy variable for social class or socioeconomic status. Revisit Stories From the Field: Asking About Economic Status in a Survey: An Odyssey from Chapter 2 for a "real world" scenario in which researchers had to determine the best way to understand their respondents' income levels for a specific purpose.

Finally, at times researchers may want to use a proxy variable, something that may at least loosely correlate with the variable of interest—in this case, income—to substitute for a more sensitive question. Education level, though not nearly a perfect proxy, can potentially be used in this way for income, because it is most likely a less sensitive topic than income and will likely feel less like an invasion of privacy to respondents.

Asking about religion. Religion may not always have been a sensitive topic. Sudman and Bradburn (1982) claim "nongovernment survey organizations have uniformly found that religion is not a sensitive topic and that reports of religious behavior are easy to obtain" (p. 25). They repeat this claim in their 2004 book (Bradburn, Sudman, & Wansink, 2004), but nearly two decades later, this has changed and we're certain that religion belongs in a discussion of potentially sensitive or threatening survey topics.

Recent research-based advice specific to designing questions around religion (i.e., whether they should be open- or closed-ended, and which specific response options should be offered) is limited; hence, for this topic, we return to our earlier emphasis on purpose and operationalizing constructs. Articulating the purpose for needing to know something about respondents' religion is critical. Will data be disaggregated by this variable, and if so, why? What research or evaluation questions will be answered by this?

Religion and religiosity are deceptively complex. McAndrew and Voas (2011) contend:

> For some people, religious affiliation is purely nominal or used as an identifier to distinguish themselves from members of other religious groups. By contrast, others have a serious personal commitment. Therefore surveys often seek to capture both religious adherence (also called religious identity or religious affiliation) and degree of religious commitment, or "religiosity." Religiosity is bound up with attitudes, behaviour and values, while religious affiliation is more like ethnicity, something that for most is part of their family, community or cultural heritage, rather than being chosen by them.

> While quantification of religiosity is possible . . . there are no clear standards regarding what aspects should be measured. A number are relevant: belief, practice, formal membership, informal affiliation, ritual initiation, doctrinal knowledge, moral sense, core values, or how you are regarded by others. Further, different aspects may relate to fundamentally different types of religiosity. (p. 2)

To operationalize religion for the purpose of a survey, researchers must carefully consider information needs. Is it important to know affiliation, such as if a respondent identifies as Christian, Jewish, or Muslim? Is it important to understand whether or how often a respondent engages in religious *worship*, *practice*, or *observance*? If a respondent believes in a god (or multiple gods) or higher power?

The 2014 General Social Survey, a telephone-administered survey, asked a number of questions around religion including the following open-ended questions:

- What is your religious preference? Is it Protestant, Catholic, Jewish, some other religion or no religion?

- Would you call yourself a strong [religious preference] or a not very strong [religious preference]?

- In what religion were you raised? (Association of Religion Data Archives, n.d.)

Probes were administered after each question, such as "What specific denomination is that, if any?" after the question on religious preference.

According to McAndrew and Voas (2011), "It has become conventional to focus on three aspects of religious involvement: belief, practice and affiliation" (p. 3). That said, for any given survey purpose, it may be sufficient to focus one or more questions on just one of these aspects.

Discussion Questions

- What topics or subjects might a researcher have to consider as potentially sensitive or threatening to people in your organization? Your culture?

- When it is necessary to ask about gender identification or sexual orientation or preference, what resources might you use to inform your question design process?

 Design Drills

1. Suppose you are designing a survey to measure attitudes toward new housing initiatives in your community and you expect that age, gender identity, and religion may be significant determining factors in respondents' attitudes. Knowing what you know about potential respondents in your community, how might you design demographic questions for this survey? What considerations will be important given potentially sensitive topics?

2. Research Scenario, Part 6 (additional parts are found in other chapters): You are developing a survey that will ask low-income senior citizens about their behaviors and thoughts related to a program delivered at local libraries. The program is intended to help senior citizens feel more engaged with their communities and to be more social, given concerns about seniors becoming too isolated.

    a. What quality control or filtering questions might be useful for your survey, if at all? Draft a few, complete with instructions needed for any resulting branching.

    b. Which types of demographic questions are needed for your survey? Draft these and consider where they will appear in the survey.

 Extended Learning

- Aday, L. A., & Cornelius, L. J. (2006). *Designing and conducting health surveys: A comprehensive guide* (3rd ed.). San Francisco: Jossey-Bass. Offers detailed advice on sensitive questions on health-related topics and specifically for hard-to-reach populations.

- Human Rights Campaign. (2016). *Collecting transgender-inclusive gender data in workplace and other surveys*. Available at http://www.hrc.org/resources/collecting-transgender-inclusive-gender-data-in-workplace-and-other-surveys.

- Human Rights Campaign. (2017). *Sexual orientation and gender identity definitions*. Available at http://www.hrc.org/resources/sexual-orientation-and-gender-identity-terminology-and-definitions.

- LGBT TIG Week: Emily A. Greytak on So . . . you want to identify LGBTQ people in your evaluation? Ask these 4 questions first. AEA365: A Tip-a-Day by and for Evaluators. Available at http://aea365 .org/blog/lgbt-tig-week-emily-a-greytak-on-so-you-want-to-include-identify-lgbtq-people-in-your -evaluation-ask-these-4-questions-first.

- The Williams Institute. (2009). *Best practices for asking questions about sexual orientation on surveys.* Available at http://williamsinstitute.law.ucla.edu/wp-content/uploads/SMART-FINAL-Nov-2009.pdf.

- Tourangeau, R., Rips, L. J., & Rasinski, K. (2000). *The psychology of survey response.* New York: Cambridge University Press. Offers a more thorough treatment of how survey respondents edit their answers in the face of sensitive or threatening questions.

Knowing WHEN a Survey Is Ready for Use

Despite our best efforts to work through all of the planning/predrafting steps prior to developing questions, we can still come up short in developing a survey that will garner the most robust and meaningful dataset. Testing (also known as pretesting) helps ensure that survey questions are indeed understandable and answerable to respondents, and strong in their ability to measure what we are attempting to measure.

The third part of this text provides guidance for the final stages of survey design: finalizing questions and the survey instrument and planning for administration while considering how results will be analyzed and used. Although this content has been relegated to the last section of this text, pretesting strategies and their variations can be used throughout the survey design process to not only refine or finalize questions but even to generate draft questions (sourcing survey questions is discussed in Chapter 4). Likewise, researchers are wise to consider and plan for administration, analysis, and use from the outset of work on a given survey.

Purposeful Survey Design

1. Planning and predrafting
   a. Determining and articulating survey purpose
   b. Understanding what surveys can measure
   c. Understanding survey respondents

2. Developing questions
   a. Sourcing questions
   b. Crafting question stems and response options

3. **Finalizing**
   a. **Pretesting**
   b. **Pulling it all together to maximize response**

Chapter 7, "Finalizing Questions and Using Pretesting Strategies," starts with a discussion of some of the advantages of pretesting survey questions and then covers in more detail many of the strategies available to help researchers refine and finalize survey questions. This chapter also includes limited discussion of testing strategies for entire survey tools (e.g., to test for overarching reliability or validity), though this is largely outside the scope of this text.

Chapter 8, "Pulling It All Together to Maximize Response," includes guidance for planning for administering a survey with considerations for analysis and use of the resulting data. The content in this chapter is found at the end of this text somewhat reluctantly. Ideally, researchers are considering administration, analysis, and perhaps especially use much earlier in the actual survey design process.

7

Finalizing Questions and Using Pretesting Strategies

Testing leads to failure, and failure leads to understanding.

—Burt Rutan, American aerospace engineer

One goal of survey research is to compare the answers of subgroups of respondents. However, when respondents interpret survey questions inconsistently or, more importantly, in ways that differ from researcher intent, they might as well be answering completely different questions. Problems with respondent comprehension and interpretation of survey questions are the most intractable problems in survey research and play a large role in our struggle to analyze and use poor-quality survey data. "The fact that respondents answer a question cannot be taken for proof that they have understood that question as the researcher intended" (Foddy, 1998, p. 103). To illustrate this point, in one study Foddy (1998) found the following:

- different respondents interpreted the phrase "half a day" to mean at least 4 hours, at least 5 hours, or at least 6 hours (p. 119);

- different respondents interpreted "children" to mean those 5–10 years old, 5–15 years old, or 5–20 years old (p. 119); and

- different respondents interpreted "social class" as pertaining to family background, present lifestyle, or as a reference to occupation or education (p. 121).

In Chapter 1, we introduced testing as a phase in the design thinking process but also noted that the design thinking process is much more iterative than it is linear. Although the detail about why and how to test a survey (also known as pretesting because it often occurs prior to finalizing a survey) is relegated to one of the last chapters of this text, pretesting strategies and their variations can be used throughout the survey design process not only to refine or finalize questions but also to generate draft questions.

Several rounds of pretesting may be needed to revise and finalize a survey, depending on the nature of the survey. A survey with more complex questions that will necessitate deeper thinking and be much more difficult for respondents to answer may require more robust pretesting than one that is simpler and more straightforward. Researchers should always anticipate the possibility that employing pretesting methods could shift their thinking about how a question is fundamentally framed or deepen their understanding of what information is knowable in such a way as to require that some draft questions are tossed out entirely in favor of new, better questions. This is not necessarily a failure of the question drafting process but an argument for considering pretesting strategies an integral part of the survey design process.

Why Pretest Surveys and Their Questions?

Testing surveys and their questions prior to administration helps ensure that questions are as well written and as clearly understood by respondents as researchers intend and that responses will result in useful data. Pretesting strategies allow us to collect specific "evidence to evaluate the performance of survey questions" (Collins, 2003, p. 230). Czaja and Blair (2005) substantiate the need for pretesting with this cautionary note:

> In designing a questionnaire, we make many decisions and assumptions, some conscious, some not. Underlying the questionnaire draft is our judgement about what kinds of things respondents will know, what words they will understand, what sorts of information they can and will provide, and what response tasks they can perform. . . . Much of our effort is subtly informed by our feelings about how people will respond to our queries, by a belief that what we ask is sensible, by some vision of how the respondents' world works. (p. 103)

Czaja and Blair (2005) remind us of just how easy it is to design a survey we're certain will perform well and will result in the type of dataset we need to answer our research question(s) effectively. But, as many of us who have engaged in survey research can report, our gut feelings alone have hardly been sufficient in ensuring those surveys and questions will work as we want them to.

Advantages of Pretesting

There are a number of advantages of pretesting prior to survey administration. Pretesting can help researchers to do the following:

- Gather others' input in order to gain new perspective
- Develop greater understanding of and empathy with desired respondents
- Ensure questions are clear, comprehensible, and relevant to respondents (Collins, 2003)
- Confirm that response options are sufficient and appropriate and that respondents can use them appropriately and consistently (Collins, 2003)

- Explore whether questions have particular forms of validity, such as **face validity**
- Make initial assessment regarding the reliability of questions
- Anticipate how the resulting data might best be analyzed
- Test the mechanics of the survey in a real-world setting

Gather input and gain perspective. It is easy for researchers writing their own surveys to become "too close" to the work and be unable to see problems that might be obvious to others. Pretesting questions, whether formally or informally, can provide the researcher with a new perspective, seeing the questions or entire survey tool through another's eyes. Often the brief break in the survey development process afforded by having the survey out for review can also help refresh a researcher's perspective. Revisit Stories From the Field: Asking About Economic Status in a Survey: An Odyssey from Chapter 2 for a "real world" example of how piloting a survey gave a set of researchers fresh perspective on a particularly sensitive set of questions.

Develop empathy and understanding. By asking potential respondents and/or informants who are familiar with potential respondents for their feedback, and by exploring their thinking when making sense of and responding to questions, researchers can gain a great deal of empathy for and understanding of respondents. When members of the desired respondent population are *not* consulted about the survey design, nor directly involved in the drafting of survey questions, engaging them during the testing phase can be critical to ensuring that a survey is reflective of their experience, language, and culture.

Ensure clarity and relevance. Pretesting questions is particularly helpful in ensuring that problematic questions, such as those that are leading or loaded, are avoided. Examining responses collected during pretesting can sometimes make potentially problematic questions immediately obvious, but researchers can also identify and troubleshoot such questions by asking respondents pretesting the survey to notify them directly when they notice such a question. Methods such as cognitive interviewing (discussed in greater detail shortly) can support this, or additional questions can be added to a pilot survey to request feedback, including feedback about particular questions, from those responding.

Confirm response options. A simple but very effective use of pretesting is to confirm that response options are sufficient and appropriate for the specific respondents identified for the survey. Pretesting may identify a need for additional response options that weren't originally anticipated or may uncover instances where there are too many response options, overlapping options, or options that are problematic in some other unanticipated way. In addition, where researchers are less certain about the needed response options for a particular question, pretesting can be used to ask an open-ended question in order to have potential respondents themselves offer appropriate response options for what will then become a closed-ended question. Researchers can conduct qualitative analysis of responses to the open-ended question to inform and subsequently craft the closed-ended version of the question. For example, asking "What are your top three reasons for choosing this model vehicle?" can elicit an appropriate set of response options for a respondent group you may later want to ask, "Which of these reasons is most important to you in choosing a vehicle model?" in a closed-ended format.

Explore validity. A survey question with validity is one that measures what it is intended to measure. A question with face validity is one that appears (to researchers, experts, colleagues, and/or respondents) to measure what it is intended to measure. In other words, it appears that respondents will understand and answer the question in the way that researchers intend and expect. As with other potential problems (like leading or loaded questions), issues related to validity may become obvious through pretest responses themselves (if those respondents testing the survey don't answer as expected), but it is far more likely that validity concerns will surface when a researcher is able to explore what respondents are *thinking* as they review or answer a question. Strategies such as "think aloud" (described shortly) can help researchers ensure that respondents are thinking about the constructs being measured in the same way as the researcher(s). Cognitive interviewing provides a particularly promising way for researchers to explore and improve the face validity of questions and therefore the quality of the resulting data (Ryan, Gannon-Slater, & Culbertson, 2012; Willis, 2005).

Assess for reliability. In some cases, pretesting can be used to explore reliability as well. Survey reliability refers to whether survey questions are answered consistently. That is to say, with a reliable survey, respondents answer similar questions in appropriately similar ways, or that results from survey administration efforts with similar populations are appropriately similar. A common analogy used to explain reliability is a dartboard. A shooter who is able to hit nearly the same spot on the dartboard each time (where the darts are closely clustered in a small area) is reliable (consistent), regardless of where the darts cluster (e.g., center, to the left, to the right). If the shooter is able to closely cluster the darts around the bullseye, then that would also demonstrate validity (think: hitting the target with regard to measuring what we want to measure).

Exploring reliability through pretesting is most likely to be accomplished through a pilot test in which enough data are collected to explore whether problematic patterns may be surfacing. There are three good indicators that survey questions may not produce reliable responses. Problems with reliability can surface when

1. a group of testers a researcher expects would answer the same way do not, in fact, answer in the same way;

2. testers provide different answers to similar questions; or

3. testers provide different answers to the same question asked at different times.

It is important to acknowledge that this is not the same as full reliability testing, which is typically done with much more robust statistical methods on full sets of response data (and often for very large-scale surveys). Although reliability testing does sometimes result in changes to versions of a survey (and so it supports refinement of survey questions and tools over time), these more complex methods are beyond the scope of this text.

Anticipate analysis. Gathering responses to draft survey questions through pretesting can also help researchers anticipate how to work with the data that will eventually be captured through a finalized survey. Sometimes the best way to set up a survey question for ease of response actually results in a more complicated analysis scenario. In fact, this may be preferable sometimes. Capturing accurate responses should usually outweigh ease of analysis. For example, "check all that apply" answer options are often the reasonable, or even ideal, choice, but this question type can present challenges for response analysis. Seeing how respondents answer these questions in a pilot effort, or learning how they think about their answers, may provide hints to the researcher about how best to analyze (or even eventually present) results. We discuss this further, and emphasize the importance of considering analysis needs ahead of time in Chapter 8.

Test survey mechanics. More formal approaches to pretesting surveys, such as pilot testing, offer an opportunity to test the logistics and mechanics of the survey tool in an approximation of the expected survey conditions (Fowler, 2014). For example, a pilot effort may follow the same approximate timeline that the researcher wishes to use with the finalized survey. Pilot participants can be asked to weigh in about the adequacy of instructions provided, the number and type of reminders used, and other aspects of the respondent experience. Feedback at this stage can help a researcher to ensure that none of these other aspects of the survey design becomes a barrier to quality survey response.

To echo our advice throughout this text, determining which pretesting methods to employ should be done thoughtfully; each survey effort may require a different approach, depending on its content and context. To illustrate this point, Dillman et al. (2014) discuss quality control and testing advice separately for various types of surveys (e.g., differentiating how to treat surveys by mail and online surveys).

How Can Surveys and Their Questions Be Tested Prior to Use?

Of course, pretesting surveys and their questions requires the researcher to devote what may be substantial time and energy to the process. Fortunately, there are several existing methods survey researchers can use, either alone or in combination. We discuss the following in this chapter:

- Survey quality assessment tools (e.g., our Checklist for Quality Question Design)
- Expert review
- Cognitive interviewing
- Focus groups
- Pilot testing

These methods can be applied either to entire survey instruments, to groups of questions, or to individual questions. Many variations of each of these methods are possible, and some share similar characteristics (e.g., the use of probing questions or think-aloud strategies in both focus groups and cognitive interviewing). Though we describe the most typical ways these strategies are used, researchers need not hesitate to adapt or combine these as needed. Survey researchers must also consider the time and resources available in determining which strategy or set of strategies is the best fit for a given survey effort. Typically, less formal efforts such as using a survey quality assessment tool (e.g., the checklist we present) are far easier and faster to implement than more formal efforts such as a full survey pilot.

Survey Quality Assessment Tools

Perhaps the simplest and easiest pretesting strategy is to use a survey quality assessment tool to guide review of and reflection on draft questions. At least a handful of survey researchers before us have compiled lists of advice or standards for question design that can be used as survey assessment tools (see, for example, Fowler and Cosenza's [2008] list in the *International Handbook of Survey Methodology* or Willis and Lessler's *Question Appraisal System QAS-99*, 1999). Lists like these can be used to review draft survey questions to ensure all of their applicable advice has been heeded, prior to finalizing a survey.

To support improved question and survey design, we have developed our own, detailed quality assessment tool, the Checklist for Quality Question Design, that can be used to reflect on the quality of draft survey questions. In developing this checklist (and this text in general) we aimed for a list of what *to do* in order to ensure quality questions, rather than a list of what *not* to do, which is the advice most commonly seen in survey and other research texts (e.g., *do not* use double-barreled questions). The Checklist for Quality Question Design brings advice found throughout this text together in one tool. For ease of use, we've included an additional copy in the appendix that can be extracted from the book.

 # CHECKLIST FOR QUALITY QUESTION DESIGN

The purpose of this checklist is to assist the survey researcher in designing an effective survey instrument that will elicit a rich, robust, and useful dataset for a respondent-centered survey aligned with the researcher's information needs. This checklist serves as a reflective self-assessment that focuses on the design of survey questions themselves and will not thoroughly inform *all* aspects of survey design. It is meant to be particularly helpful for researchers who are drafting questions from scratch, though it could also be applied to assist the review and finalization of questions adapted from existing tools.

This tool will be of greatest use if the following has already been determined:

- That a survey is indeed the appropriate tool to meet data collection needs

- The research or evaluation questions and information

- The population or sample of desired respondents

- How the survey will be administered: online, paper, by phone, in person, or some combination of these

We recommend going through the checklist for *each* survey question. Use the space to the right of each item to jot down notes about why you are checking yes or no and/or any edits needed. Note that not every item will apply to every question; use N/A as needed.

Checklist Item	Yes	No	N/A	Notes
Question type is appropriate:				
Question type will result in the type of data needed given research question(s)	☐	☐	☐	
Researcher is prepared to analyze results from this type of question	☐	☐	☐	
Question design is centered around respondents:				
Question asks for information respondent is likely to know, or respondent will have access to the information needed	☐	☐	☐	
Question focuses on respondent and respondent experiences (and not what respondent thinks about others)	☐	☐	☐	
Researcher can anticipate how a respondent might answer the question	☐	☐	☐	
Question is focused:				
Question relates closely and clearly to one (or more) research question(s)	☐	☐	☐	
Question is as specific and narrowly focused as possible	☐	☐	☐	
Question asks about only one concept (i.e., is not double-barreled)	☐	☐	☐	
Question is concise, using as few words as possible to convey meaning	☐	☐	☐	
Question phrasing is consistent with language used in other places in the survey	☐	☐	☐	

(Continued)

[Continued]

Checklist Item	Yes	No	N/A	Notes
Question wording supports respondent understanding:				
Question is written in semantically valid, plain, straightforward language	☐	☐	☐	
Question is syntactically correct, employing correct grammar and usage	☐	☐	☐	
Question wording reflects the language and culture of respondents	☐	☐	☐	
Question is specific enough for respondents to know exactly what information is being requested	☐	☐	☐	
Question requires as little inference or mental math as possible	☐	☐	☐	
Question is phrased using active voice	☐	☐	☐	
Question is phrased as neutrally as possible	☐	☐	☐	
Instructions and contextual cues are included as needed:				
Question itself includes any necessary instructions for answering	☐	☐	☐	
Explanations are included for any terms that might require clarification	☐	☐	☐	
For an open-ended question, question instructions note how long or detailed answers should be	☐	☐	☐	
Reference periods correspond to the information needed (e.g., shorter time periods for more common occurrences)	☐	☐	☐	

Checklist Item	Yes	No	N/A	Notes
Reference periods are clear and specific (e.g., *since last Tuesday* as opposed to *in the last week*)	☐	☐	☐	
If question is sensitive (e.g., a demographic question), question instructions include information about why the question is being asked and/or how responses will be used/useful	☐	☐	☐	
Closed-ended questions feature appropriate instructions and response options:				
Question instructions make it clear how to answer (e.g., *check all that apply*, *select the top three*)	☐	☐	☐	
Response options are exhaustive; that is, they fully cover the range of expected responses	☐	☐	☐	
Response options are mutually exclusive; that is, they do not overlap	☐	☐	☐	
Response options are labeled (either numerically, pictorially, verbally, or a combination) where appropriate	☐	☐	☐	
Closed-ended scale questions feature appropriate response options:				
Response options are aligned with wording of question stem (i.e., direct labeling or item-specific response options are used)	☐	☐	☐	
Bipolar response options are balanced with the same number of positive and negative options	☐	☐	☐	
5–7 options are used for scaled responses (unless desired level of precision requires fewer or more options)	☐	☐	☐	

(Continued)

[Continued]

Checklist Item	Yes	No	N/A	Notes
Don't know, neutral, N/A, or similar response options are used only as needed and have a clear purpose	☐	☐	☐	
A midpoint is used when a neutral option is needed or when forcing respondents to "choose a side" may result in measurement error	☐	☐	☐	
The order of scaled response options is consistent (e.g., left to right, least to greatest) with other questions	☐	☐	☐	
Numeric scales are ordered least to greatest	☐	☐	☐	
Response options start with least desirable and move to most desirable (to mitigate possible primacy effect)	☐	☐	☐	
Demographic questions reflect deep understanding of and respect for respondents:				
Question uses appropriate terminology for the specific respondent population (check with members of respondent population whenever possible)	☐	☐	☐	
Response options reflect all desired respondents (i.e., respondents can see themselves in the options) and avoid use of the term *other*	☐	☐	☐	
Question includes a *prefer not to answer* or *prefer to describe* response option when question topic is sensitive or potentially threatening	☐	☐	☐	
Response options reflect a balance of the need for accuracy, granularity, and respondent sensitivity (e.g., a question about age asks for year of birth or offers a series of age ranges depending on context)	☐	☐	☐	

Finally, we would be remiss not to note that using the Checklist for Quality Question Design or other like question assessment system does have its limitations. Whenever possible, researchers should strive to use such checklists in combination with other methods to test and refine survey questions (and survey tools more broadly). Willis (2005) outlines three key reasons to test questions by using methods more extensive than the application of a checklist; we have added our own explanations of each here:

1. "Question design rules are by themselves not specific enough" (p. 28). Guidance about how to write quality questions is simply not sufficient to ensure that question will work in the real-world survey context. There are also, of course, exceptions to any rule and cases in which a researcher may legitimately decide to break with the general guidance for how to write quality questions.

2. "Design rules are blind to the bigger picture" (p. 29). As Willis (2005) states, "because they focus somewhat microscopically on each question in isolation, rather than on the questionnaire as a whole, they fail to provide an overall assessment" (p. 27).

3. "Rules help us to fashion the question, but is it the right question?" (p. 29). As we discussed earlier in this text, it is first critical to be sure that measurement objectives, stemming from the research question and survey purpose, are clear so that only the "right" questions are included in a given survey.

Expert Review

Soliciting input or feedback from experts (in addition to respondents) can be critical in ensuring that surveys and questions will be appropriately understood by our respondents. Experts can provide a fresh look at draft survey tools and are also often able to ask questions about language choices or otherwise challenge assumptions we may not realize we are making. Although this may feel uncomfortable at times (we can certainly recall those *duh, I should have seen that* feelings after asking experts for feedback on our own drafts), it is a relatively informal and potentially fast way to get feedback on an entire survey tool, or even on specific questions.

Who are "experts"? Experts may be fellow researchers, typically those with survey design or with content knowledge on the topic at hand (e.g., behavioral psychologists or public health experts if we are asking respondents to report about their behaviors related to health and wellness). Experts may be approached individually or pulled together as a panel or advisory group, which has the added benefit of generating discussion among the experts that can result in even richer reflection, especially when a mixture of those with different types of expertise are engaged (Collins, 2014). Existing groups may come in handy for expert review. For example, when developing a survey for students, an existing leadership or advisory group may be tapped to review and provide feedback on the survey, even if only tangential to the purpose of the group.

The greatest risk in soliciting only expert review is that experts are not at all guaranteed to think like desired respondents. Although expert feedback may help uncover critical issues with survey questions or overall design, it may not illuminate the same challenges that respondents would face. The remaining methods all require engaging with at least a subgroup or strategic sample of desired respondents. As such, these strategies are more time and resource intensive but are likely to result in more useful information about how respondents will handle the survey.

Cognitive Interviewing

Cognitive interviewing is intended to help a researcher understand more deeply how respondents think about their survey questions. Cognitive interviewing is usually conducted once survey tools are drafted and typically after some initial review and revision have taken place. A strategic sample of respondents (typically drawn from volunteers) is asked a set of survey questions (or potentially one question at a time) and asked to reflect on their understanding of the question, either while answering each question or retrospectively once they've answered a set of questions. It represents a "direct study of the question-and-answer process—identifying how and where the question fails to achieve its measurement purpose" (Collins, 2003, p. 230). This can be especially helpful when researchers anticipate potential comprehension challenges due to the survey content or characteristics of the respondent pool (e.g., a language-related challenge) or when the survey includes questions that could be sensitive or perceived as potentially threatening to respondents.

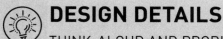

DESIGN DETAILS
THINK-ALOUD AND PROBING STRATEGIES

Two of the most common (and related) strategies used in cognitive interviewing are

1. asking participants to "think aloud" either as or after they review questions, and

2. asking probing questions about the participants' experience in understanding and responding to a question.

Although associated with cognitive interviewing, these strategies can also be used in other pretesting methods, such as focus groups.

Think-aloud typically requires that participants are trained in how to reflect on their own cognitive processes. During the think-aloud process the researcher captures what participants report they are thinking and any contextual notes that may be helpful in reviewing and refining questions (e.g., if

a participant's nonverbal gestures such as facial expressions indicate that a question is particularly challenging) (Ryan et al., 2012; Willis, 2005).

The probing strategy is somewhat similar but also distinct from the think-aloud process. In this case a researcher asks specific questions of the participants that prompt them to reflect on their experience in answering the question, or their feedback about the question more generally. Probes, because they can focus on specific aspects of the question-answering process, can help researchers ensure they have avoided particular issues of concern (e.g., whether a question might present too much challenge related to memory), whereas with think-aloud, the researcher relies only on what participants share of their own volition (Ryan et al., 2012; Willis, 2005).

Formal cognitive interviewing requires additional time and resources, and to do it well also requires significant experience and expertise. Cognitive psychologists are often employed to conduct the interviews, which often take place in formal survey laboratory settings. In addition to an understanding of the human thought process, interviewers must also have enough content knowledge to help interviewees reflect on the questions appropriately (Fowler, 2014; Willis, 2005). While full, formal implementation of cognitive interviewing may not be feasible in many circumstances (e.g., due to resource constraints or researcher expertise), survey researchers can use cognitive interview strategies such as think-aloud interviewing and probing to expose respondents' thought processes to support survey revision.

Both think-aloud interviewing and probing strategies involve an interviewer asking respondents how they go about answering survey questions. With the think-aloud strategy, respondents are asked to verbalize to the interviewer their thinking process while they read, interpret, and answer a question. Probing involves the interviewer asking specific questions ("probes") of respondents about how they go about answering questions (see Figure 7.1 for examples of cognitive probes). This can happen during the answering process or after, and the two strategies can be used in conjunction with one another to elicit even more depth of understanding of how respondents answer questions.

Foddy (1998) found that the most successful probes were also the most specific to the question, such as "What did you take the words 'having no religion' to mean? [and] How many hours did you take 'half a day' to mean?" (p. 123). The least successful probes were more general in nature, such as "Could you tell me a little more about that?" (p. 129).

FIGURE 7.1 ● **Examples of Cognitive Probes**	
Comprehension/interpretation probe	What does the term *dental sealant* mean to you?
Paraphrase	Can you repeat the question in your own words?
Confidence judgment	How sure are you that your health insurance covers . . .
Recall probe	How do you remember that you went to the dentist 3 times?
Specific probe	Why do you think that cancer is the most serious health problem?
General probe	How did you arrive at that answer? Was that easy or hard to answer? I noticed that you hesitated before you answered. What were you thinking about?

Source: Willis, G. B., 1994.

STORIES FROM THE FIELD
USING THINK-ALOUD AND PROBING STRATEGIES IN COGNITIVE INTERVIEWS

No Child Left Behind (NCLB) was a relatively controversial education reform effort in the 2000s intended to make schools and teachers more accountable for student success. It is viewed by some as placing unrealistic expectations on both teachers and schools more broadly; the sanctions levied on schools that didn't meet standards may have only perpetuated the challenges faced by those teachers and students. As part of an evaluation of the implementation of NCLB practices and policies in school districts throughout a single state, Ryan, Gannon-Slater, and Culbertson (2012), researchers from the University of Illinois, were tasked with surveying teachers and administrators about their experiences and perspectives. This included efforts to measure perception of change, such as whether collaboration among teachers improved. This survey (and broader evaluation effort) was to be conducted during implementation of NCLB practices and policies (sanctions were already in place for some schools), and measurement repeated over time in order to track ongoing implementation. Not only was the context sensitive enough to merit a testing process like cognitive interviewing, the researchers anticipated that respondents may not interpret the language used to describe some aspects of NCLB and its implementation consistently (within as well as across schools) in good part because much of it was abstract—such as the concept of collaboration.

The researchers employed a hybrid model of cognitive interviewing—including both think-aloud and probing strategies—before and after a pilot of the survey tool. Participants were strategically selected to represent different types of respondents (principals and teachers) and selected from districts that were struggling to meet NCLB standards. When at least two participants had trouble with a question, revisions were considered, and if made, tested again prior to finalization. Revisions were typically adjustments to wording or the way a survey item appeared on the page. For example, the initial draft survey did not include a "don't know" response option for select questions because of concerns that respondents would choose that option rather than go through the more difficult cognitive processes to select a more accurate response (satisficing). However, the survey pilot revealed that respondents were answering these questions differently than others on the survey—half selecting "no change" (where researchers believed there was change) and a substantial number skipping these questions all together. Cognitive interviewing revealed that teachers actually didn't know the answer to that particular question and were marking "no change" because it was as close to neutral as possible. Given this was generating inaccurate results, a "don't know" option was genuinely warranted and added to the next draft of the survey.

Source: Ryan et al. (2012).

In *Cognitive Interviewing: A Tool for Improving Questionnaire Design,* Willis (2005) notes that many variations of cognitive interviewing are used to test surveys and that cognitive interviewing is usually conducted as part of a broader testing process, inclusive of steps such as reviewing earlier draft questions and pilot processes. Willis (2005) outlines a number of general features of cognitive testing that are helpful in defining and understanding what these entail, including the following:

- Cognitive interviewing focuses on the thought processes of respondents, including their comprehension, recall, and decision making.

- Respondents are often chosen to represent desired respondents, and potentially those the researcher is concerned will be challenged in responding to the survey.

- Probing and verbal reporting procedures are used. (For example, Fowler [2014] notes that the interviewer typically asks the respondent to "think aloud" as they answer the question, "to ask respondents to say in their own words what they think the question is asking [or] to ask respondents to explain how they chose a particular answer over others" [p. 103].)

- Cognitive interviewers aim to uncover both the obvious problems as well as more subtle problems with particular questions; by doing so, much more valuable information is gathered than can be seen through typical pretesting or pilot testing efforts.

- The process is often iterative; multiple rounds of cognitive interviewing may be done as survey revisions are made.

- Cognitive interviewing itself does not generate survey revisions, nor is it a formal validation process; a researcher must use the information generated to make judgments about how best to revise a particular survey. Cognitive interviewing does not typically result in statistical proof of a question or tool's validity (p. 6).

Focus Groups

Focus groups can be used to pretest questions with a strategic sample of potential respondents just as they can be used to source or develop draft questions (see Chapter 4). These two uses of focus groups are distinctly different, and different strategies may be appropriate for each usage. For example, group brainstorming or word association exercises might be used to *design* questions, and when a focus group is used to *pretest* questions, probing questions might be used to gain insight about how participants might answer drafted questions. Exploring how participants think about questions can be especially effective in determining what language will be most familiar to respondents (e.g., whether respondents will be more familiar with "trash collection" or "garbage pick-up") (Collins, 2014). In this way, using focus groups to pretest questions can seem quite similar to conducting cognitive interviews. However, both Willis (2005) and Krueger (1994) note ways in which the two methods differ:

- Researchers typically use focus groups to explore topics more generally, rather than to review participants' thought processes about questions in detail. Think-aloud strategies may be adapted for use in focus groups, but the same degree of detail may not be solicited.

- Focus group protocols are likely to be more flexible than those typically used in cognitive interviewing. Researchers usually conduct focus groups with a fairly short set of key questions they want to ask participants, and employ probing questions as needed to clarify and solicit additional detail, depending on what participants share.

- Focus groups, because they are conducted socially, allow for and encourage interaction between participants. This can result in rich information surfacing that might not have surfaced during an individual interview, when one individual's comments prompt another's response and so forth.

Focus groups do have some limitations. Some researchers caution that focus groups are unlikely to result in information as robust as that gathered through more rigorous cognitive interviewing or pilot testing processes. In particular, focus group participants may be reluctant to openly ask their own questions or acknowledge something they don't understand (Collins, 2014), especially when in the presence of researchers, or other respondents with whom they do not feel comfortable, or when survey questions are of a potentially sensitive or threatening nature. Willis (2005) also notes that research comparing focus groups and cognitive interviews has found focus groups unsuited to evaluating specific questions and more appropriate for understanding more general dynamics of potential respondent thinking. Focus groups can, however, offer even more insight into respondents as part of the testing phase of the design thinking process. "Testing is another opportunity to build empathy through observation and engagement—it often yields unexpected insights" (Hasso Plattner, n.d.).

> *Testing is another opportunity to build empathy through observation and engagement—it often yields unexpected insights.*
>
> *–Hasso Plattner*

Pilot Testing

A full pilot test, sometimes referred to as a field test, is perhaps the most rigorous way to pretest a survey. Running a draft survey through a pilot testing process can help test the survey content, design, and process. Pilot tests can also be done in conjunction and even concurrently with cognitive interviewing. In fact, Collins (2003) argues:

> Whilst pilots may detect overt problems that disrupt the response elicitation process they often do not provide evidence of causes, nor do they provide evidence of covert problems. Thus we need to use question-testing methods derived from social and cognitive psychology, which will help us to systematically look at the question-and-answer process. (p. 231)

In a true survey pilot, a small but strategic sample of desired respondents is drawn, and those respondents are asked to complete a draft of the survey, typically using the exact process the researcher intends to use when the survey officially launches. As with all other things survey related, it is useful to first articulate the *purpose* for a given pilot effort before committing to or launching such an endeavor. Pilots can help achieve the following:

- *Determine needs for survey instructions.* Survey respondents may need more context or instructions for the entire survey or for particular sections in order to understand (or appreciate) what information the researcher is trying to capture.

- *Identify questions that are problematic.* This can sometimes be seen in the survey responses themselves, or respondents can be asked whether they had trouble with particular questions or have suggestions for better wording or response options.

- *Determine preferences regarding question order or identify other order issues (e.g., skip logic problems).* Order effects may be seen in pilot responses themselves if a sufficient number of respondents are included in the pilot and survey versions with different question orders are included so that analyses can be run (see later in this chapter for more on order effects). Likewise, pilot responses will often illuminate issues of skip logic in electronic surveys that may have been missed in internal testing.

- *Identify changes needed in the survey process itself.* Pilot respondents may indicate that more time is needed or that invitations aren't being received in the manner intended (e.g., ending up in junk email folders). They may also be able to provide feedback on what incentives may be most appropriate for the full survey.

Feedback on survey questions and the survey process can also be solicited through questions embedded in the survey tool or through a separate follow-up process. Pilot testing often includes an interview of the respondent following (or even during) completion of the survey tool. Although it may be easiest for respondents to react to particular questions and their experiences as they answer them and complete a survey, this obviously changes the amount of burden placed on the respondent. Survey content changes (as in the addition of questions specific to the pilot) can also result in a pilot survey experience that doesn't provide a legitimate "dry run" of the survey. If the pilot's purpose is to find out how long it will take a respondent to reply, a separate follow-up process (e.g., a short second survey triggered by submission of the first) may be preferable.

Important considerations when pilot testing a survey include the following:

- There are many ways to adapt a survey process for pilot testing purposes, such as by shortening the timeline for response, but the more closely the pilot mirrors the intended survey process, the more we can potentially learn about what works, and what doesn't work, about that process.

- Being strategic about which respondents to include in a pilot is smart. It is not uncommon to use a convenience or quota sampling strategy for a survey pilot. We suggest considering whether it is most helpful to include respondents who are more likely to provide more helpful information about how the process worked (or did not work) or are more likely to struggle with some or all of the survey questions.

- Informing participants of the valuable input they are providing is an important part of incentivizing participation in a pilot effort (and is useful for the eventual final survey administration too). Developing "buy-in" from pilot respondents is likely to result in a quicker response and more useful feedback. And the pilot respondents can then be asked (when appropriate) to help encourage others to respond (e.g., by noting that they were engaged in the survey design or by talking about how the information will be valuable to their community).

 ## Discussion Questions

1. How might you determine which pretesting strategies to use for a given survey effort? What specific factors might inform your decision about which to use?

2. What might you do differently if using one or more of these strategies to draft questions, as opposed to testing questions?

3. What might you anticipate are the greatest challenges in implementing pretesting strategies? Do they present any ethical challenges?

 ## Design Drills

1. Pick five questions from your draft survey or a survey example found online. Go through the Checklist for Quality Question Design for each of the questions. What edits do you want to make as a result, if any? What was challenging about using the checklist?

2. Research Scenario, Part 7 (additional parts are found in other chapters): You are developing a survey that will ask low-income senior citizens about their behaviors and thoughts related to a program delivered at local libraries. The program is intended to help senior citizens feel more engaged with their communities and to be more social, given concerns about seniors becoming too isolated.

   a. Write a brief plan for pretesting your survey, answering the following questions:

      i. What pretesting strategies will you use, and why?

      ii. Who will you include in any pretesting efforts?

      iii. What challenges do you anticipate in implementing these pretesting strategies? How will you mitigate those challenges?

Extended Learning

- Collins, D. (2014). *Cognitive interviewing practice.* Thousand Oaks, CA: Sage; and Willis, G. B. (2005). *Cognitive interviewing: A tool for improving questionnaire design.* Thousand Oaks, CA: Sage. For a thorough review on cognitive interviewing and related strategies (including "think aloud").

- Dillman, D., Smyth, J. D., & Christian, L. (2014). Internet, phone, mail, and mixed-mode surveys: The tailored design method. Hoboken, NJ: Wiley.

- Krueger, R. A. (1994). *Focus groups: A practice guide for applied research* (2nd ed.). Thousand Oaks, CA: Sage.

- Ryan, K., Gannon-Slater, N., & Culbertson, M. (2012). Improving survey methods with cognitive interviews in small- and medium-scale evaluations. *American Journal of Evaluation, 33,* 41. Includes examples of the use of cognitive interviewing in small- to medium-scale research projects, including discussion of the advantages of doing so.

- Sudman, S., Bradburn, N. M., & Schwarz, N. (1996). *Thinking about answers: The application of cognitive processes to survey methodology.* San Francisco: Jossey-Bass. For more about think-aloud strategies.

- For more on validity and reliability:

  o Litwin, M. (1995). *How to measure survey reliability and validity.* Thousand Oaks, CA: Sage.

  o Trochim, William M. (2016). *The research methods knowledge base.* Available at http://www .socialresearchmethods.net/kb.

  o Vogt, W. P., & Johnson, R. B. (2016). *Dictionary of statistics & methodology: A nontechnical guide for the social sciences* (5th ed.). Thousand Oaks, CA: Sage.

8

Pulling It All Together to Maximize Response

It's not just what it looks like and feels like. Design is how it works.

—Steve Jobs, co-founder of Apple

Though questions are the heart of any survey, it is not until those questions are pulled together into the actual survey instrument that data can be collected. In this section, we discuss some of the considerations key to putting together a questionnaire to maximize the usefulness of resulting data. We start with aspects of the survey tool itself, such as how best to order questions, and then review guidance about how best to communicate with desired respondents. Finally, we touch briefly on the value of incentivizing survey response. Notably, other survey texts cover this aspect of the survey design and administration process in far greater detail than we do; the resource list at the end of this chapter includes a few texts we have found particularly helpful.

Pulling a set of well-crafted questions into a well-composed survey requires intention and at least a few key considerations:

- The survey will need a clear and concise introduction that prepares the respondent to provide accurate and useful information.

- Questions should be compiled in a strategic and meaningful order (even a randomized order is strategic!).

- Survey formatting should attend to visual appeal that supports engagement and understanding by the respondents.

- A final review of the survey for reading comprehension is usually warranted.

Before diving into these details, we want to pause to revisit the fact that survey design, especially undertaken with a design thinking approach, is an iterative process. This chapter in particular may make the process appear linear. We urge readers to keep this in mind as we discuss survey administration modes in particular because decisions about survey administration mode can impact the way questions are designed and vice versa.

Survey Instructions

Just as clues provided in question stems and response options help respondents understand what information researchers want to collect, instructions that precede the survey or introduce groups of questions provide critical information to respondents. Our best advice for composing effective instructions is the same advice we've offered for designing quality questions. Keeping instructions as simple and brief as possible while also giving respondents the information they need will result in their providing the most accurate and useful responses.

In particular, we like to include a short page of contextual information that precedes the survey, and likely mirrors language in the survey invitation. This preamble should include information about the purpose of the survey, the deadline for responding, any information respondents might need to answer the questions, and researcher contact information in case the respondent has questions or technical challenges. Headings at the top of each section of questions (typically each page in an online survey) can also provide context specific to those questions. A phrase such as "The questions in this section ask you to share information about . . ." or "Your responses to questions in this section will help us understand . . ." placed below the heading but above the questions can also provide helpful guidance and encouragement for respondents.

Finally, parenthetical instructions may be needed after a question stem but should only be used when absolutely necessary. Ideally, questions are written clearly and concisely enough that this is not necessary, but occasionally a simple "check all that apply," "choose up to 3 options," or "select the best fit" following the question stem can ensure that respondents will fully understand what the researcher is asking them to do in responding to a question.

Order Effects

"Question order plays an enormous role in setting [the] larger context" for a survey (Dillman et al., 2014, p. 229). Research on surveys suggests that question order can play an important role in the quality of survey responses. Order effects occur when answers to later questions on a survey are influenced by earlier questions (for a review of early research on this see Sudman et al., 1996). In general, surveys should be organized with a logical flow that is likely to make sense to and appeal to respondents. A poorly organized survey "can confuse respondents, bias their responses, and jeopardize the quality of the entire research effort" (Rea & Parker, 2014, p. 35).

As with many other aspects of the survey design process, the order in which questions appear in a survey largely depends on the specific research objectives; hence, our advice may apply perfectly to a given survey effort, or there may be valid reasons to break with this advice and order questions differently. Nevertheless, we offer the following general recommendations:

1. Order questions in a way that minimizes the potential for order effects. In other words, consider whether earlier questions are likely to influence answers to later questions (Babbie, 1990; Bradburn, Sudman, & Wansink, 2004; Czaja & Blair, 2005; Dillman et al., 2014).

2. Order questions in a way that will be likely to keep respondents engaged and discourage them from satisficing, giving low-quality data, or quitting the survey. In other words, place at least some of the most interesting or relevant (to respondents) questions early in the survey (Babbie, 1990; Bradburn et al., 2004; Dillman et al., 2014). Identify questions that appear more obviously central to the research effort and therefore feel worthwhile for a respondent to answer. This also supports rapport building and "buy in" for the respondent.

3. Begin with less sensitive or threatening questions before moving on to more sensitive questions (Babbie, 1990; Bradburn et al., 2004; Czaja & Blair, 2005; Dillman et al., 2014). This also allows the researcher to achieve some degree of positive rapport with respondents as they answer less threatening questions first. It helps ensure that even if respondents refuse to answer sensitive or threatening questions, or quit the survey altogether, researchers may still end up with some usable data from earlier questions.

4. Related to the previous advice is a recommendation to place certain demographic questions (e.g., questions asking about gender identity or sexual preference) later in a survey, for these can potentially be the most sensitive questions included. Although some researchers choose to begin surveys with these questions, because they seem so fundamental and are typically easy and quick to answer, we advise that they are left to the end whenever appropriate for two reasons: a) to avoid asking potentially sensitive questions at the beginning of a survey, thus making respondents uncomfortable, and b) to ensure that the survey can start with more engaging questions, thus encouraging respondents to persist in answering subsequent questions. It is also possible, and sometimes helpful, to break up demographic questions if several will be included. For example, asking about job position and educational level could be grouped together but separated (and perhaps appear earlier in a survey) from more sensitive questions such as those on gender, race, or ethnicity. Additional considerations for designing and using demographic questions are discussed in Chapter 6.

5. Begin with questions that are relatively easy to answer (Czaja & Blair, 2005; Rea & Parker, 2014).

6. Put questions of high importance to the researcher(s) early in the survey so that if respondents quit the survey early, some useful data will be preserved (Bradburn et al., 2004).

7. Group questions that are related into meaningful categories or topics (Czaja & Blair, 2005; Dillman et al., 2014; Rea & Parker, 2014; Weisberg et al., 1996). Questions should be grouped strategically, so that those related to one another are adjacent or flow in a logical manner. There are instances, however, where it is not only feasible but ideal to randomize the order of questions in a survey. Though this is far more often done with online surveys, it is possible to generate multiple versions of a paper-based or telephone survey so that question order is not only randomized once but multiple times with different question orders. This effort may be necessary when researchers are concerned that order effects will play a significant role in how respondents will answer questions.

Of course, it would be all but impossible to do all of these all of the time, so it is important to prioritize according to the purpose and context for the research and survey itself. Pretesting strategies such as providing different forms of a survey with different question orders to separate groups of respondents can also be used to uncover and assess order effects.

Formatting the Survey

Survey formatting often depends on the survey administration tool selected. Some online tools are more restrictive, with "canned" formatting and layout options, whereas others offer more customization options. Several researchers have conducted studies on various visual or formatting elements of surveys, some comparing paper-based to web-based administration and others focusing on one or the other administration mode. Regardless of administration mode, it is important to recognize that formatting choices such as question layout and font size and color can influence response in similar ways to other question features.

Research on survey formatting is closely related to research on question design, so much so that it is challenging to provide advice that applies only to the visual layout and formatting of a survey. Consider research on choice and placement of response option labels, for example. Much like other aspects of survey design, here too, we must take into account the ways in which respondents make sense of what they see when they encounter a question. It may sound surprising, but respondents in fact "have difficulty in using response scales and they rely on a range of cues to assign meaning to the scale points" (Tourangeau et al., 2007, p. 93). Hence, even after devoting significant time to understanding respondents in order to craft well-worded question stems and appropriately aligned response options, survey researchers still need to consider how visual and formatting elements may influence response.

Formatting for Respondent Understanding

Toepoel, Das, & van Soest (2009) found that "respondents draw meaning from nonverbal as well as verbal cues in a web survey" (p. 522). Respondents pay attention to and make inferences about labels—the words they see as they read through response options—as well as additional features, such as the shape of the scale (i.e., whether it is vertical or horizontal) and even the spacing of the response options (Tourangeau et al., 2007).

Tourangeau et al. (2007) claim that respondents use "five interpretive heuristics" (p. 94) to interpret what they see in a survey question:

- Middle means typical.

- Left and top mean first.

- Near means related.

- Up means good.

- Like (in appearance) means close (in meaning) (p. 94).

The first heuristic in particular carries implications for questions that feature an odd number of response options and consequently, a midpoint. "Respondents expect the middle option of a scale to be special in some way—to represent the most typical category, a neutral point, or the conceptual midpoint. As a result, they may use the visual midpoint as an anchor in formulating their answers" (Tourangeau et al., 2007, p. 94). Respondents also expect that the response options they see are logically ordered by the survey designer in some sort of meaningful progression from left to right or top to bottom.

In general, survey questions and their response options should be grouped together to make it apparent that the question stem and response options together constitute one survey item. This is consonant with Tourangeau et al.'s (2007) third heuristic, "near means related" (p. 94). Response options should be evenly spaced, whether they are presented vertically or horizontally, with one key exception. When a response scale includes a range of options along with a nonsubstantive option such as *don't know*, *no opinion*, or *not applicable*, these should be visually separated from the other scale options (see Figure 8.1).

One reason to visually separate nonsubstantive response options has to do with sets of options that contain a midpoint. When a nonsubstantive response option appears in line with other options, it can shift the conceptual midpoint— the response option the researcher intended as the midpoint—thereby confusing respondents and ultimately influencing response. For example, in Figure 8.2 at first glance, it would appear that *fair* is the midpoint in what seems like a 5-point scale. It is the visual midpoint between *excellent* and *no opinion*. But *excellent* and *no opinion* are not polar opposites. The poles are, in fact, *excellent* and *poor*. Separating the nonsubstantive response option (in this example, *no opinion*) would reduce the possibility of measurement error that would result from substantive options being directly in line with nonsubstantive options (Artino & Gelbach, 2012).

Visual text features such as bold text, italics, underline, boxes, indentation, and color should be used with caution and with the understanding that these can serve to assist respondents in completing a survey but also have the potential to distract or signal them in a way that departs from the researcher's intent.

FIGURE 8.1 ● Separating a Nonsubstantive Response Option

1. How would you rate the quality of the materials you received?

   O Excellent
   O Good
   O Fair
   O Poor

   O No opinion

2. How often do you change your bedsheets?

O	O	O	O	O
Once per week or more often	About every 2 weeks	About every 3 weeks	About once per month or less often	Prefer not to answer

3. How often do you mow your lawn in the summer months?

   O About once per week or more often
   O About 2–3 times per month
   O About once per month or less often

   O Not applicable

FIGURE 8.2 ● Visual Midpoint Interferes With Conceptual Midpoint

How would you rate the quality of the materials you received?

   O Excellent
   O Good
   O Fair
   O Poor
   O No opinion

Separating the nonsubstantive option from the substantive options:

How would you rate the quality of the materials you received?

   O Excellent
   O Good
   O Fair
   O Poor

   O No opinion

Online Platforms

Smyth et al. (2009) explored whether a larger answer box for an open-ended question on a web-based survey would result in an increase in the length and quality of responses. They compared early and late responders, under the assumption that those who respond later in the survey window are likely somewhat less motivated than those who respond earlier. The researchers found no effects for early responders, but the increased box size was effective for late responders and associated with increased response quality. Smyth et al. (2009) report being encouraged that "a visual design manipulation can stimulate less motivated respondents to give more complete responses" (p. 336). In addition, the researchers experimented with adding the following explanation to the question stem: "You are not limited in the length of your response by the size of the box" (p. 331). This explanation made it clear to respondents that the size of the box they saw on their screens did not necessarily limit the length of their answers. The researchers found that the added explanation increased the length of responses for both early and later responders (p. 332).

Although not strictly a visual matter, specific features of online platforms can be problematic for respondents to use with accuracy. For example, Healy and Gendall (2007) found that using a drop-down feature for a question about age resulted in significant response error. When respondents were asked to select their age range from a drop-down menu of options, especially when using a computer mouse with scrolling, it resulted in a high degree of input error as they inadvertently selected the wrong range. Healy and Gendall's (2007) findings were corroborated by similar studies that tested different questions using a drop-down response feature. The authors conclude with the advice to avoid drop-down response menus when possible. Instead, questions can be designed such that all response options appear on the screen, or in the case of a question about age for example, a fill-in box appears for year of birth. Although this study is now more than a decade old and technology hardware and software has certainly improved along with many people's facility with them, it is reasonable to believe that drop-downs can still result in mistakes. We advocate for erring on the side of caution avoiding drop-downs in favor of presenting all response options on a screen wherever possible.

Mobile-Friendly Formatting

It is increasingly important for researchers to consider what their surveys will look like on a smartphone or other mobile device. Some electronic survey tools, such as SurveyMonkey or SurveyGizmo, are capable of ensuring that a survey will be functional on mobile devices and in fact offer apps for mobile devices. As with all surveys, here again it is crucial to know the desired respondents well enough to anticipate how they will be responding. Are respondents likely to answer via smartphone and might they stop responding due to frustration if the survey isn't formatted well? Or will most respondents be answering through email at work where they are more likely to be on a full-sized screen?

Attending to Visual Disabilities

The Blind Foundation (2018) in New Zealand has offered a set of recommendations for presenting text-based information (e.g., surveys) in a way that is supportive of those with low vision or blindness. Their recommendations for printed text (which many with low or no vision will use adaptive technologies to read) include the following:

- Using a 12-point font size or larger

- Selecting colors with a high level of contrast (black type on white paper always works well)

- Avoid too much formatting; use bold for emphasis rather than italics, which are more difficult to read

- Provide a narrative description for any images, tables, or charts used and avoid using images of text (e.g., scanned documents)

Recommendations for web-based text are based on the Web Content Accessibility Guidelines developed by W3C (2008) and are very similar to those for print. Fortunately, web-based surveys often provide good solutions, assuming that respondents use devices that are compatible with such surveys. Providing text alternatives is a particularly good way to ensure that those with low vision or blindness will be able to respond accurately to a survey. Text alternatives can come in the form of assistive technology such as text readers or screen magnifiers, but for most survey researchers, who aren't able to provide these technologies directly, making text alternatives available may look like ensuring that the electronic systems we select are compatible with those technologies. At bare minimum, following as many of the guidelines for print as possible (see earlier list) and making it possible to enlarge the font size in an electronic survey is often warranted.

Reviewing for Reading Comprehension

It is always wise to give everything one final read-through to ensure the survey is easy for respondents to both read and comprehend. Fortunately, many tools now exist that assess written documents for reading comprehension, including tools embedded in Microsoft Word. Two tests of readability can be enabled in Microsoft Word (this requires a change in settings related to grammar and spelling checks; see Microsoft Word help online for instructions). The Flesch Reading Ease Test produces a score up to 100, with higher scores indicating easier reading. The Flesch-Kincaid Grade Level Test produces an approximate (United States) grade level; a 4.0 indicates a fourth-grade reading level, a 4.5 somewhere between fourth and fifth grade, and so on. A number of online tools are also now available, such as Readable.io (https://readable.io), which provides several comprehensibility tests for an uploaded text (including the Flesch-Kincaid Grade Level Test).

Tests like these should be used as just one indicator of readability, as opposed to the only way readability is determined. Nothing beats having others review your survey and provide feedback, especially if they are similar to or from the respondent population. It is also worth exploring resources for writing in "plain language," a government mandate for U.S. federal agencies (see the site Plain Language: Improving Communication from the Federal Government to the Public [http://www.plainlanguage.gov]). That said, when using tests like the Flesh-Kincaid, a good rule of thumb is to aim for at least a grade level or two below where most respondents are likely to be in order to ensure maximum readability for all respondents. Conventional wisdom calls for keeping any writing for the general public no higher than about ninth-grade reading level (the average reading level of U.S. adults is estimated to be between about seventh and eighth grade). Surveys on more technical subjects (e.g., health-related issues) may benefit from a somewhat lower-grade reading level (ideally fifth grade or lower) to ensure readability by all respondents.

Contacting Potential Respondents

Any communication researchers send to desired respondents should be carefully crafted, including invitations and reminder messages. Invitations and reminders set the stage for the survey, letting desired respondents know what to expect if they choose to participate. A poorly worded or poorly timed invitation or reminder has the potential to increase nonresponse just as easily as poorly crafted questions. Most survey efforts at the very least include the following:

- An invitation

- One or more reminders

- A thank-you or acknowledgment

For an online survey, four or five total points of contact with desired respondents are likely needed: an initial invitation, three or four reminders, and an acknowledgment of survey completion.

It was once common to recommend that researchers send a "pre-notice" as well, letting potential respondents know that a survey is coming, but this has largely fallen out of favor given how inundated most people are with emails and how likely they are to ignore postcards or other mail notifications. Dillman et al. (2014) note exceptions, of course. In particular, when a survey is coming from an entity that the desired respondent is *unfamiliar* with (e.g., when a research firm is conducting a client survey for an organization) it can be useful for the organization to first send a notice letting clients know to expect the request, effectively verifying that the survey is a legitimate request.

In composing survey invitations and reminders, we often draw on Robert Cialdini's (2007) principles of persuasion, recounted in his classic book *Influence*, first published in 1984. The six principles, along with very brief descriptions, are as follows:

1. *Reciprocation.* "We should try to repay, in kind, what another person has provided us" (p. 17).

2. *Commitment and consistency.* "Our nearly obsessive desire to be (and to appear) consistent with what we have already done. Once we have made a choice or taken a stand, we will encounter personal and interpersonal pressure to behave consistently with that commitment" (p. 57).

3. *Social proof.* "One means we use to determine what is correct is to find out what other people think is correct. . . . We view a behavior as more correct in a given situation to the degree that we see others performing it" (p. 116).

4. *Liking.* "We prefer to say yes to the requests of someone we know and like" (p. 166).

5. *Authority.* "A deep sense of duty to authority (p. 213). . . . We are trained from birth that obedience to proper authority is right and disobedience is wrong" (p. 216).

6. *Scarcity.* "Opportunities seem more valuable when their availability is limited" (p. 238).

We describe how we use these principles and offer examples in the following sections. Before we do so, it is important to note that no contact can be made with potential respondents until after institutional review board (IRB) approval, whenever it is required (more about IRB approval later). However, rules and processes will vary by institution.

Compelling Invitations

Writing a compelling invitation for a survey is a craft in itself. It is best to keep the invitation as short and direct as possible, while also including all the most important information needed for a respondent to make an informed decision about participation. A comprehensive invitation typically includes the following:

- Who is asking for a survey response and who is conducting the survey/analysis (using our titles and affiliations lends credibility to the survey but also draws on the principle of authority)

- The topic/purpose/intended use for the survey and its results (hint: this is where our survey purpose statement can come in handy!)

- The deadline for response

- Why the respondent should care about responding, including any incentives being offered (using incentives draws on the principle of reciprocation)

- Any promises of anonymity or confidentiality (remember, these are different!)

- Any detail needed to ensure proper informed consent/assent is provided

- Notification of any information they might like to have on hand to help them respond

- Researcher contact information in case a respondent has questions or needs help responding

Using a conversational and personal tone in a survey invitation (as well as in reminders) can draw on Cialdini's (2007) principle of "liking" as we attempt to establish a positive rapport with respondents. By emotionalizing our appeal for survey participation, we can also draw on the principle of "commitment and consistency." For example, sharing with respondents that survey results will help organizers improve a program for the next generation of program participants presupposes that respondents would want to help future participants. Given the need for people to be consistent (and assuming they have done other helpful things in their lives), this may subtly persuade them to complete the survey.

freshspectrum.com

Sufficient and Engaging Reminders

Our experience with and expert advice on the use of reminders varies. Dillman et al. (2014) generally suggest three or four reminders but emphasize that there is no perfect system; the right number, content, and timing of all contacts, including reminders, depends on the context for the survey and the characteristics of the respondents. It is more important that reminders (and all contacts, for that matter) are actually engaging, that they encourage a potential respondent to complete the survey. The content of reminders can and should vary, to help catch the attention of the desired respondent. Not all information about the survey needs to be included in each reminder, but a few basic details are usually necessary:

- A brief overview of the purpose of the survey and why responses are needed and/or will be useful

- Instructions for how to respond and a link if the survey is to be completed online

- Information about incentives (discussed shortly)

- The deadline for response

- Contact information should the desired respondent have questions about the survey

In addition, it can be motivating to include information about how the survey results will be used. Whenever possible, personalizing contacts (by addressing individuals) is ideal, though when survey responses are to be anonymous, this may not be wise because it could indicate to the desired respondent that the researcher knows their identity and could track their response individually. Often we address all respondents with reminders and again take the opportunity to capitalize on some principles of persuasion. For example, by thanking "all of you who have already completed the survey" before reminding respondents about it, we are taking advantage of Cialdini's (2007) principle of "social proof." In the following story, Kylie Hutchinson draws on two principles of persuasion: "liking" and "reciprocation." She uses humor to personalize survey reminders and pretends to offer a wildly generous gift in return for participation. Even though the gift is a joke, we think the principle of reciprocation may indeed be activated.

STORIES FROM THE FIELD
THE IMPORTANCE OF REMINDERS

iStock.com/Viktor_Kitaykin

For my undergrad thesis I surveyed 300 members of the general public at a local tourist attraction. My professor bugged and bugged me to read Dillman, Smyth, and Christian's *Tailored Design Method*, which stressed the importance of sending three reminders. I kept ignoring her, but when I finally did it, I was able to get a final response rate of 84%. Not bad from the general public! Over the years I've grown more creative when sending my reminders. For a group of busy lawyers I promised to send them their very own pony (see left). For a steering committee of busy physicians, I offered a pretend Hawaii vacation. They both knew I was kidding, but it increased the responses dramatically. I realize this isn't official survey practice, but if you know the respondents well, a sense of humor can go a long way toward prompting them to complete your survey.

—Kylie Hutchinson

Planning for extensions. It may seem a bit sneaky, but we have found it useful to plan for extensions to survey deadlines when appropriate and feasible. By extending the survey window briefly (i.e., keeping the survey open for a few more days or even a week) and offering respondents additional opportunities for input, we are using Cialdini's (2007) principle of "scarcity." This means setting an initial (usually ideal) deadline and using that for initial invitations and reminders but planning to extend the deadline if additional responses are needed/desired. The final reminder can then be used to announce the extension with a statement with intentionally compelling language like "we've decided to extend the survey by X days in order to give everyone an opportunity for input," or "we have decided to keep the survey window open just a bit longer so that everyone will have the chance for their voice to be heard on this important issue."

Informed Consent/Assent

Many research efforts that involve human subjects (i.e., research participants) are subject to specific legal and ethical guidelines determined by an institutional review board (IRB). This includes most graduate or university-based research as well as most research funded through federal grants. IRB guidelines are specific to each institution and dictate how research participants (such as survey respondents) must be informed of the risks involved in their participation and subsequently provide written **informed consent** or be provided opportunity to decline to participate. For research participants who are younger (the specific age varies by IRB guidelines), a parent or guardian may need to provide consent in writing in addition to the young person's approval, which is called **assent**, because they are not capable of being fully informed or consenting legally.

Regardless of whether a given survey effort is technically subject to IRB or other legal guidelines, it is our strong belief that survey researchers are ethically compelled to inform anyone involved of the risks (and rewards) of participating by responding to a survey. The basic principles of informed consent can be followed regardless of what is required more formally. These principles include the following:

Chris Lysy, Fresh Spectrum

- Providing a complete and honest picture of a survey's purpose and contents

- Letting respondents know whether survey responses will be confidential or anonymous

- Informing respondents of how the information will be stored, used, and shared

- Disclosing to respondents who will have access to the information collected

All of this should be done prior to asking for someone's response. In particular, it is important to note whether the survey may contain questions that could be alarming or in any way inflict or reinflict trauma for a respondent.

Survey Incentives

Researchers can also consider incentivizing survey response. Dillman et al. (2014) outline several ways to incentivize survey response, building on the premise that people are more willing to respond to surveys when the "social exchange" is in their favor—that the benefits of responding to the survey outweigh the costs experienced. Ways to increase these benefits, and therefore response, include the following:

- Specifying how the survey results will be useful

- Piquing the respondent's interest by asking interesting questions

- Stressing that opportunities to respond are limited

- Using cash and material incentives to encourage, but not require, reciprocity

DESIGN DETAILS
CONFIDENTIALITY AND ANONYMITY

Confidentiality and anonymity are easily and often confused but are in fact two different concepts. Survey responses are *confidential* when a survey researcher promises not to share any identifying information (whether captured in a survey or not) or to reveal enough detail in survey reporting that could be used to identify who responded (or who responded in a particular way). In contrast, survey responses are *anonymous* when the researcher does not capture any information that is identifying of specific respondents. In other words, confidentiality means that a researcher may know the identity of specific respondents (including but not only when surveys ask for contact information), whereas anonymity means that researchers do not (and cannot) know the identity of respondents. Survey researchers must be careful about what they promise to potential respondents and about what data they capture and/or share in survey reporting that might jeopardize confidentiality or anonymity. It is possible to inadvertently capture or report on identifying information either in how surveys are administered (e.g., if responses are collected online and the dataset includes contact information such as email addresses as a result) or in the detail captured by particular questions or combinations of questions (e.g., very specific responses are captured regarding demographic details and/or a respondent's participation in particular events).

Additionally, researchers can decrease the "cost" to respondents by doing the following:

- Reducing the length and complexity of the survey

- Using visual design principles to make questionnaires easier to complete

- Avoiding subordinating, alienating, or excluding language

- Avoiding collection of sensitive or threatening information unless absolutely necessary to answer the research or evaluation question(s)

Planning for Administration

At this point in the text, it's likely quite obvious that we are proponents of thorough and thoughtful planning. This extends well beyond planning for and developing survey content to planning for survey administration, analysis, and eventual use of the survey results. Despite relegating this content to the last chapter, we strongly suggest plotting out the details of administration, analysis, and use (to the extent feasible) at the outset of planning a survey. The following is a suggested outline for such a "mini plan" (a moniker we use because these planning documents are specific to individual data collection efforts and are therefore smaller than the broader researcher or evaluation plan to which an individual data collection effort contributes). When fleshed out, this can serve as a working, internal plan for a survey used to help keep the effort focused and on track. This can be especially helpful when researchers are working in collaboration with others such as in team-based research efforts or when planning collaboratively with stakeholders is critical (as in participatory research).

SURVEY MINI PLAN
OUTLINE AND INSTRUCTIONS

Use this outline to flesh out as much detail as is useful prior to developing the actual survey, updating it as needed throughout the planning process. It can be especially helpful to use a framework such as this when more than one researcher is working on a survey or the survey timeline is lengthy in order to ensure that the plan is clear to all involved and that critical details aren't lost over time.

Overview of survey. It can be helpful to articulate and have on hand a very basic description of the survey: the who, what, when, where, and how. We often write this last when drafting a survey plan. Hint: this can be very useful later in the process when composing introductory and reminder language to send to respondents.

Purpose. As we described in Chapter 2, clearly articulating survey purpose is critical. A purpose statement should indicate why the data are being collected and how the survey results will be used, briefly. Additional details about how the researcher will support survey use can also be outlined separately below.

Related research questions. Surveys are usually conducted as part of broader research efforts. At the very least, a researcher is trying to answer a few bigger-picture questions with the help of the data the survey will capture. Having a copy of those broader research questions here can help keep a survey effort focused appropriately.

Other contextual notes. This is effectively a reminder to consider and note any other contextual issues that could influence respondents or the survey design and administration more generally. For example, if researchers need to share drafts with stakeholders prior to finalization, or need to remember to consider particular types of respondents (e.g., those with disabilities or those with a primary language different from the researcher), including those details here will help ensure they are not forgotten.

Administration

Mode. Note how the survey will be administered. On paper? By phone? Online? Some combination of these modes?

Timeline. When will the survey be administered? How long will the survey window remain open? When will reminders be needed? This is a good place to insert a detailed timeline; see the worksheet that follows for help in fleshing out this part of the plan.

Data management and analysis. It is critical to consider how survey responses will be analyzed, preferably prior to finalizing survey questions, but certainly prior to administering the survey. It is useful to write down a general plan for working with the survey data, from how it will be cleaned and stored, to who will have access to it, to what analysis will be conducted. Specific notes may also be needed for questions that will be particularly tricky to analyze (e.g., *choose all that apply* questions).

(Continued)

(Continued)

Use. Building on the purpose statement written for this plan, articulate how the survey results will be used here. With whom will they be shared, how, and when? How will researchers support stakeholders' use of the results?

Draft text/content notes. Use this section of the working plan to capture any early notes about content for the actual survey and/or introduction or reminder text, prior to drafting the actual survey questions.

STORIES FROM THE FIELD
THE TROUBLE WITH A LACK OF PLANNING

Read! is a program dedicated to helping at-risk youth improve their reading level. There are 35 chapters of this organization across the United States. Each chapter implements the program in 10 to 26 elementary schools. Each school has a teacher who is a volunteer site coordinator. This includes identifying students to participate and coordinating tutoring schedules.

A university conducted a national evaluation of Read! The evaluation consisted of documenting tutoring activities in terms of length and frequency as well as a site coordinator survey.

The survey included *300 questions* for the volunteer site coordinator to complete.

The survey had no input from chapter organizations or their volunteers. The national evaluation team required each volunteer coordinator to complete the survey. The Oregon program director tried, calling volunteers and asking them to complete the survey. The national evaluation team pressured the director to complete the survey administration to ensure they had the data needed.

Can you guess what happened? Very low return rate (3%). Frustration experienced by everyone—a program director who couldn't meet the national evaluation team's unrealistic requirements, and the evaluation team didn't get the data they needed for their national evaluation.

This is an extreme example, where the national evaluation team overcommitted to the amount of data that could be *realistically* collected.

Why does this happen? A group of data enthusiasts puts a plan on paper, with no action plan of who is doing what and/or without talking to those on the front lines collecting the data. Or leadership decides what will be collected, with no input from others. It occurs in silo. It's mandated, leading to the likelihood of no data being collected.

–Chari Smith

Note: The actual name of the program is confidential; therefore, the fictitious program name Read! is used instead. Read! to our knowledge, is not a real program and not affiliated with the true story above.

Selecting a Survey Administration Mode

There are several survey administration modes for researchers to choose from, and many online survey administration tools. Attempting to review all of the possibilities would put our text out of date before it was published, but this section provides some considerations for determining the best way to administer a survey.

First, we note that surveys are most commonly "self-administered": respondents are left to complete the survey on their own, with only the guidance sent with or embedded into the survey itself (as opposed to researcher-administered surveys, such as those conducted by phone). Self-administered surveys are typically conducted by mail (on paper) or online. Determining whether to use a paper-based survey or other mode typically depends on the researcher's access to desired respondents. Will we see them in person? Do we have the ability to send them a survey electronically? Are they able to respond electronically, given their own circumstances and/or the content of the survey itself?

Using paper-based surveys. Despite the increased use of online surveys, many examples of surveys on paper and by mail are still present. For example, paper surveys are still administered for the U.S. Census. Even comment cards on restaurant tables are a form of paper-based, self-administered survey. Paper-based surveys can be administered in person with a researcher or other individual present to read questions aloud or answer questions from respondents if part of the research plan. More commonly though, paper surveys are distributed by mail, and a key consideration for this administration mode is the cost of printing, paper, envelopes, and postage. Although they also may require the effort to fold, stuff, and seal envelopes, much of this process can now be completed by machines. The larger the population or sample, the more costs that will be incurred. Mail surveys may also bear the additional cost of reminders, such as second copies of the survey that go out to nonresponders.

Both mail and online surveys can reach much larger pools of respondents than telephone or in-person researcher (i.e., interviewer) administered surveys. Both can also be translated into other languages if needed, and pretesting with the target population can ensure that the survey will be answerable by desired respondents.

Using online or web-based surveys. Web-based surveys are often "distributed" to potential respondents via a link in an email or embedded on a website. For example, shoppers often receive links to surveys on retail receipts or receive emails asking for feedback following a shopping experience. Many online survey systems are now available that make the researcher's job easier than ever before, with predesigned survey formats to select from and semiautomated administration options (e.g., automatic email reminders to nonrespondents), along with built-in analysis tools. Online surveys are usually the most time-efficient administration mode. Time considerations include how long a window to allow respondents to complete the survey and when to schedule reminders. Reminders are easy to implement once an email list of respondents is generated. Online surveys generally incur the cost of the survey platform itself, but the cost does not change with the number of respondents, as is the case with mail surveys.

STORIES FROM THE FIELD
MOVING FROM PAPER TO TABLET ADMINISTRATION

In 2012, I had the opportunity to volunteer in Zambia with an organization working to enhance primary education through the use of online learning and tablets. One of my first tasks was to survey approximately 2,000 primary school students on their literacy and numeracy levels. Thanks to recent developments in online survey software, my team and I were able to move the existing survey from a 10-page double-sided paper version to a mobile tablet. We immediately noticed a number of benefits. There were significantly reduced photocopying expenses and fewer boxes of heavy surveys to transport. Entering the data directly onto the devices made for easier analysis and fewer data entry errors. At the end of each day, I was able to download and easily review the data for any inaccuracies. Best of all, the data collection staff quickly learned to use the mobile version in less than an hour and strongly preferred it to the paper version.

—Kylie Hutchinson

Using telephone and in-person surveys. Surveys can also be administered more directly by researchers (or their delegates), most commonly by phone or in person. Survey researchers still go door-to-door in some communities with written questionnaires (or surveys on tablet computers), and many surveys (e.g., political polls, marketing surveys) are conducted via telephone. This mode of administration typically requires a team of staff (or volunteers) who administer the survey to respondents; depending on the size of the target population or sample, it can be difficult or impossible for the principal researcher(s) to do all of the survey administration. Additional considerations for using telephone or in-person surveys include the following:

- Ensuring that those administering the survey are adequately trained so that all respondents are receiving the same explanations and that responses are recorded consistently and accurately

- That the larger the population or sample, the greater the cost may be regarding survey administrator training and wages

- That these survey administration modes are limited in their ability to reach larger or more geographically diverse populations; in-person surveys in particular can typically only be administered in limited geographical areas

- That telephone and in-person interviewers will need to be able to speak the same language as respondents and understand important cultural context factors in order to help respondents understand questions if needed

- That time is needed to train in-person interviewers and to schedule sessions, especially if survey administrators are expected to conduct multiple sessions

Although more resource-intensive, telephone and in-person surveys can be a desirable option when respondents may not be able to accurately or easily respond to a paper or web-based survey. For example, Schaeffer and Presser (2003) describe research from the mid-1990s that found self-administered surveys more likely to result in higher social desirability bias and therefore inaccurate responses.

Mixed-mode administration. Survey administration modes are not limited to those already described, and they may also be combined in ways that capitalize on the advantages of and minimize the disadvantages of each. The Tailored Design Method (TDM) was developed by Dillman et al. (2014). TDM is a robust approach to survey design that provides guidance about mixing modes of survey adminis-tration and is built on an understanding of respondent ability and willingness to answer survey questions and provide useful information. As Dillman et al. note, TDM was developed

> using an understanding of what causes people to behave in certain ways and not others. Specifically, we use a social exchange perspective on human behavior, which suggests that respondent behavior is motivated by the return that behavior is expected to bring, and in fact, usually does bring, from others. It assumes that the likelihood of responding to a questionnaire, and doing so accurately, is greater when the person trusts that the expected rewards for responding to a survey will outweigh the anticipated costs of responding. (p. 17)

Determining a Survey Timeline

The time required to complete a survey research project is highly dependent on the specific context and scope of the project. A number of factors can influence the timeline, including population or sample size, the extent of pretesting or piloting that needs to be done, the administration mode (e.g., in person, telephone, mail, online), and the analysis techniques, not the least of which is how long the data collection period will remain open, something that can significantly affect response rate.

The survey design process we outlined in Chapter 1 can be used to create a timeline for a specific project. The design process is a series of phases that high-light the importance of such activities as planning and predrafting; understanding our survey respondents; sourcing and designing questions; and finalizing a survey by using pretesting strategies and preparing a final draft for administration, anal-ysis, and use. These phases are not just linear but in fact overlapping and iterative. These elements all *precede* survey administration, data collection, analysis, and reporting. It's not that we privilege these phases or want to imply that they are in any way more important than the later phases of survey research. Rather, we posit that these preadministration design steps are critically important for oth-ers to achieve their purposes and result in the highest-quality dataset in service to answering key research or evaluation questions. So, although we cannot offer specific advice as to how long each phase will take (as would be the case in any endeavor in which quality is desired), adequate time *must* be allotted to each step to achieve desired results.

TIMELINE WORKSHEET

Task	Date/Deadline	Who Is Responsible
Draft survey tool completed		
Testing/piloting survey tool Details here:		
Survey launches Details here:		
Reminder # 1		
Reminder # 2		
Reminder # 3		
Survey closes		
Last possible extension date for survey responses		
Any specific efforts to follow up for responses (e.g., with particular desired respondents) Details here:		
Data cleanup/organization		
Survey analysis		
Draft report		
Solicit report feedback		
Finalize report		

DESIGN DETAILS
REVIEWING TYPES OF MEASUREMENT

Social scientists measure people and their attributes, behaviors, and thoughts in four ways. These ways inform different types of survey questions, respondent tasks, and data analysis. Although data analysis is beyond the scope of this text, it is critical for the researcher to understand measurement and be able to anticipate the types of analyses needed for a given survey effort. Nominal, ordinal, interval, and ratio variables help us classify what we wish to study (e.g., people, places, events) into categories and understand how those categories relate to one another.

Nominal

Nominal literally means "in name only." Nominal measurement is used to sort people into categories with no particular order. Response options for nominal variables are categories and have no inherent order. Examples of nominal response options might be countries of origin, favorite sports, or religions. These response options can be randomized if need be. Nominal variables are commonly used in surveys but provide limited understanding of the phenomenon of interest.

Ordinal

Ordinal means "relating to things in a series." Response options for ordinal variables do have an inherent order and for this reason, cannot be randomized. Ordinal variables have no numeric qualities, and it is not assumed that the distance between any two successive options are the same as between any other two. For example, the distance between *frequently* and *very often* is not assumed to be the same as the distance

between *very often* and *somewhat often*. Agree-disagree response scales are a well-known example of an ordinal scale. Ordinal variables allow us to place categories on a continuum, for example, from lowest to highest educational degree earned.

Interval

Interval measurements include response options that are not only ordinal but also feature an equal distance between each option. Interval scales typically feature numbers, in that the distance between 2 and 3, between 3 and 4, and between any other two consecutive options is the same. True interval scales are rare. The Fahrenheit temperature scale is a commonly cited example of a true interval scale. Agree-disagree scales are often mistakenly believed to be interval, but it cannot be assumed that the distance between *strongly disagree* and *disagree* and the distance between *agree* and *strongly agree* are the same. Interval scales allow us not only to place categories on a continuum but also to understand the exact differences among them.

Ratio

Ratio measurements have the same characteristics as interval but also include a true zero. Age is an example of a true ratio measurement, for not only is the distance between age 31 and 32 the same as between 32 and 33, but someone who is 50 is twice as old as someone who is 25. Height is another commonly cited example of a ratio scale, as is distance and time.

Figure 8.3 offers examples of nominal, ordinal, interval, and ratio questions.

(Continued)

(Continued)

FIGURE 8.3 ● Examples of Nominal, Ordinal, Interval, and Ratio Questions

Nominal measurement:

What is your favorite type of entertainment?

- ○ Movie
- ○ Concert
- ○ Television show
- ○ Radio program
- ○ Podcast
- ○ Live comedy show
- ○ Other

Ordinal measurement:

What is the highest level of education you have completed?

- ○ High school
- ○ College
- ○ Graduate school
- ○ Postgraduate studies

Interval measurement:

Rate the movie *Gone With the Wind*

- ☆
- ☆ ☆
- ☆ ☆ ☆
- ☆ ☆ ☆ ☆
- ☆ ☆ ☆ ☆

Ratio measurement:

What is your age? _____

Note: Interval and ratio measurements do not generally need to be distinguished for survey researchers, because the choice of statistical techniques will not be impacted, but it is important to recognize the differences among nominal, ordinal, and interval/ratio.

Planning for Analysis

If not done already, now is the time to think carefully through how to work with the responses to each survey question. Think of this as a last chance to ensure that the questions and response options are going to result in responses that are as useful as possible, particularly given the time and resources available for analysis. Remember that there is no point in collecting information that can't be analyzed!

It is important to be aware that some types of survey questions are particularly challenging to analyze, such as ranking/ordering questions, Likert and Likert-like questions, "check all that apply" questions, and open-ended questions. Researchers should use these types of questions only after ensuring that they are worthwhile given the research purpose and information needs and that these are indeed the best question formats for respondents. Determining how to analyze responses to these questions will depend in part on the researcher's technical capabilities and the intended use of the resulting information. A comprehensive review of analysis is beyond the scope of this text; we recommend that researchers who need to use these types of questions take care to study analysis strategies prior to survey administration to adequately prepare and ensure it will be feasible to use the data being collected.

That said, we recommend erring on the side of designing questions that work well for respondents as opposed to those that will make analysis easy. Recall the example from the mini interview with Jara Dean-Coffey in Chapter 6:

> *Take gender identify as an example—it is especially challenging to capture in an authentic way. During a recent survey administration, staff noticed that more than half of students didn't identify with a particular gender or sex (they checked "none apply"). While an obvious challenge for data collection and analysis, RYSE views this positively for young people's identities—young people are less confined by traditional (biased) conceptions of gender identity. Changing these questions to ensure we're capturing how young people see themselves, with the current best language, is difficult. It may be we don't even have the right language for the way that young people view gender now. We strive to collect information in a way that honors who they are, and shift the burden to analysis—to prioritize getting the options right over how complicated it may make analysis later.*

This is a great illustration of why it is important to ensure questions are designed for respondents and not for researchers. Clearly this is a balancing act that requires planning ahead as much as possible, and determining how responses to each question will be analyzed.

Jara's example also illustrates the importance of consulting with respondents or other informants (e.g., experts or other stakeholders) in interpreting survey results. Just as a researcher cannot craft quality survey questions while sitting alone at her desk, it is best to interpret survey results (and in some cases even analyze results) in collaboration with others, such as those who might better understand the respondent population. There are many creative ways to do this, including participatory evaluation methods that support analysis and interpretation of data, subsequently driving use of that data. For example, see Innovation Network's *Participatory Analysis: Expanding Stakeholder Involvement in Evaluation* (Pankaj, Welsh, & Ostenso, 2011).

Discussion Questions

- What are the pros and cons of self-administered versus researcher-administered surveys?

- What is a researcher's responsibility to ensure results from a survey are actually used? How can researchers support the use of survey results to improve programs? To support better understanding of respondents?

 ## Design Drills

1. Research Scenario, Part 8 (additional parts are found in other chapters): You are developing a survey that will ask low-income senior citizens about their behaviors and thoughts related to a program delivered at local libraries. The program is intended to help senior citizens feel more engaged with their communities and to be more social, given concerns about seniors becoming too isolated. Complete a "mini plan" for your draft survey. Be sure to address the following questions in doing so:

   a. What is the best way to administer a survey to this population? What challenges do you anticipate regarding administration?

   b. Given what you have drafted per earlier chapters, what analysis challenges do you anticipate?

   c. How will you help support use of the survey results to improve the program?

 ## Extended Learning

- For more on focus groups
  - R. A. Krueger, & M. A. Casey. (2014), Focus groups: A practical guide for applied research. Thousand Oaks, CA: Sage.

- For a more thorough treatment of survey administration modes, including order effects, and how to combine modes, along with more on visual layout and formatting.
  - Dillman, D., Smyth, J. D., & Christian, L. (2014). *Internet, phone, mail, and mixed-mode surveys: The tailored design method* (4th ed.). Hoboken, NJ: Wiley.

- Krosnick, J. A. (1999). Survey research. *Annual Review of Psychology, 50*(1), 537–567.
  - Response rates have been the subject of many studies. See also Pew Research http://www.people-press .org/2012/05/15/assessing-the-representativeness-of-public-opinion-surveys) for more information.

- For more about survey fatigue and other response-related challenges.
  - Porter, S. R., Whitcomb, M. E., & Weitzer, W. H. (2004). Multiple surveys of students and survey fatigue. *New Directions for Institutional Research*, 121, 63–73.
  - Chapter 2, "Reducing People's Reluctance to Respond to Surveys," in Dillman et al. (2014).

- Robinson, S. B. (n.d.) *Six fab formatting tips for surveys*. Evergreen Data. Available at http://stephanieevergreen.com/6-tips-for-surveys.

• Appendix •

Checklist for Quality Question Design

This checklist was created as a companion to *Designing Quality Survey Questions* and will be most helpful to survey researchers who have read the text. The purpose of this checklist is to assist the survey researcher in designing an effective survey instrument that will elicit a rich, robust, and useful dataset for a respondent-centered survey aligned with the researcher's information needs. This checklist serves as a reflective self-assessment that focuses on the design of survey questions themselves and will not thoroughly inform *all* aspects of survey design. It is meant to be particularly helpful for researchers who are drafting questions from scratch, though it could also be applied to assist the review and finalization of questions adapted from existing tools.

This tool will be of greatest use if the following has already been determined:

- That a survey is indeed the appropriate tool to meet data collection needs

- The research or evaluation questions and information needs

- The population or sample of desired respondents

- How the survey will be administered: online, paper, by phone, in person, or some combination of these

We recommend going through the checklist for *each* individual survey question. Use the space to the right of each item to jot down notes about why you are checking yes or no and/or any edits needed. Note that not every item will apply to every question; use N/A as needed.

Checklist Item	Yes	No	N/A	Notes
Question type is appropriate:				
Question type will result in the type of data needed given research question(s)	☐	☐	☐	
Researcher is prepared to analyze results from this type of question	☐	☐	☐	
Question design is centered around respondents:				
Question asks for information respondent is likely to know, or respondent will have access to the information needed	☐	☐	☐	
Question focuses on respondent and respondent experiences (and not what respondent thinks about others)	☐	☐	☐	
Researcher can anticipate how a respondent might answer the question	☐	☐	☐	
Question is focused:				
Question relates closely and clearly to one (or more) research question(s)	☐	☐	☐	
Question is as specific and narrowly focused as possible	☐	☐	☐	
Question asks about only one concept (i.e., is not double-barreled)	☐	☐	☐	
Question is concise, using as few words as possible to convey meaning	☐	☐	☐	
Question phrasing is consistent with language used in other places in the survey	☐	☐	☐	
Question wording supports respondent understanding:				
Question is written in semantically valid, plain, straightforward language	☐	☐	☐	

Checklist Item	Yes	No	N/A	Notes
Question is syntactically correct, employing correct grammar and usage	☐	☐	☐	
Question wording reflects the language and culture of respondents	☐	☐	☐	
Question is specific enough for respondents to know exactly what information is being requested	☐	☐	☐	
Question requires as little inference or mental math as possible	☐	☐	☐	
Question is phrased using active voice	☐	☐	☐	
Question is phrased as neutrally as possible	☐	☐	☐	
Instructions and contextual cues are included as needed:				
Question itself includes any necessary instructions for answering	☐	☐	☐	
Explanations are included for any terms that might require clarification	☐	☐	☐	
For an open-ended question, question instructions note how long or detailed answers should be	☐	☐	☐	
Reference periods correspond to the information needed (e.g., shorter time periods for more common occurrences)	☐	☐	☐	
Reference periods are clear and specific (e.g., *since last Tuesday* as opposed to *in the last week*)	☐	☐	☐	

[Continued]

(Continued)

Checklist Item	Yes	No	N/A	Notes
If question is sensitive (e.g., a demographic question), question instructions include information about why the question is being asked and/or how responses will be used/useful	☐	☐	☐	
Closed-ended questions feature appropriate instructions and response options:				
Question instructions make it clear how to answer (e.g., *check all that apply, select the top three*)	☐	☐	☐	
Response options are exhaustive; that is, they fully cover the range of expected responses	☐	☐	☐	
Response options are mutually exclusive; that is, they do not overlap	☐	☐	☐	
Response options are labeled (either numerically, pictorially, verbally, or a combination) where appropriate	☐	☐	☐	
Closed-ended scale questions feature appropriate response options:				
Response options are aligned with wording of question stem (i.e., direct labeling or item-specific response options are used)	☐	☐	☐	
Bipolar response options are balanced with the same number of positive and negative options	☐	☐	☐	
5–7 options are used for scaled responses (unless desired level of precision requires fewer or more options)	☐	☐	☐	
Don't know, neutral, N/A, or similar response options are used only as needed and have a clear purpose	☐	☐	☐	

Checklist Item	Yes	No	N/A	Notes
A midpoint is used when a neutral option is needed or when forcing respondents to "choose a side" may result in measurement error	☐	☐	☐	
The order of scaled response options is consistent (e.g., left to right, least to greatest) with other questions	☐	☐	☐	
Numeric scales are ordered least to greatest	☐	☐	☐	
Response options start with least desirable and move to most desirable (to mitigate possible primacy effect)	☐	☐	☐	
Demographic questions reflect deep understanding of and respect for respondents:				
Question uses appropriate terminology for the specific respondent population (check with members of respondent population whenever possible)	☐	☐	☐	
Response options reflect all desired respondents (i.e., respondents can see themselves in the options) and avoid use of the term *other*	☐	☐	☐	
Question includes a *prefer not to answer* or *prefer to describe* response option when question topic is sensitive or potentially threatening	☐	☐	☐	
Response options reflect a balance of the need for accuracy, granularity, and respondent sensitivity (e.g., a question about age asks for year of birth or offers a series of age ranges depending on context)	☐	☐	☐	

• Glossary •

A

Autobiographical memory is how people store and retrieve the events, people, and places in their lives, as well as general knowledge of the world. It is generally divided into lifetime periods and general events such as "The time I lived in California" or "When I worked at headquarters."

B

Bias is an inclination or prejudice in favor of or against a thing, person, idea, or group as compared with another. Bias is the tendency to believe that some things, people, ideas, or groups are better than others. In general, biases are considered unfair. Numerous types of biases can potentially affect survey research, including social desirability bias, order effects (or question order bias), and the primacy effect (or primacy bias).

Branching (also known as conditional branching, branch logic, or skip logic) allows researchers to customize a survey based on a respondent's answer to one or more questions. Branching determines which subsequent questions a respondent will answer. Branching allows the researcher to skip respondents from one page to another in the survey or to terminate or finish the survey based on a respondent's answer to a question.

Bipolar rating scale is a type of rating scale used to measure a construct from one polar opposite to the other (e.g., dissatisfaction to satisfaction). Bipolar rating scales tend to feature midpoints and therefore have an odd number of response options.

C

Case record reviews are a data collection method that involves systematically examining (reviewing) documents related to program participants or beneficiaries (case records), typically to learn about and look for patterns in the experiences of those participants or beneficiaries in a system or program.

Census is everyone in a population, as opposed to a **sample**.

Closed-ended questions (sometimes called structured questions) are composed of a **question stem** and a set of response options.

Cognitive interview is a particular kind of individual interview, intended to explore the thinking processes that respondents go through in answering draft survey questions.

Cognitive load is mental effort, or the amount of information that working memory can hold at any one time. Heavy cognitive load can interfere with the ability to complete tasks and can lead to error.

Construct is something to be measured that cannot be directly observed. Examples of constructs include intelligence, health, and happiness.

Cultural responsiveness refers to practice that effectively and respectfully relates to people of various cultures. Culturally responsive researchers value and honor the languages, customs, life experiences, and contributions of people, especially those from whom data are collected.

Culturally responsive evaluation (CRE) is a specific approach to evaluation in which the planning and implementing of evaluation efforts draws on the cultural strengths and is relevant to the range of needs and experiences of culturally diverse populations.

D

Demographic questions are questions that measure and help the researcher describe the *characteristics* of a population or sample. These questions measure respondents' attributes such as age, gender, sexual orientation, race, ethnicity, occupation, education level, or religion.

Design thinking is both a process and a mindset that can be broadly applied to problem-solving challenges. Design thinking is characterized by a human or user-centered approach that involves empathizing with users, understanding and defining the problem, brainstorming (or ideating), and finally building and testing prototypes in response to feedback from users.

Dichotomous questions are those that feature just two response options (e.g., yes/no, true/false).

E

Evaluation is the use of social science research methods to determine the merit, worth, significance, or impact of a social intervention. Evaluation is a systematic way to collect, analyze, and use data to answer questions about programs, projects, or policies—particularly about their implementation or effectiveness.

Evaluation questions serve as the research questions for evaluation studies (see also **research questions**).

Extreme response style (ERS) is the tendency for survey respondents to answer questions with rating scales using the endpoints. ERS is considered a source of survey error because it is believed to represent a distortion of people's "true" attitudes and opinions.

F

Face validity is the degree to which something (in our case a survey or survey question) appears to measure what it intends to measure.

Focus group (or focus group interview) is a qualitative research strategy using a small group of people (often around 4 to 10 people) who are invited to participate in a guided discussion about a particular topic. In survey research, focus groups can be used to help researchers generate survey questions by learning more about potential respondents' perspectives or to test survey questions and provide feedback to researchers.

Frequency scales are ordered sets of response options for survey questions that ask about frequencies or rates, as in "how often" or "how many times." Frequency scales can be labeled with numbers (e.g., *1–2 times, 3–4 times*) or words (e.g., *rarely, sometimes, always*).

I

Item-specific (IS) refers to a set of response options or rating scale whose labels are designed specifically for the question stem. This approach is also called "direct labeling" and is contrasted with using a standard set of response options such as an agree-disagree (AD) rating scale for multiple question stems.

Indicators tell us the state or level of something. An indicator is a measurement that shows the level of a particular construct. For example, cholesterol level, heart rate, and blood pressure are indicators of the construct "health."

Informed consent/assent involves respondents granting their permission to participate in research with full knowledge of the possible risks and benefits of their participation. **Assent** is the term used to express willingness to participate by minors, who are too young to give **consent** but who are old enough to understand the research (including the possible risks and benefits) and the activities expected of them as participants.

Interview is most often a face-to-face (or telephone) conversation between a researcher and research subject or respondent used in qualitative research. Interviews can range from highly structured to unstructured but often include the opportunity for the researcher to probe the respondent with additional questions to gain additional insights.

L

Likert-type (or Likert-like) item is a single survey item or question that features a specific set of response options (see also **Likert scale**).

Likert scale is a psychometric scale (i.e., a carefully crafted combination of questions devised using the science of scaling) that allows a researcher to measure respondents' attitudes about particular topics. A Likert scale is a cluster of survey items related to each other that probe a particular construct of interest with a specific set of consistent response options (*strongly disagree, disagree, neither disagree nor agree, agree, strongly agree*).

M

Measurement error occurs during the data collection process (as opposed to sampling error or nonresponse error, or other types of error) and is how and to what extent a survey result differs from the "true" value due to imperfections in the way the data are collected. Measurement error can result from such circumstances as poor wording (leading to respondents misunderstanding questions or interpreting them differently from researchers' intent) or problems with response options (e.g., no options accurately match the respondent's actual circumstance). Measurement error is essentially the difference between the value of a variable as given by the respondent and the "true" (unknown to the researcher) value of the variable.

N

Needs assessment is a systematic process (often considered a form of research or evaluation) for identifying and measuring needs or "gaps" between current and desired conditions.

Nonresponse is the result of survey respondents being unwilling or unable to complete surveys or individual survey items. Nonresponse bias is the result of nonresponse and is problematic because it introduces survey error due to the fact that respondents differ from nonrespondents in meaningful ways that may be unknown to researchers.

O

Observation is a systematic data collection approach that involves direct observation of people and their behavior in natural settings.

Open-ended questions (sometimes called unstructured questions) have no response options and generally allow respondents to answer without specific parameters. Open-ended questions are essentially question stems with no response options.

Operationalize is to define or describe something in such a way that it can be measured.

Order effects (also known as question order bias) are the result of respondents being influenced by the order in which questions appear on a survey. Questions that appear earlier than others can prime respondents by impacting their thoughts, feelings, and attitudes, which in turn affects answers on subsequent questions.

P

Population includes *all* members of a defined group studied by researchers. Population can be contrasted with **sample**, which is only part of the population being studied.

Positivity bias results when respondents tend not to use the negative end of a response scale (they are reluctant to assign negative ratings). It also refers to the general tendency for people to remember pleasant items or events more accurately than unpleasant ones.

Primary data are data collected firsthand or directly by the current researcher (as opposed to secondary data that are collected in the past by those other than the current researcher).

Probe is a follow-up question designed to elicit additional data from respondents as the researcher encourages them to add, expand, or revise their initial answers (e.g., "What makes you say that?" "What do you mean by that?" "Can you say more about that?").

Primacy effect occurs when the first item or items seen, read, or heard are best remembered or more influential than later items.

Psychometric scale is a carefully crafted combination of questions devised using the science of scaling.

Q

Qualitative data are almost any information that can be captured that is not numerical and can include transcripts of interviews and focus groups, completed observation protocols, responses to open-ended survey questions, journal entries, letters, documents, video, or photographs.

Question stem is the part of the survey item that contains the question or statement to which people respond. An open-ended question is simply a question stem, whereas a closed-ended question includes both a question stem and a set of response options.

Questionnaire is synonymous with *survey* and is often used interchangeably with *survey* (see also **survey**).

R

Reference period is a time frame presented in a survey question for which respondents are asked to report behaviors, activities, or experiences of interest to the researcher(s).

Reliability is generally the repeatability and consistency of a test. In survey research, reliability is concerned with the degree to which the questions we ask on a survey generate the same types of information each time they are used under the same conditions.

Research questions make up the core of a research project or study. Research questions focus the work, inform the methodology, and guide all stages of inquiry, analysis, and reporting.

Respondent is a person who participates in or answers questions on a survey.

Response contraction (or response contraction bias) happens when survey respondents tend not to choose the extremes or endpoints of a set of response options. Responses are therefore biased or "contracted" to the middle options.

Response effects are changes or differences in survey responses that occur due to various aspects of survey design or administration. Response effects can arise from what seem like minor or inconsequential design decisions.

Response options (or response categories, response alternatives, answer choices) are the structured set of answers that accompany a question stem a respondent can use to complete a survey item.

Response rate (or completion rate or return rate) is simply the number of people who completed the survey divided by the number of people in the sample or population surveyed, resulting in a percentage.

Retrieval cues appear in survey instructions or question stems and are usually in the form of examples or definitions provided to stimulate respondents' memories.

S

Sample includes those members of a defined population being studied by researchers. Sample can be contrasted with **population**, which includes *all* members of the defined group being studied.

Satisficing refers to respondents giving minimally acceptable answers to survey questions, rather than expending more effort to give higher-quality responses.

Secondary data are data collected by other researchers (as opposed to primary data, which are data collected firsthand by the current researcher). Sources of secondary data for social science may include censuses, information collected by government agencies, organizational records, or other datasets that may have originally been collected for other research purposes.

Skip logic (see **branching**)

Social desirability bias involves respondents answering questions or editing their answers in ways that make them "look good" to the researcher behind the survey (or to the in-person or telephone interviewer), thus providing possibly inaccurate and lower-quality data and contributing to survey error.

Survey (see also **questionnaire**) is an instrument or tool used for data collection composed of a series of questions administered to a group of people either in person, through the mail, over the phone, or online.

Survey error refers to the set of problems and biases that can interfere with a survey's accuracy. Survey error can arise from nearly any facet of the survey design and administration process, including question wording, response options, question order, sampling procedures, and even nonresponse.

Survey fatigue (or respondent fatigue) happens when respondents become disengaged, bored, tired, or otherwise uninterested in the survey and either provide low-quality data, quit the survey partway through, or refuse to participate at all, resulting in nonresponse.

U

Unipolar rating scale is a type of rating scale used to measure a construct, quality, or attribute from its absence to its presence (e.g., never to always).

V

Vague quantifiers are words and phrases used to communicate uncertain or approximate amounts (e.g., *few, some, many, most*).

Validity generally refers to the degree of truthfulness or accuracy of a measure or item; in other words, whether and how well an item measures what it is intended to measure. Validity is a complex concept that has many definitions and types.

Variance in statistics is the measure of the spread of scores in a distribution of scores. In survey research, variance can be thought of as the spread of responses over a set of responses from different individuals. Variance is the range of responses received to any survey question.

• References •

Alreck, P. L., & Settle, R. B. (2004). *The survey research handbook* (3rd ed.). Chicago: Irwin.

American Anthropological Association. (1998). *Statment on race*. Available at www.americananthro.org/ConnectWithAAA/Content.aspx?ItemNumber=2583.

American Evaluation Association. (2011). *Public statement on cultural competence in evaluation*. Fairhaven, MA: Author. Available at http://www.eval.org/p/cm/ld/fid=92.

American Psychological Association. (n.d.). *Education and socioeconomic status*. Available at http://www.apa.org/pi/ses/resources/publications/education.aspx.

ANES. (2016). *2016 time series post-election questionnaire*. Available at http://www.electionstudies.org/studypages/anes_timeseries_2016/anes_timeseries_2016_qnaire_post.pdf.

Artino, A. R., Jr., & Gehlbach, H. (2012). AM Last Page: Avoiding four visual-design pitfalls in survey development. *Academic Medicine, 87*(10), 1452. Available at https://www.researchgate.net/publication/231210670_AM_Last_Page_Avoiding_Four_Visual-Design_Pitfalls_in_Survey_Development.

Association of Religion Data Archives. (n.d.). *General Social Survey 2014: Cross-Section and Panel Combined—Instructional Dataset*. Available at http://www.thearda.com/Archive/Files/Codebooks/GSS14ED_CB.asp.

Babbie, E. (1990). *Survey research methods* (2nd ed.). Belmont, CA: Wadsworth.

Belli, R. F., Schwarz, N., Singer, E., & Talarico, J. (2000). Decomposition can harm the accuracy of behavioural frequency reports. *Applied Cognitive Psychology, 14*(4), 295–308.

Berger, Warren. (2014). *A more beautiful question: The power of inquiry to spark breakthrough ideas*. New York: Bloomsbury.

Blind Foundation. (2018). *Making your communications accessible*. Available at https://blindfoundation.org.nz/how-we-can-help/businesses-and-professionals/accessible-documents-and-websites.

Borgers, N., de Leeuw, E., & Hox, J. (2000). Children as respondents in survey research: Cognitive development and response quality. *Bulletin de Méthodologie Sociologique, 66*, 60–75.

Bowen, M. L., & Tillman, A. S. (2015). Developing culturally responsive surveys: Lessons in development, implementation, and analysis from Brazil's African descent communities. *American Journal of Evaluation, 36*(1), 25–41.

Bradburn, N. M., & Sudman, S. (1988). *Polls & surveys: Understanding what they tell us*. San Francisco: Jossey-Bass.

Bradburn, N. M., Sudman, S., & Wansink, B. (2004). *Asking questions: The definitive guide to questionnaire design—for market research, political polls, and social and health questionnaires* (2nd Rev. ed.). San Francisco: Jossey-Bass.

Brown, L. X. Z. (2016). Ableism/language. Available at http://www.autistichoya.com/p/ableist-words-and-terms-to-avoid.html.

Brown, T. (2009). *Change by design: How design thinking transforms organizations and inspires innovation*. New York: Harper Business.

Cena, F., & Vernero, F. (2015). A study on user preferential choices about rating scales. *International Journal of Technology and Human Interaction, 11*(1), 33–54.

Centers for Disease Control and Prevention. (n.d.). *National health interview survey*. Available at https://www.cdc.gov/nchs/nhis/rhoi/rhoi_history.htm.

Chan, J. C. (1991). Response-order effects in Likert-type scales. *Educational and Psychological Measurement, 51*(3), 531–540.

Cialdini, R. B. (2007). *Influence: The psychology of persuasion*. New York: Collins.

Clark, H. H., & Schober, M. F. (1992). Asking questions and influencing answers. In J. M. Tanur (Ed.), *Questions about questions: Inquiries into the cognitive bases of surveys* (pp. 15–48). New York: Russell Sage Foundation.

Cohn, D. (2017). *Seeking better data on Hispanics, Census Bureau may change how it asks about race.* Pew Research Center. Available at http://www.pewresearch.org/fact-tank/2017/04/20/seeking-better-data-on-hispanics-census-bureau-may-change-how-it-asks-about-race.

Collins, D. (2003). Pretesting survey instruments: An overview of cognitive methods. *Quality of Life Research, 12*(3), 229–238.

Collins, D. (2014). *Cognitive interviewing practice.* London: Sage.

Consortium of Higher Education LGBT Resource Professionals. (n.d.). *Suggested best practices for asking sexual orientation and gender on college applications.* Available at http://www.lgbtcampus.org/policy-practice-recommendations.

Conti, G., & Pudney, S. (2011). Survey design and the analysis of satisfaction. *Review of Economics and Statistics, 93*(3), 1087–1093.

Courneya, K. S., Jones, L. W., Rhodes, R. E., & Blanchard, C. M. (2003). Effect of response scales on self-reported exercise frequency. *American Journal of Health Behavior, 27*(6), 613.

Cox, E. P., III. (1980). The optimal number of response alternatives for a scale: A review. *Journal of Marketing Research, 17*, 407–422.

Czaja, R. F., & Blair, J. (2005). *Designing surveys: A guide to decisions and procedures* (2nd ed.). Thousand Oaks, CA: Sage.

DeVellis, R. F. (2017). *Scale development* (4th ed.). Thousand Oaks, CA: Sage.

Dillman, D., Smyth, J. D., & Christian, L. (2014). *Internet, phone, mail, and mixed-mode surveys: The tailored design method* (4th ed.). Hoboken, NJ: Wiley.

Dimensions of gender. (n.d.). Genderspectrum. Available at https://www.genderspectrum.org/quick-links/understanding-gender.

Flowers, A. (2016). How we undercounted evictions by asking the wrong questions. FiveThirtyEight. Available at https://fivethirtyeight.com/features/how-we-under counted-evictions-by-asking-the-wrong-questions.

Foddy, W. (1998). An empirical evaluation of in-depth probes used to pretest survey questions. *Sociological Methods & Research, 27*(1), 103–133.

Foden-Vencil, K. (2016). Neither male nor female: Oregon resident legally recognized as third gender. NPR. Available at http://www.npr.org/2016/06/17/482480188/neither-male-nor-female-oregon-resident-legally-recognized-as-third-gender.

Fowler, F. J. (1995). *Improving survey questions.* Thousand Oaks, CA: Sage.

Fowler, F. J. (2014). *Survey research methods* (5th ed.). Thousand Oaks, CA: Sage.

Fowler, F. J., & Cosenza, C. (2008). Writing effective questions. In E. De Leeuw, J. Hox, & D. Dillman (Eds.), *International handbook of survey methodology* (pp. 136–160). New York: Erlbaum.

Frierson, H. T., Hood, S., Hughes, G. B., & Thomas, V. G. (2010). Strategies that address culturally responsive evaluation. In J. Frechtling (Ed.), *The 2010 user-friendly handbook for project evaluation* (pp. 75–96). Arlington, VA: National Science Foundation.

Gaskell, G. D., O'Muircheartaigh, C. A., & Wright, D. B. (1994). Survey questions about the frequency of vaguely defined events. *Public Opinion Quarterly, 58*(2), 241.

The GenIUSS Group. (2014). *Best practices for asking questions to identify transgender and other gender minority respondents on population-based surveys.* Los Angeles: The Williams Institute.

Goetz, E. G. (2008). Words matter: The importance of issue framing and the case of affordable housing. *Journal of the American Planning Association, 74*(2), 222–229.

Goodrich, Richelle E. *Slaying Dragons.* Smashwords, Inc., 2017.

Gray, D. (n.d.). Empathy map: Understand your customer. *The Toolkit Project.* Available at http://thetool kitproject.com/tool/empathy-map#sthash.yQPop9v2.dpbs.

Greytak, E. A. (2015). LGBT TIG Week: Emily A. Greytak on So . . . you want to identify LGBTQ people in your evaluation? Ask these 4 questions first. AEA365: Tip-a-Day by and for Evaluators. Available at http://aea365.org/blog/lgbt-tig-week-emily-a-greytak-on-so-you-want-to-include-identify-lgbtq-people-in-your-evaluation-ask-these-4-questions-first.

Guy-Ryan, J. (2016). *In Indonesia, non-binary gender is a centuries-old idea.* Atlas Obscura. Available at http://www.atlasobscura.com/articles/in-indonesia-nonbinary-gender-is-a-centuriesold-idea?utm_source=facebook.com&utm_medium=atlas-page.

Hasso Plattner Institute of Design. (n.d.). *An introduction to design thinking process guide.* Available at https://dschool-old.stanford.edu/sandbox/groups/design

resources/wiki/36873/attachments/74b3d/ModeGuide-BOOTCAMP2010L.pdf.

Healey, B., & Gendall, P. (2007). Asking the age question in mail and online surveys. *International Journal of Market Research, 50*(3), 309–317.

Hinsdale, M., McFarlane, E., Weger, S., Schoua-Glusberg, A., & Kerwin, J. (2009). *Cognitive testing of the American Community Survey content test items.* Report submitted to U.S. Census Bureau. Research Triangle Park, NC: RTI International.

Hood, S., Hopson, R., & Kirkhart, K. (2015). Culturally responsive evaluation. In K. E. Newcomer, H. P. Hatry, & J. S. Wholey (Eds.), *Handbook of practical program evaluation* (4th ed., pp. 281–317). San Francisco: Jossey-Bass.

Howe, M. L., & Knott, L. M. (2015). The fallibility of memory in judicial processes: Lessons from the past and their modern consequences. *Memory, 23*(5), 633–656.

Human Rights Campaign. (2016). *Collecting transgender-inclusive gender data in workplace and other surveys.* Available at http://www.hrc.org/resources/collecting-transgender-inclusive-gender-data-in-workplace-and-other-surveys.

Human Rights Campaign. (2017). *Sexual orientation and gender identity definitions.* Available at http://www.hrc.org/resources/sexual-orientation-and-gender-identity-terminology-and-definitions.

Igou, E. R., Bless, H., & Schwarz, N. (2002). Making sense of standardized survey questions: The influence of reference periods and their repetition. *Communication Monographs, 69*(2), 179–187.

Jansen, W., Verhoeven, W., Robert, P., & Dessens, J. (2013). The long and short of asking questions about income: A comparison using data from Hungary. *Quality & Quantity, 47*(4), 1957–1969.

Krosnick, J. A. (1999). Survey research. *Annual Review of Psychology, 50*(1), 537–567.

Krosnick, J. A. (2000). The threat of satisficing in surveys: The shortcuts respondents take in answering questions. *Survey Methods Newsletter, 20*(1), 4–8. Available at https://pprg.stanford.edu/wp-content/uploads/2000-The-threat-of-satisficing-in-surveys-The-shortcuts-responde.pdf.

Krosnick, J. A., & Alwin, D. F. (1987). An evaluation of a cognitive theory of response-order effects in survey measurement. *Public Opinion Quarterly, 51*(2), 201–219.

Krueger, R. A. (1994). *Focus groups: A practice guide for applied research* (2nd ed.). Thousand Oaks, CA: Sage.

Lavrakas, P. J. (2008). Respondent fatigue. *Encyclopedia of survey research methods.* Available at http://srmo.sagepub.com/view/encyclopedia-of-survey-research-methods/n480.xml.

Lenzner, T. (2012). Effects of survey question comprehensibility on response quality. *Field Methods, 24*(4), 1–20. Available at http://fmx.sagepub.com/content/early/2012/08/31/1525822X12448166.

Lenzner, T., Kaczmirek, L., & Galesic, M. (2011). Seeing through the eyes of the respondent: An eye-tracking study on survey question comprehension. *International Journal of Public Opinion Research, 23*(3), 361–373.

Lenzner, T., Kaczmirek, L., & Lenzner, A. (2010). Cognitive burden of survey questions and response times: A psycholinguistic experiment. *Applied Cognitive Psychology, 24*, 1003–1020.

Lipka, S. (2011). Want data? Ask students. Again and again. *Chronicle of Higher Education, 57*, 43.

Livingston, G. (2017). *The rise of multiracial and multiethnic babies in the U.S.* Pew Research Center. Available at http://www.pewresearch.org/fact-tank/2017/06/06/the-rise-of-multiracial-and-multiethnic-babies-in-the-u-s.

Lozano, L. M., García-Cueto, E., & Muñiz, J. (2008). Effect of the number of response categories on the reliability and validity of rating scales. *Methodology, 4*(2), 73–79.

Malhotra, N., Krosnick, J. A., & Thomas, R. K. (2009). Optimal design of branching questions to measure bipolar constructs. *Public Opinion Quarterly, 73*(2), 304–324.

McAndrew, S., & Voas, D. (2011). Measuring religiosity using surveys. *Survey Question Bank: Topic Overview, 4*(2), 1–15.

Meadows, K. A., Greene, T., Foster, L., & Beer, S. (2000). The impact of different response alternatives on responders' reporting of health-related behaviour in a postal survey. *Quality of Life Research, 9*(4), 385–391.

Moors, G., Kieruj, N. D., & Vermunt, J. K. (2014). The effect of labeling and numbering of response scales on the likelihood of response bias. *Sociological Methodology, 44*(1), 366.

Pankaj, V., Welsh, M., & Ostenso, L. (2011). *Participatory analysis: Expanding stakeholder involvement in evaluation.*

Innovation Network. Available at https://www.innonet.org/media/innovation_network-participatory_analysis.pdf.

Patton, M. Q. (2008). *Utilization-focused evaluation* (4th ed.). Thousand Oaks, CA: Sage.

Payne, S. L. B. (1951). *The art of asking questions.* Princeton: Princeton University Press.

Pearse, N. (2011). Deciding on the scale granularity of response categories of Likert type scales: The case of a 21-point scale. *Electronic Journal of Business Research Methods, 9*(2), 159–171. Available at www.ejbrm.com.

Peterson, R. A. (1984). Asking the age question: A research note. *Public Opinion Quarterly, 48*(1), 379–383.

Pettit, F. A. (2016). *People aren't robots: A practical guide to the psychology and technique of questionnaire design.* Charleston, SC: CreateSpace.

Pew Research Center. (n.d.-a). *The problem of declining response rates.* Available at http://www.peoplepress.org/methodology/collecting-survey-data/the-problem-of-declining-response-rates.

Pew Research Center. (n.d.-b). *Questionnaire design.* Available at http://www.pewresearch.org/methodology/u-s-survey-research/questionnaire-design/#open-and-closed-ended-questions.

Porter, S. R., Whitcomb, M. E., & Weitzer, W. H. (2004). Multiple surveys of students and survey fatigue. *New Directions for Institutional Research, 121*, 63–73.

Preston, C. C., & Colman, A. M. (2000). Optimal number of response categories in rating scales: Reliability, validity, discriminating power, and respondent preferences. *Acta Psychologica, 104*(1), 1–15.

QUAID Tool. (n.d.). University of Memphis Institute for Intelligent Systems. Available at http://quaid.cohmetrix.com.

Rasinski, K. A., Mingay, D., & Bradburn, N. M. (1994). Do respondents really "mark all that apply" on self-administered questions? *Public Opinion Quarterly, 58*(3), 400–408.

Rea, L. M., & Parker, R. A. (2014). *Designing and conducting survey research: A comprehensive guide* (4th ed.). San Francisco: Jossey-Bass.

Reja, U., Manfreda, K. L., Hlebec, V., & Vehovar, V. (2003). Open-ended vs. close-ended questions in web questionnaires. *Developments in Applied Statistics, 19*(1), 159–177.

Robison, J. (2015). Different demographic groups must be managed differently. *Gallup Business Journal.* Available at http://www.gallup.com/businessjournal/181205/different-demographic-groups-managed-differently.aspx?g_source=demographic&g_medium=search&g_campaign=tiles.

Rugg, D. (1941). Experiments in wording questions: II. *Public Opinion Quarterly, 5*(1), 91–92.

Ryan, K., Gannon-Slater, N., & Culbertson, M. (2012). Improving survey methods with cognitive interviews in small- and medium-scale evaluations. *American Journal of Evaluation, 33*, 41.

Saris, W., Revilla, M., Krosnick, J. A., & Shaeffer, E. M. (2010). Comparing questions with agree/disagree response options to questions with item-specific response options. *Survey Research Methods, 4*(1), 61–79.

Schaeffer, N. C., & Dykema, J. (2011). Questions for surveys current trends and future directions. *Public Opinion Quarterly, 75*(5), 909–961.

Schaeffer, N. C., & Presser, S. (2003). The science of asking questions. *Annual Review of Sociology, 29*(1), 65–88.

Schuman, H., Ludwig, J., & Krosnick, J. A. (1986). The perceived threat of nuclear war, salience, and open questions. *Public Opinion Quarterly, 50*, 518.

Schuman, H., & Presser, S. (1977). Question wording as an independent variable in survey analysis. *Sociological Methods & Research, 6*(2).

Schuman, H., & Presser, S. (1979). The open and closed question. *American Sociological Review, 44*(4), 692.

Schuman, H., & Scott, J. (1987). Problems in the use of survey questions to measure public opinion. *Science, 236*(4804), 957–959.

Schwarz, N. (2007). Cognitive aspects of survey methodology. *Applied Cognitive Psychology, 21*(2), 277–287.

Schwarz, N., Hippler, H., Deutsch, B., & Strack, F. (1985). Response scales: Effects of category range on reported behavior and comparative judgments. *Public Opinion Quarterly, 49*(3), 388–395.

Schwarz, N., & Oyserman, D. (2001). Asking questions about behavior: Cognition, communication, and questionnaire construction. *American Journal of Evaluation, 22*(2), 127–160.

Schwarz, N., Strack, F., Müller, G., & Chassein, B. (1988). The range of response alternatives may determine the meaning of the question: Further evidence on informative functions of response alternatives. *Social Cognition, 6*, 107–117.

Seidman, I. (2013). *Interviewing as qualitative research: A guide for researchers in education and the social sciences* (4th ed.). New York: Teachers College Press.

Sexual Minority Assessment Research Team (SMART). (2009). *Best practices for asking questions about sexual orientation on surveys.* Los Angeles: The Williams Institute.

Simons, D. J., & Chabris, C. F. (2011). What people believe about how memory works: A representative survey of the U.S. population. *PLOS ONE, 6*(8), e22757.

Singer, E., Von Thurn, D. R., & Miller, E. R. (1995). Confidentiality assurances and response: A quantitative review of the experimental literature. *Public Opinion Quarterly, 59*(1), 66–77.

Smyth, J. D., Dillman, D. A., Christian, L. M., & Mcbride, M. (2009). Open-ended questions in web surveys. *Public Opinion Quarterly, 73*(2), 325–337.

Stein, P. (2017). Meet the first person in the country to officially receive a gender-neutral driver's license. *Washington Post.* Available at https://www.washingtonpost.com/local/meet-the-first-person-in-the-country-to-officially-receive-a-gender-neutral-drivers-license/2017/06/30/bcb78afc-5d9a-11e7-9fc6-c7ef4bc58d13_story.html?tid=sm_fb&utm_term=.0b7f106ccf30.

Sturgis, P., Roberts, C., & Smith, P. (2014). Middle alternatives revisited: How the neither/nor response acts as a way of saying "I don't know"? *Sociological Methods & Research, 43*(1), 15–38.

Sudman, S., & Bradburn, N. M. (1982). *Asking questions: A practical guide to questionnaire design.* Hoboken, NJ: Wiley.

Sudman, S., Bradburn, N. M., & Schwarz, N. (1996). *Thinking about answers: The application of cognitive processes to survey methodology.* San Francisco: Jossey-Bass.

Swierzbin, B. (2014). What's in a noun phrase? Judging the difficulty of a reading text by understanding the complexity of noun phrases. *MinneTESOL Journal.* Available at http://minnetesoljournal.org/spring-2014/whats-in-a-noun-phrase-judging-the-difficulty-of-a-reading-text-by-understanding-the-complexity-of-noun-phrases.

Symonds, P. M. (1924). On the loss of reliability in ratings due to coarseness of the scale. *Journal of Experimental Psychology, 7*(6), 456–461.

Tanur, J. M. (Ed.). (1992). *Questions about questions: Inquiries into the cognitive bases of surveys.* New York: Russell Sage Foundation.

Toepoel, V., Das, M., & van Soest, A. (2009). Design of web questionnaires: The effect of layout in rating scales. *Journal of Official Statistics, 25*(4), 509–528.

Tourangeau, R. (2003). Cognitive aspects of survey measurement and mismeasurement. *International Journal of Public Opinion Research, 15*(1), 3–7.

Tourangeau, R., Conrad, F. G., Couper, M. P., & Ye, C. (2014). The effects of providing examples in survey questions. *Public Opinion Quarterly, 78*(1), 100–125.

Tourangeau, R., Couper, M. P., & Conrad, F. (2007). Color, labels, and interpretive heuristics for response scales. *Public Opinion Quarterly, 71*(1), 91–112.

Tourangeau, R., Rips, L. J., & Rasinski, K. (2000). *The psychology of survey response.* New York: Cambridge University Press.

Tourangeau, R., & Yan, T. (2007). Sensitive questions in surveys. *Psychological Bulletin, 133*(5), 859–883.

United States Census Bureau. (n.d.-a). *American Community Survey: Why we ask: Age.* Available at https://www2.census.gov/programs-surveys/acs/about/qbyqfact/Age.pdf.

United States Census Bureau. *Race.* (n.d.-b). Available at https://www.census.gov/topics/population/race/about.html.

United States Census Bureau. (n.d.-c). *American Community Survey: Why we ask: Income.* Available at https://www.census.gov/acs/www/about/why-we-ask-each-question/income.

Viswanathan, M., Sudman, S., & Johnson, M. (2004). Maximum versus meaningful discrimination in scale response: Implications for validity of measurement of consumer perceptions about products. *Journal of Business Research, 57*(2), 108–124.

Wamsley, L. (2017). *Oregon adds a new gender option to its driver's licenses: X.* NPR. Available at http://www.npr.org/sections/thetwo-way/2017/06/16/533207483/oregon-adds-a-new-gender-option-to-its-driver-s-licenses-x.

Weijters, B., Cabooter, E., & Schillewaert, N. (2010). The effect of rating scale format on response styles: The number of response categories and response category labels. *International Journal of Research in Marketing, 27*(3), 236–247.

Weisberg, H. F., Krosnick, J. A., & Bowen, B. D. (1996). *An introduction to survey research, polling, and data analysis* (3rd ed.). Thousand Oaks, CA: Sage.

Weng, L. (2004). Impact of the number of response categories and anchor labels on coefficient alpha and test-retest reliability. *Educational and Psychological Measurement, 64*(6), 956–972.

Weng, L., & Cheng, C. (2000). Effects of response order on Likert-type scales. *Educational and Psychological Measurement, 60*(6), 908–924.

Weprin, M. (2016). *Design thinking: Empathy maps.* Available at https://uxdict.io/design-thinking-empathy-map-c69ab5d6b22.

Willis, G. B. (1994). *Cognitive interviewing and questionnaire design: A training manual.* Office of Research and Methodology, National Center for Health Statistics. Washington, DC: U.S. Department of Health and Human Services.

Willis, G. B. (2005). *Cognitive interviewing: A tool for improving questionnaire design.* Thousand Oaks, CA: Sage.

Willis, G. B., & Lessler, J. T. (1999). *Questionnaire Appraisal System QAS-99.* Research Triangle Park, NC: Research Triangle Institute.

Winkielman, P., Knaüper, B., & Schwarz, N. (1998). Looking back at anger: Reference periods change the interpretation of (emotion) frequency questions. *Journal of Personality and Social Psychology, 75,* 719–728.

Wouters, K., Maesschalck, J., Peeters, C. F. W., & Roosen, M. (2013). Methodological issues in the design of online surveys for measuring unethical work behavior: Recommendations on the basis of a split-ballot experiment. *Journal of Business Ethics, 120*(2), 1–15.

W3C. (2008). *Web content accessibility guidelines (WCAG) 2.0.* Available at https://www.w3.org/TR/WCAG20.

Yorke, M. (2001). Bipolarity . . . or not? Some conceptual problems relating to bipolar rating scales. *British Educational Research Journal, 27*(2), 171–186.

• Index •

Note: The letter *f* after the page number indicates a figure